MUM'S T KT-420-107 RD

Also published by Cassell:

Change for the Better, by Elizabeth Wilde McCormick

Counselling Supervision, by Michael Carroll

Effective Thinking Skills, by Richard Nelson-Jones

Issues in Professional Counsellor Training, by Windy Dryden, Ian Horton and Dave Mearns

Levels of Personality, by Mark Cook

Lifeskills, by Richard Nelson-Jones

Practical Counselling and Helping Skills, fourth edition, by Richard Nelson-Jones

Skills Training for Counselling, by Francesca Inskipp

The Theory and Practice of Counselling, by Richard Nelson-Jones

You Can Help! by Richard Nelson-Jones

MUM'S THE WORD

THE MAMMA'S BOY SYNDROME REVEALED

Arlene Gorodensky

CASSELL

The author and publisher wish to thank:

Woody Allen, Orion Pictures Corporation and
Touchstone Pictures for permission to quote from
'Oedipus Wrecks' (1989) and *Crimes and
Misdemeanors* (1989).

Jason Aronson Inc., Northvale, NJ 07647, for
permission to quote from Robert J. Stoller, *The
Transsexual Experiment* (1975).

Reed Books Ltd for permission to quote six lines of
A. A. Milne's poem 'Disobedience' (from *When We
Were Very Young*, published by Methuen
Children's Books).

Cassell

Wellington House, 125 Strand, London WC2R 0BB

PO Box 605, Herndon, VA 20172

First published 1997

**British Library Cataloguing-in-Publication
Data**
A catalogue record for this book is available from the
British Library.

ISBN   0-304-33883-4 (hardback)
        0-304-33884-2 (paperback)

Typeset by Ben Cracknell Studios
Printed and bound in Great Britain by
Redwood Books, Trowbridge, Wilts

Contents

Acknowledgements

I would like to acknowledge first Brett Kahr, who supervised the dissertation which formed the basis of this book. Without his unwavering support, encouragement and inexhaustible guidance, his vast knowledge and willingness to share it, this book would not have been as easily born. I thank you.

I would also like to thank Dr Ernesto Spinelli, Teresa and François di Matanga, Dr Holli Schauber and Dr Jussi M. Hanhimaki, Dr Steve Ticktin, Dr Stella Acquarone of The Parent Infant Clinic, Stefan Durlach, Lynn Sullivan, Veronica Denby, Jan Halstead and Dr Joe Halstead, James Talbot, Peggy Murawnik, Jennifer Goodwin, Glenn Garrett, Dr Barry Rubin, Dr Nina Couvaras, Carrie Heppner, Bruno Grunfeld, Marsha Jacobs Shmuckler, Anthony Moran, Jojo Zimmerman, Adel Darwish of *The Independent*, Marion Malkin, Howard Shaw, the staff of Regent's College Library (Geoff, Anne, and especially Chris Diachuk), Natasha Maty, Jeffrey and Andrea Farkas, Barrie and Emmanuel Roman, Jan Simpson, the late Russell B. Rivera, and Mary Ann Somerville.

I am grateful to Dr Charles Socarides for his unfaltering interest and encouragement, and to my agent, Sugra Zaman of Watson, Little Limited, for her optimism and hard work.

Special thanks to all those who took part in my research and remain nameless. Your honesty and personal experiences have added to the richness of this work and I am grateful for your contributions.

Indirectly, I am also compelled to thank Oprah Winfrey for her popular contribution to mental health. She has inspired me in the writing of this book with the hope of bringing its subject matter to public awareness.

Last but not least, I thank my brothers, Marvin and Jeffrey, and my parents, Helen and Hy, for their love and support.

Foreword

This book, with its semi-whimsical title, is to be taken seriously. It should rival Philip Wylie's *Generation of Vipers*, published over fifty years ago, a stunning runaway best-seller of the 1940s and 1950s which underwent twenty-seven printings. Gorodensky describes in psychological terms what Wylie did in sociological terms: the state of a society, after World War II, in which a 'megaloid mom-worship had gotten completely out of hand', making the world a worse place for individuals and society. Gorodensky dares to describe the *inner psychological world* in which boys become mother's playthings, with a loss of independence of thought, of separateness, masculinity, and leadership which is then reflected in our social customs and behaviour. She reminds us, in restrained yet compelling psychological detail, of the adage 'the hand that rocks the cradle is the hand that rules the world', the truth of which psychoanalysts are well aware of on a daily basis, yet which is infrequently presented in such bold and compelling prose to the general public.

Within these pages the reader will find an engrossing and stimulating scientific work by a brilliant young psychotherapist who probes this neglected yet astonishing aspect of the effects of certain patterns of child-rearing. By studying the male's relationship to his mother, from his earliest years into adulthood, and to some extent the father's relationship to his son, she details what makes for the health and enrichment of the self and what makes for its impoverishment. With an admirable absence of psychoanalytic jargon, she tells us of mothers' need to control their sons, how a mother's psychopathology and her inability to allow a male child to separate from her *intrapsychically* (not just in terms of actual distance) have a crucial influence over whether or not a boy will grow up to be a productive, active citizen operating with his full capacities to benefit not only himself but others about him. In simple, incisive, yet elegant language, she makes it all highly readable and understandable.

So often society overlooks or casually dismisses an individual's poor performance or failure in functioning, viewing it as a tragic-comic aspect of life. In actuality it represents a forfeiture of self-fulfilment for countless numbers of people caught in the 'dark side' of motherhood. I know of no book – whether in the field of psychoanalysis, psychiatry or psychology, or in popular literature, both fiction and nonfiction – or film which not only taps the salient features of this condition but also captures the subtle balance of forces which lead mothers to steal the lives of their sons, making those lives their own. Reading this book may well make it possible to make 'choices' to escape, or at least mitigate, some of the tragic inhibitions caused by this unfortunate predicament. One may find aspects of one's own life-situation within these pages – one's own relationship to his family, and the possible fate which may lie in store if no correction is made.

This particular mother–son relationship generates what the author calls the 'Mamma's Boy Syndrome', a syndrome which has often been encouraged, in fact even socially sanctioned and applauded during various periods of history, but at a terrible price both for the individual and for society itself. It consists of an overweening control of a son's psychological life so that it is interwoven and enmeshed with that of the mother. The bond between mother and son may become relentless – a form of bondage – used to 'shackle her son so that he exists only in relation to her – his every limited movement corresponds to her wishes and he cannot take a step to separate without finding Mother attached to the end of the chain that binds them'. And what is the effect of all this? It is one of slavish proportions involving all areas of endeavour – work, social, group membership, competition, sexuality and the capacity for the enjoyment of all pleasures.

Gorodensky's clinical examples are particularly incisive and convincing. The interlocking pathologies between mother and son are clear, as well as those, to some degree, between son and father, and are captured in every detail. She demonstrates that such individuals grow up as appendages of their mothers, with little sense of their identity, their gender, their sexuality or their ability to compete with others. Of central importance is the derailment of the ability to relate to the opposite sex, first in adolescence and then in maturity, with consequent deformations in their sexual functioning.

While this book superbly describes the 'dark side' of motherhood, it is self-evident that in so doing it brings the 'bright side' into sharp relief. In praise of motherhood, George Bernard Shaw (1926) said in

The Admirable Bashville, 'God could not be everywhere, and therefore, he made mothers'; Edna Ferber (1927) made popular the three-word phrase 'Mother Knows Best', still in popular jocular use; Emerson, in his 'Conduct of Life', announced that 'men are what their mothers made them' (1860); Napoleon Bonaparte is credited with saying, 'The future destiny of the child is always the work of the mother'; and John Quincy Adams is said to have said, 'All that I am, my mother made me'. Abraham Lincoln himself didn't give that credit to his mother but to his step-mother, a widow whom Thomas Lincoln married the year after his first wife's death. Lincoln was fond of saying, 'all that I am or hope to be I owe to my angel mother', and Jay Phillips (1942) popularized a song which began with the phrase 'A boy's best friend is his mother'. And where would the English-speaking world be today if it were not for Winston Churchill? According to psychoanalyst S. Donald Coleman (who carefully detailed the British leader's early development in a 1995 essay entitled 'Winston S. Churchill: special resolutions of childhood deprivations helped form the heroic character of the statesman'), Churchill's most particularly influential relationship was *not* to his mother, but to a devoted nanny, Mrs Everest, who became his surrogate mother. From the earliest stage of his infancy, Churchill grew up against the background of severe maternal neglect and a father's remoteness and overt hostility. These conditions were successfully overcome by the surrogate mother's loving influence: the nanny allowed both parents to become objects of a conflict-free idealization, especially an idealization of his father which indeed seems to have been largely responsible for Churchill's playing a heroic role in the future of not only Britain, but of the world itself.

With consummate tact, Gorodensky reminds us that the purpose of her book is not to *blame* mother, and, as a professional therapist, she asserts that this would be unproductive for both. It is a confluence or concatenation of events which makes both mother and son victims; she the victim of her own unresolved childhood complexes and childhood experiences which are then translated into a form of 'smothering-mothering' – a form of deep intrusion and, in my opinion, a form of child abuse, with resultant deformations of the son's character, personality, endeavours and ability to grow and learn from experience.

Charles W. Socarides, M.D.,
Clinical Professor of Psychiatry,
Albert Einstein College of Medicine,
New York City.

Dedicated to the memory of my grandparents,
Chana and Haskel Gorodensky
and
Alta Aiga and Meyir Basch-Farkas

Who Is the Mamma's Boy?

The following have given their own definitions of who the Mamma's Boy is:

Joanne, age 42: 'A Mamma's Boy looks after his mother at the cost of his own life, and society says, "Oh, what a good boy!" A generation ago, it was expected that one of the children would have that role.'

Nicola, age 40: 'A Mamma's Boy is someone whose mother is overly concerned and has her finger in every aspect of his life. She does not let him live his own life.'

Judith, age 44: 'A Mamma's Boy is created by a woman who doesn't dare allow her son to take possession of his penis.'

Gemma, age 43: 'A Mamma's Boy is asexual or his orientation is towards the mother.'

Daniel, age 38: 'The Mamma's Boy receives messages from his mother that say, "I'll die if you leave me or you will die if you leave me ... It is a dangerous world out there."'

David, age 17: 'A Mamma's Boy is like a "teacher's pet". He has to get one up on everyone else. He is precious and very annoying!'

Mark, age 23: 'The Mamma's Boy is not self-obsessed or wrapped up in himself. He is able to take on his mother's problems and empathize and identify with her.'

Natasha, age 34: 'A Mamma's Boy is a man who is basically controlled by his mother. He won't move out of the house and his whole life is focused on her.'

Fabio, age 35: 'A Mamma's Boy's primary concern is his mother at all times. He will give up having a family and wife to support his mother.'

Julius, age 32: 'A Mamma's Boy is someone who is close to his mother. It is not such a bad thing if that is how he chooses to live his life.'

Meris, age 34: 'A Mamma's Boy never has to grow up or do his own laundry. Mother is always there to take care of him and all his needs. It is a better deal than living on your own and taking responsibility.'

Helen, age 60: 'A Mamma's Boy looks like a man but is effeminate and weak.'

Gregory, age 51: 'A Mamma's Boy is a man who can't make a meaningful attachment to a woman because of his mother's influence.'

What is your definition of a Mamma's Boy?

Introduction

We had been dating for seven months when the decision was made to become engaged to be married. Together, the ring was selected which was to symbolize the shining life we were to lead and his commitment to me as his wife, the woman he would justly turn to as his partner, confidant and lover. My elation and plans for our impending marriage and future together were abruptly brought to a halt by the searing words which rang in my ears when, as a unit, we went to share our news with his mother. She scanned my ringed finger momentarily, turned to penetrate her son's eyes and blurted not what I had anticipated would be her blessing but her spontaneous expression which revealed the naked manifestation of the concealed nature of her relationship with her son: 'You should have bought me one too!'

Undoubtedly, he was, in a sense, already married to his mother. My position as his future wife was, in my mind at least, made redundant.

It was this personal experience which piqued my passionate interest and subsequent research into the relationship between mothers and sons. Initially, I thought that what I had encountered was an oddity, a surreal portrait of the mother–son bond. However, I soon discovered that it was, indeed, not an isolated example. As the following accounts will illustrate, the engulfing mother and her son who remains under her thumb and skirt are far more prevalent than I could have ever imagined:

Donna and Bruce were dating for one and a half years. At her flat, early on a Sunday evening, with the answering machine left to intercept any interruptions, they were engrossed in a game of Scrabble. The phone rang persistently and after the fourth call, Donna checked her messages fearing an emergency. To her amazement as well as horror, as she played back the recorded calls with Bruce by her side, his mother's voice was heard blaring over the speaker. She sounded 'possessed' as she screeched that she 'knew we were there and knew what we were doing!' As

Bruce telephoned his mother, Donna could hear her shouting invectively at him. He seemed unaffected as he coldly said, 'No, mother, don't worry, we weren't making love.' Bruce quickly left Donna without an explanation or apology and went back to his mother, with whom he still lived. He was thirty-eight years old.

Similarly, Tess told me,

'When I didn't cook his favourite dish or fold his laundry exactly as his mother had done it for him, my husband would become abusive with me. It was especially explosive after he would return from visiting his mother, who would continually tell him, as she had since he was a young child, "Frankie-boy, you could have twelve wives, my son, but remember, you only have one mother." I filed for divorce after he threw his dinner at me – his mother had prepared the same thing when he was there that day for lunch. How was I to know?'

I was propelled into investigating the abusive power of motherhood, albeit an unconscious enactment, which is executed in the guise of motherly love. Not only do mothers use their power to control their sons' independence or, more aptly, their lack of it, but as their son's first love object, mothers are granted the power to influence his subsequent relationships with both women and men, as well as the formation of his personality, gender identity and self-esteem, as an individual out in the world at large.

Sanctioned by society, women as mothers are applauded for bearing sons who are stunted indefinitely into maintaining a dependence on those who have borne them. The son who dutifully remains an appendage of his mother, unable or not allowed to separate from her far beyond appropriateness, is wrongfully viewed as a testament to a mother's vocation well done. The blurred and sometimes non-existent boundaries, which are evident in other forms of abuse, are ignored in the instance of the mother–son relationship. How often do we look at the bond between mother and son and catch a healthy glimpse of a boy who will grow into an independent man rather than a man–boy who must indefinitely meet his mother's needs, desires and expectations?

This book explores the unconscious as well as conscious mechanisms which contribute to the creation and perpetuation of the son who is dwarfed by his mother's inability to see him as an individual, separate from herself. This type of excessive mothering or 'smothering-mothering' leads to our sons being popularly referred to as 'Mamma's Boys'.

From my research, I have identified a phenomenon which I have labelled the Mamma's Boy Syndrome (MBS). The Mamma's Boy Syndrome – a collection of symptoms that are expressed by specific patterns – is a dysfunction which occurs in males on a continuum from mild to extreme and which is always stimulated by the interactive relationship with Mother. There is no textbook definition of a Mamma's Boy, yet we each hold a caricature of this male in our mind: 'A Mamma's Boy is a son who is needed to give his mother a purpose in life'; 'He is someone who cannot find his own sexuality as he is not let free to discover it. Mother has chosen it for him and perhaps his orientation is towards her and maybe he will be freed when she is dead'; 'A Mamma's Boy has a problem because he can't differentiate between being supportive of his mother and being totally engulfed by the relationship'; 'On one hand, the Mamma's Boy strongly loves his mother and accepts her influence. On the other hand, he hates her authority and wants to be free'; 'A Mamma's Boy is a male who has never cut the apron strings and doesn't even know that they are there. He is weak and dependent.'

The Mamma's Boy Syndrome is by no means life-threatening but it will affect the sufferer socially, sexually, and psychologically with concrete and debilitating effects.

Symptoms include: an identification with Mother which arrests his ability to develop a separate and independent identity; a deficiency in masculine identity, feelings of femininity or a questioning of one's male gender identity; blurred roles and a loss of clear boundaries whereby the son is demanded to become responsible for Mother's emotional state and sense of purpose; impaired relationships embodied by an avoidance of women due to a fear of engulfment, avoidance of men because of a mistrust which defends against possible homoerotic feelings or, conversely, enactment of homosexual desires; a sense of inferiority and worthlessness due to a lack of self-identity and an inability to function appropriately and independently; and guilt, shame and self-hate caused by an overwhelming sense of ambivalence towards Mother.

The Mamma's Boy Syndrome has for too long been trivialized in order to protect against the startling implications closer examination of it would provide. It has been wrongly regarded as a by-product of a healthy, loving mother–son relationship rather than acknowledging Mother's own hidden agenda. It is more palatable to protect the sanctity of motherhood than to recognize the engulfing mother's decisive role in her son's ultimate defence against her. Blindly viewed as being unaffected in his functioning, the Mamma's Boy has to suffer its crippling effects without his predicament being acknowledged or marked as anything more than a joke played on him by society.

For my research on MBS, 100 mothers and sons (also included in this total are women interviewed on their relationships with Mamma's Boys) were asked prepared questions in semi-structured interviews. They were uninstructed as to my brief except that my investigation was in the context of the mother–son relationship. Their experiences, feelings and insights may appear sensationalized but they have not been altered except to protect confidentiality. By no means is this method to serve a quantifiable function but rather as concrete illustrations of the concepts put forward. I hope that their case histories and stories will act as a means by which identification and awareness are inspired.

My intention is to examine the Mamma's Boy Syndrome from the perspective of its basis, Mother. The emphasis of this book will detail the unconscious as well as conscious needs, motivations and often faltered development of the Mother that moves her to handicap her son. The Mamma's Boy Syndrome should be viewed as more than a son who has chosen to remain attached to his mother emotionally and psychologically – he has never been given the opportunity to make a conscious choice.

This book will be especially illuminating for those mothers who are unaware of their potent influence and so adamantly believe that they have their son's best interest at heart – it is their own best interest to which they are unknowingly catering. It is for sons who are unaware of the dynamics which are responsible for their feelings of alienation, anger and ambivalence towards Mother and their inability to form meaningful relationships. It is for fathers who are unaware of the crucial contribution they must make in facilitating their sons' separation from Mother and their unconscious collusion in their sons' eventual situation. It is for anyone who wants to gain a better understanding of the Mamma's Boy who remains attached to, and suffocated by, his mother's apron-strings.

CHAPTER ONE

What Is the Mamma's Boy Syndrome?

My mother usually assumed that I was mentally far beyond my age, and she would talk to me as to a grown-up. It was plain that she was telling me everything she could not say to my father, for she early made me her confidant and confided her troubles to me.

C.G. Jung, *Memories, Dreams, Reflections*, p.41

Who is the Mamma's Boy, celebrated as the 'good son' yet mocked and undermined by his unending obedience to Mother? Why does he resign himself to Mother's control instead of fighting to liberate himself from her influence? Is it his conscious and knowing choice to cast himself in this role or has he been manipulated into handing over his power to a Greater Being? What is it that differentiates him from other males? In exploring the answers to these questions, the aim is a better understanding of who the Mamma's Boy is and what the Mamma's Boy Syndrome represents for those males entangled within its web.

There is little known psychologically about the dynamics of the Mamma's Boy Syndrome. Until now, there has been little or no research to investigate it as a condition of epidemic proportion which causes severe emotional, gender and relationship problems. It has not been viewed as a dysfunction, yet it has created generations of boys who have been intimidated into a symbiotic trance paralysing their healthy development and individuation.

The Mamma's Boy Syndrome is a multi-faceted phenomenon which is learned, internalized and adopted by a boy from an early age as a means of self-protection. As a mechanism, the MBS serves to protect him primarily from the real or fantasized recriminations of Mother and secondly, as a consequence of his acquiescence to her, as protection from the outside world which he has not been prepared to function within. Most simply put, the Mamma's Boy is unable to separate appropriately from Mother in relation to his developmental age and, therefore, he learns to survive by remaining dependent on her. Ironically, the overprotective mother, who assumes she is shielding her son from the dangers of the big, bad world, is leaving him unprotected and unsuited to the realistic demands of life (Welldon, 1988, p.9). As a result, the Mamma's Boy must remain reliant on mother – as he was as a helpless infant – if he is to survive.

The Mamma's Boy does not easily lend himself to one concise definition. Rather, the MBS is manifested in varying degrees in direct correlation to the covert and often overt degrees of expectation, manipulation, encouragement, inconsistent behaviour, reward or threat of loss of the one constant variable of this phenomenon, Mother. Her behaviour and attitude towards her son is instrumental to his development as a Mamma's Boy.

A composite image of the Mamma's Boy would merely relegate it to the absurd – not all traits could exist in one living boy and not all circumstances would be experienced by him. The following cases illustrate the gradations of the Mamma's Boy Syndrome and the role Mother plays in its creation and perpetuation.

THE EXTREME MAMMA'S BOY

The case of Harold

Harold, a single man of sixty-four, was the third of five children. His mother 'was powerful, dominating and the decision-maker in the house'. According to Harold, 'she was very depressed, antagonistic and very displeased with her circumstances and role as mother'. She is described as 'resenting having to cater to me and the other offspring although I knew she implicitly loved me'.

His father, a warm, gentle, comforting and friendly man, was never really around. 'He virtually worked around the clock. When he was at home, I felt close to him.' Harold explains:

> My father was a placid man, passively strong in the sense that he resisted the pressure of my mother by saying nothing. He failed by never putting his foot down. He was not a real man as it were. I sometimes acted as the father in the family, a husband to my mother. When we were evacuated during the war, he wasn't with us so I was given the role of pseudo-husband. My mother would talk to me about things I never had to consider before. Such things as whether to take the decision to go back to

London to be with our father again. She actually asked me my views on this! And things like what name should we give the new baby. I was very happy because for the first time I had become important. As I got older I felt that I had replaced my father. I had more formal education than him and therefore I did things like explaining letters and giving simple economic advice to my mother which she regularly asked for. As my older brother left home I was the only man in the house and my mother would depend on me even more. I was happy to be her husband in a sense. It gave me the feeling that I was able to please her and make her happy.

Harold was a lonely child and adolescent. He found it difficult to make friends because of his mother's 'bullying, hectoring and control expressed as love'. This caused definite withdrawal symptoms which made it difficult for him to communicate with others. Harold elaborates:

My mother derided me for not living up to her expectations and therefore did not regard me as a person. I was simply her object that was fed and sent to school. I still find it difficult to communicate with others and that has had a great negative effect on my personality. I am increasingly aware that I have become like my mother. I tend to be short-tempered and quick to become emotional and I treat people roughly as a result. Not very roughly of course. I have unfortunately emulated her but only up to a point. I don't claim to have performed quite as well as she!

His mother was overbearing, although Harold did not realize it until his teens. Before then, it didn't occur to him that he was separate from her because, as Harold explains,

I had no power, no say in my life. I was not permitted to make a decision, I was unaware that I could. It had seemed a natural thing for her to command everything. She never took me into her thoughts when what she had planned concerned me. So in that sense, intrusive is not a strong enough word. She was in total control! I had no affairs to which she could poke her nose, nothing that was private or mine. I was completely under her thumb as a child, I was her possession. The only thing I had control of was playing with the other children in the street and she used to have to lean out the window to call me for meals and I just ignored her. It was the only way that I could exercise any power over her. That was the only set of circumstances in which I could say 'no'. It was complete and utter control. When I reached my teens and started going out more on my own, she would make inquiries and insist that I tell her exactly what I was up to. She didn't like me going out because she didn't want me to ever leave her.

Communication in Harold's family consisted of shouting and screaming. His mother's moods were erratic and inconsistent. As Harold puts it, she was 'inconsiderate, short-tempered and all around disagreeable. She was unpredictable.' He was never spoken to directly but was made to feel that he was the cause of his mother's frustrations. As a result, Harold attempted to protect himself from blame by trying to please her.

Even after he had finally left home at the age of thirty, he would desperately try to win his mother's affections:

I would give her all the things I thought a good son should give his mother like money for a holiday or a present for her birthday. I would take her out on trips in the car. I understood from her that this is what she wanted so I increasingly tried to give her what she wanted but the more I gave her, the more I did for her, the less happy she seemed to be. She had expectations of me that I would become a professional, become wealthy and maintain her in the custom that she was anxious to acquire. I never felt that I could live up to her expectations, that nothing I ever achieved or gave her was ever enough.

Sexuality, a taboo subject in his family, was never discussed. However, the message Harold received from his mother was clear – he somehow did not measure up to her notion of what a man should be:

When I was sixteen, at my mother's request, my father, a tailor by profession, was pretending to be measuring me up for a pair of trousers. What he was doing in fact, was checking if I had a penis of adequate size. Even at my age, I understood that my mother had some doubts as to whether or not I was going to be a 'man'. When my father happily reported back with some glee in his voice that yes, in fact I was a real man, my mother seemed to accept this with a certain amount of pleasure. Of course, this was done without talking to me about it.

Harold was frightened of his mother. He never knew when she would explode or when he would be made to take the brunt of her anger. 'I am scared of all women,' he confessed, 'because I was made to fear her.' He continues:

I see all women as scary. It is a ridiculous thing for a man my age to say but that is how I feel. My fear quenches any sexual desire. You cannot make love to something you are afraid of, can you?

As a child, Harold was often told how much his mother loved him and that he should be 'grateful to have been fed and have a bed to sleep in'. He confesses:

I feel a certain resentment and depression that I had to go through her indignities. But on reflection, it must be pretty intolerant of me because she was never violent. There must be worse cases than mine.

The case of Carlos

Carlos, thirty, is the only child born to Portuguese parents. He describes his mother as 'a glamorous, powerful, strong-willed woman who always gets what she wants. She has a hard life and is not a very happy woman.'

His father, who spent a lot of time at home, is described as 'a horrible man' with whom Carlos was never able to get close. Carlos explains:

I don't like my father very much because he is a very traditional man who pushes women around. He believes women shouldn't think, that their place is in the home. He didn't treat my mother very well at all and he totally ignored me. I never felt that we had any kind of a relationship and I can't remember ever playing or spending time with him. He never gave me anything, neither attention nor money for books or anything. I never expected anything at all from him.

According to Carlos, his parents' marriage is one of convenience. They don't like one another and barely even speak. He is, as he explains, his mother's whole life:

My mother is proud of me and thinks I am beautiful. She spoils me and always gives me the best of everything even if it is a sacrifice for her. I am hers, her little baby and slept in her bed until the age of eight. Until the age of ten, I drank from a baby's bottle which she would prepare. I am her whole life, her whole reason for living. I am her comfort and joy and ally against my father.

Growing up, Carlos did not have many friends. He blames himself for his lack of interest in playing with other children even though he proclaims:

My mother was protective of me and still is. She didn't let me have very much contact with other people. She wanted to keep me to herself. No one was ever good enough for me. So, while the other children were playing on the street, I was dressed up in nice clothing talking to my mother or accompanying her to the movies or shopping. It wasn't easy for me to make friends.

Sexuality was never discussed in this religious Catholic family. While his parents were not, by any means, affectionate towards one another, his mother's love and attention was lavished solely on her son. His father expressed his jealousy and hostility in a manner which left Carlos questioning his own masculinity:

My father would refer to me in the feminine, 'ela', when I was with my mother. Instead of using the masculine plural, he would refer to us both as women. This confused me. I was forced into feeling that I had no choice but to identify with my mother because that is how he saw me. I believed that others would see me in the same way. I couldn't identify with my father, with men, because of the harsh and indifferent way he treated my mother and me. I am left wondering about my maleness and sexuality, whether I am masculine enough or perhaps, too feminine. It is clear what my father thinks of me. Somehow, I don't feel comfortable within myself and have never been with a woman in the sexual sense.

After he completed college, Carlos attempted to leave home and forge a life of his own. His plans were abruptly quashed by the overwhelming guilt he felt at his mother's reaction. Carlos explains:

I wanted to become a priest. My mother was shocked at my decision and took it really badly. She cried and wailed and asked me how I could leave her. I thought she would be proud of me. I realized that it had nothing to do with me wanting to be a priest. It was that she never wanted me to leave her.

It has only been two years since Carlos was successfully able to move away from the home he shared with his parents. He packed two suitcases and told his mother he was going on holiday. A week later he called to tell her that he had moved to England permanently.

> When I moved away from my mother I felt free for the first time in my life. She is my mother and I love her but what is important to her is not important to me. I could never lie to her. She would always know what I was thinking or doing almost like she was inside of me. That is why I think it was important for me to move away from her so I could have my own life. Now, when I go back home to visit, it seems that nothing has changed. She still spoils me by giving me money and cooking for me. She is always happy to have me and cares for me like I'm still a little baby. I think my mother knows it was important for me to move away.

Carlos feels close to his mother 'because she loves me unconditionally'. He adds:

> I can have long conversations with my mother although it is she who does most of the talking, usually about my father. She also tends to place a lot of demands on me which she seems to think is advice. She often tells me that she would like me to move back home again to be her little boy. However, it seems that she respects my decision to have moved away.

THE MODERATE MAMMA'S BOY

The case of Julius

Thirty-two-year-old Julius was born to an English single mother whom he describes as a tomboy, because he 'can't ever recall seeing her in a dress or wearing make-up'. He expresses that 'she is outgoing, warm and caring. She can be irrational and often suffers from a lack of confidence. Once she sets her mind to something though, she gets it done and no one can stand in her way.'

Characterizing his relationship with his mother as 'eccentric', he explains:

> My mother is different. All my friends think she is wonderful but she isn't the image of a mother that I hold. I would like to have the mother who looks after the house better than she does,

cooks and goes out to the women's club so that I wouldn't have to explain her ways to other people.

He elaborates:

Being the only child, I am very important to her and she tries to treat me like a best friend although I don't always want that. All my friends are her friends and she goes out with me whereas I do occasionally like to have my friends separate from her. She acts as though we are a couple and treats me like a partner rather than a son. I know that she will never be the traditional role model mother and I wouldn't want that either, but she is very untypical. Ironically, she is the liberated one in terms of attitudes and lifestyle so there is a role reversal there.

Julius tells me that his childhood was full and enjoyable because his mother made sure that he was allowed to play with toys and other children of his own age.

My mother would play with me all the time. She didn't have much of a childhood as it was wartime, her father was hardly there because he worked overseas and her mother was emotionally distant. She was brought up in an immaculate house and my mother didn't dare breath in case she disturbed something. It wasn't a place for children. As a result of her awful childhood, it was very important to her that mine was happy and it certainly was.

While he was growing up, his mother's job demanded that she travelled the world, so Julius was cared for by a nanny of whom he was 'quite fond of and vice versa'. She was 'strict but fair' and it was her influence, he believes, that instilled in him 'old-fashioned ideas, rules of behaviour and morals'. Julius feels that his mother was not very happy in her role of mother because she struggled very hard to bring him up on her own:

She had no support at all from the family which must have been very hard. My mother left home at eighteen because of the difficult relationship she had with her mother. In fact, my grandmother died never knowing about me because my mother said that she would have totally disapproved. It was only at my grandmother's funeral, when I was eleven, that my mother admitted to the rest of the family that I existed.

He adds:

It makes me angry that my mother kept me hidden because I missed out on having a family when I was young. I was lucky in that I eventually got to know my grandfather and we had a wonderful relationship. My mother doesn't like it at all that I get on much better with the rest of the family than she does. It makes her feel insecure. I almost get the impression that she kept me a secret so she wouldn't have to share me.

He believes that his needs – love, security and approval – were met primarily by his nanny, and later by his houseparents at boarding-school. His mother was able to meet his needs only sporadically, when she was around. Of his mother, Julius says:

She was a good role model in terms of the way she cared for others rather than the way in which she cared for me. I don't think she has done any damage to me – she had a difficult experience of bringing me up and didn't have the support to be a typical mother.

Julius never knew his father. He often wondered what effects this had on him. He elaborates:

I don't know exactly what I missed by not having a father but I feel there is just something I didn't have, something I know I have missed. Perhaps I didn't get socialized into the things that so-called men do like going down to the pub or to football. Maybe the reason that I ended up in my profession is because I have had more of that maternal caring influence than the paternal side of things. I am also quite happy with doing things like cooking, sewing and decorating. I will wear things like silk shirts and waistcoats simply because I like them or the feel of the cloth, which is quite feminine. In fact I have been accused of being gay on several occasions which ties in with the fact that I don't meet the masculine role.

To this he adds:

I find it much easier to get along with women than men. I don't have good relationships at all with men and I find them extremely insensitive. Most of my good friends are women. On certain occasions when I have liked a woman, it has been awkward because she has turned around and said, 'Oh, shock horror, I thought you were gay!' If I turned out to be genuinely gay, I don't think my mother would mind it. She would happily accept it. I think I have missed out on something by not having a father but I am not sure what it is.

Sexuality was openly discussed to the extent that it was almost embarrassing for Julius. He explains:

My mother is very open about sex. She has a totally liberated attitude and, actually, she isn't even entirely sure who my father is! Right from when I was six or seven she was quite keen to make sure that I knew absolutely everything about the facts of life. I guess it didn't do me any harm. As a teenager, she always kept contraceptives in the house for me.

He continues:

She is very, very open about sex although I don't really think she understands the way a lot of modern relationships work. She has a very anti-feeling about marriage and has even said that if I ever did such a stupid thing, as she put it, she wouldn't come to the wedding. Her view doesn't make me rule out marriage entirely. It just makes me feel that I have to be very careful to choose someone that would meet her specifications. I find her attitudes embarrassing.

From the time Julius was a child, his mother consulted him on all major decisions. He viewed this as 'irritating'.

I wished she would have made up her own mind. I saw it as a big responsibility but in some ways flattering. When I got older, she would especially ask my advice on major financial issues. She tends to defer important decisions to me. It often feels like I am her parent particularly when it comes to sorting out her legal or financial affairs. She just doesn't understand about these things or at least pretends that she doesn't. I feel that I have an obligation to look after her. It is something that has to be done. It makes me feel a bit irritated that she doesn't have a husband or boyfriend to share the burden with.

Julius likes to see his mother happy, he tells me, and does go out of his way 'to sometimes please her'. He explains:

I tend to avoid causing her grief because I don't see the point in upsetting her. I know when she is unhappy with me, she makes it obvious. Perhaps it is the way she looks at me, a facial expression, but usually, she will ignore me. So, if an issue doesn't have to be confronted, I will skirt around it because it is just not worth the confrontation. I avoid causing friction at any cost. I feel that I have to protect her – she is someone special.

Julius feels that his mother allowed and encouraged him to develop as his own person. Although she dissuaded him from playing sports, she supported some of his other interests. Of his mother's encouragement, he proclaims:

> She has always encouraged me with music, playing the violin and intellectual things. She was very proud when I got my degree and professional qualifications. I think, to a certain extent, she has encouraged me to do things she didn't do and gets enjoyment when I have been able to achieve them. She has instilled in me a self-esteem and confidence which perhaps, she doesn't have, so through me, she is living out some of those accomplishments. It is not in a way that I think is bad or damaging. She just didn't have the same opportunities.

His mother, he believes, is overly affectionate and dependent on him. He illustrates this point as follows:

> When I go to her because she demands a hug, I will give it to her but sometimes I think she wants a bit too much. I think perhaps, it isn't good to have too close a relationship with one's mother. Close is important but I think I do have to have another life and she should not be encouraged to be dependent on me. I would be much happier if she had a boyfriend. Sometimes I feel she puts too much onto me rather than onto someone else. It is a huge drawback.

Between the ages of eleven to seventeen, Julius was 'packed off and sent away' to boarding-school. Although he chose the school he was to attend, the decision that he was to go was made for him. He thinks the separation was 'a reasonable progression' from his nanny and mother, whom he saw only on weekends and holidays:

> There is an element of my mother sending me to boarding school in order to hide me away from the family. She felt it very important that I find a school that could give me stability which she couldn't give me because she was always away working. The fact that I was happily out of the way was a plus. In retrospect, I can understand why she did it but I don't necessarily forgive it.

Julius moved out on his own at twenty-seven although, as he notes, he hardly ever really lived with his mother. After boarding-school, he travelled for a year and then went to university. He found the long summer holidays which he spent at his mother's to be 'torturous at times'.

I couldn't bear living with my mother any longer. She lives in absolute chaos and mess. Although she wanted to be my partner and best friend, I found her habit of staying up late and making sure I was in safely, quite irritating.

Julius explains that he knows exactly where he stands with his mother:

Being an only child I am very fond of her but at the same time I like to maintain a sense of distance. I like to have my own life and sometimes, I think, she would like me to be closer with her than I am. She is very fond of me and almost possessive perhaps, but I don't think it has damaged me. I am the only one she can count on. I definitely feel that I have to be there for her because sadly, there is no one else.

The case of Mark

The second of two sons born to English parents, twenty-three-year-old Mark was treated differently from his brother eight years his senior 'because of the complications of my birth'. Mark was born prematurely and was a sickly infant and child.

He explains that he was very much a wanted child and that his mother had had a miscarriage two years before he was born. Mark describes his mother as 'incredibly down-to-earth and practically minded'. He adds:

My mother is maternal. She is sort of the typical Jewish mother and although my brother would say she is clawing, I don't think she is any more prying than any other mother. She has a lot of respect and has always fought for me. She is like all mothers and will ask, 'what's wrong' and if I answer, 'nothing' she will not press too hard. She has always been very keen to cultivate a warmth and bond which is the main thing in her life that she is so proud of. We are very close. On the whole, I have never felt wanting for attention. I was fairly easy about getting on with my own thing but whenever I wanted attention, my mother was there for me. I think she loves being a mother although I don't know if she enjoyed the 'whole trip'. I don't know if any mother really does.

Mark portrays his relationship with his mother as 'stable, warm and open'. He tells me:

We have a rare ability to be open and honest with each other. There is not a lot of resentment from either side. There is a lot of humour. It is a fairly rare relationship in terms of my peers who don't have any respect for their mothers. As a result, I have very few illusions about relationships. I have lived with a good relationship and I know what the general criteria are.

Mark would listen as his mother complained to him about his father. He believes his mother confided in him because 'my father didn't really listen to her. Now that he is getting older, he is listening more which probably means that she doesn't have to confide in me as much.'

Mark characterizes his father as 'a man with an incredible sense of responsibility, who has always been a rock'. He is 'always there when he is required'. As Mark explains, by the time he was born, his father had lost his ability to 'get irritable on key'. His father, in later years, had become 'sappy' because 'it was easier than verbalizing what was bothering him'. He sees his father as losing face and explains:

My father has no patience. It has come to the point now that he will be feverishly demanding me to do a simple job which he should be doing and I will just look at him and say, 'no'. I am not disrespectful to him but if I know that he is wrong, I will confront him with it and that usually shuts him up. He is like Joan of Arc ... a martyr.

Mark remembers playing with his father and states, 'I never knew when he would "lose it". I remember building models with him and I smashed to bits the ones that he had worked hours to make.' Mark also recounts that his father was more concerned about the garden being torn to pieces than enjoying the time with his son.

His parents' marriage is a happy one. Mark confirms this belief with the following:

My mother was very young and had very little confidence when she married my dad. He was strong and sure. Over the years, they have compensated each other. Now, my dad is like an old woman and my mother has taken over. I don't think anything happens unless my mum really wants it to. She is not assertively manipulative but she does always get what she wants out of him. I think their marriage is stable and they are very happy.

Mark slept with his parents until the age of seven and explains:

I slept in my parents' bed, on my mum's side. She would roll over and my dad would land up on the floor! This went on until I had a tonsil operation with the idea being that I would be more contented to sleep on my own. One night though, after the operation, I went into their bed and my mother rolled over and my dad fell out and smashed his head on the way down. He went into a rumble and in wanting to lash out, he hit the wall and started crying. Mum started laughing at him. I ran out of the room in a terror. That was the last time I ever dared step foot into their bed.

Mark considers himself spoiled and special. He tells me that his mother instilled self-esteem in him by always highlighting what he was good at. 'She hated when I was criticized and has always been quite defensive of me. She would always stick up for me.' He continues:

I was made to feel confident about myself. I am comfortable within myself and from the age of fifteen, I didn't go out with girls. I wasn't part of that scene. I was always more eccentric and had a lot of time to develop myself. I didn't have the need to sort of be attached to any other female. Not being reliant on being in a relationship goes back to being comfortable with Mum, not needing a surrogate.

Mark was not an athletic child. He was precocious and liked performing and drawing. It was 'in these things which I tended towards anyway' that his mother encouraged him.

Up to the age of eight or nine, I would put on shows using the sofa as a stage. I would get dressed up in my mother's clothes ... bits of whatever she wasn't wearing. She didn't seem to mind. Women's clothes are always more theatrical! My mother reacted with amusement. I don't think she was ever embarrassed and she certainly never deterred me from expressing myself.

Mark also has fond memories of playing with his mother. He helped her clean the house and says, 'She would make a game of it.' He now understands his mother's cleanliness to be an obsession. He feels that he is more balanced when it comes to tidiness, where with her, 'it is an unhealthy preoccupation'.

Mark believes that his mother never pressured him into meeting any expectations she might have had for him. He explains:

My parents come from a middle-class working family and I am sure my mother would have loved me to become a doctor. It is the Jewish thing ... the next step on the ladder! I can remember when I was fifteen telling her that I was going into the arts. She wasn't very happy. She saw it as playing around, not really something serious. So, when I did my A-levels, I did economics partly to be taken seriously. When I went to university my father was not at all pleased that I was going into the arts but my mother thought it was only fair that they give me a chance to do what I want.

Although there is open communication in the family, Mark is careful of what he says and prefers to avoid confrontation with his mother. 'My mother is prone to thinking that any argument or criticism is directly pointed at her ... but she is not as paranoid as my dad.' When Mark's mother is upset with him, she will tell him directly, 'she will not put a guilt trip on me.'

The 'birds and the bees' were never explained to him by his parents. However, Mark concedes that there was 'a sense of the usual family neurosis about anything which is sort of remotely deviant from heterosexuality'. He believes that the message he received from his parents about sex was that it should be fun.

At twenty-one, Mark moved out of the family home to attend university. He is now living at home again.

I found that when I was away, I was more communicative with my mother. When we saw each other it was fresh and there was a lot to talk about. When I am living at home I tend to want to keep things to myself. I tend to sit on things and not blurt them out. I enjoy living at home and appreciate the cleanliness, and the portions, quality and frequency of food my mother prepares for me. I have a general respect for the home environment my mother has created.

Mark admits that his mother is 'ideal'. He clarifies this statement with the following:

There are very few other qualities that I would want my mother to have. In my mind, if her glitches were taken away, she would be 'perfect'. It is the imperfections that make the mother thing and nothing else. If those were taken away, she would be someone whom I would feel totally attracted to.

THE MILD MAMMA'S BOY

The case of Adam

Adam, thirty-one, is the second of two sons born to Austrian parents. He was a popular child, he recalls, with many friends. He enjoyed a full social life and participated in various sports.

His mother was a 'typical housewife' who had no interests outside the immaculately clean home she kept. Adam describes his mother:

> She was emotionally barren and still is. Yet, she was able to provide a sense of stability by the very fact that she was basically there all the time. I was raised entirely by my mother without much support from my father or anyone else. Her whole life revolved around her children. She had little contact with other women, and had few friends. She was quite isolated and had little peer contact. She must have been very lonely.

His mother did virtually everything for him. He jokes:

> The only thing I was allowed to do for myself was go to the loo when I was at that age. If she could have done it for me, she would have!

His father was very strict. 'It was the role delegated to him,' Adam notes. He was the authority figure 'Mother would turn to if she couldn't handle something on her own'. Adam speaks of his father:

> He was very much absent in my life. He was busy with his work and other things, such as women. With that said, he was still very much the power force in the house who made all the decisions. I don't ever remember playing with him as a child. He was completely unemotional and uninvolved in my life. He was merely a financial provider.

Adam characterizes his parents' marriage as 'pragmatic':

> My parents basically married because my brother was born. I find it difficult to believe that there was ever anything I would describe as love between the two of them. Although my mother confided in me that she did love my father, I don't understand it – he was emotionally abusive in the sense that he cruelly withheld love from her.

The only love Adam feels that he received from his mother was in the form of material things. 'Money was really important to her,' Adam explained, 'because it was used to control me. My mother would threaten to take away my pocket money or refuse to buy me that something special if I dared to displease her. Ironically enough, the only expectation she had of me was that I would go out and make money. Unfortunately, I am still dependent on her financially.'

From what Adam tells me, his mother clearly longed for communication. There was none between her and her husband. She desperately turned to her son:

> My mother needed to feel that someone was there for her, someone who would acknowledge and listen to her. As a result, she had no boundaries, no sense of my need for privacy. Often in the morning, without knocking, she would walk into my room and start having a conversation with me. My bed was hidden from view so she didn't even know whether I was up or not. This did not deter her. She would keep on talking until I had no choice but to respond to her. This is indicative of the kind of relationship I had with my mother.

He continues:

> I resented my mother imposing herself on me and experienced it as engulfment. I felt that she didn't let me breathe or have a thought of my own. She looked to me as being there for her but I did not want that responsibility, I did not want to care for her needs. I protected myself from her intrusions by withdrawing emotionally. I completely cut myself off from her. I relate to all women as demanding me to be open and emotional with them. As a result – by cutting off – I react to them as I did to my mother. It is the only way I have learned to cope.

At seventeen, Adam went to Los Angeles for a year. On his return he moved back home to attend a nearby university. He then travelled to India for a year and again, on his return, moved back into the family home. His permanent move came about when he was twenty-six.

> In my late teens I felt a contempt for my mother. I had to get away from her. Basically, I think it is part of the reason I chose to move permanently to London. I had to separate from her once and for all. I had to get away from her for good.

His parents divorced shortly after his move. 'I feel that I am not there for my mother even though her whole life centered around me,' he says with a tinge of guilt in his voice. 'My brother lives in a different town and I am here. It is pretty sad. She put all her energies into her sons and what does she get at the end of her life? She must be very lonely.'

The case of Fabio

An only child, thirty-five-year-old Fabio was born to Canadian parents who had tried for seven years to have a baby. When Fabio was born, even though his mother had secretly hoped for a girl, 'she was ecstatic and thought I was the greatest thing'.

He describes his mother as a 'feminine woman, compassionate, understanding and supportive'. She is also 'shy and withdrawn' and because of that, Fabio tells me, 'people tend to hurt her although they don't mean to. It is just the way she interprets things.' He reckons, 'She is not very strong where she will stand up to people. With my prompting, she has become a little more so, but it is just not her character. She is pretty reserved and she kind of stands behind my dad.'

Of his relationship with his mother he says:

I think she was a little over-protective but it is understandable since I am her only child. I was very close to my mum and we got along very well. To this day we have a pretty good relationship. I have a special bond with my mother and she thinks the same. There is something special between the two of us.

Fabio was an athletic, popular child who had many friends but was discouraged from bringing them home. Left on his own to play, he was confined to the kitchen so that he would not disturb the order of the rest of the house. He does not remember ever actually playing with his mother, though he does recall spending entire days with her as she cleaned. He expands:

It felt normal to me but I am a neat freak now. My mother did virtually everything for me. She did my bed. She insisted on it and I know why. Simply because I wouldn't do it as well as her.

Fabio's mother did not intrude upon his privacy. He had his own room and his mother never went through his things. He thinks for a moment and adds, 'and if she did, she never told me about it!'

Fabio describes his father as a 'stubborn, hard-working individual who doesn't expect support from anyone. He never complained and would silently shoulder responsibility. He is very independent and that is probably where I got my sense of independence from.'

Fabio's father was very much present when he was growing up; 'I guess he was around physically but not emotionally. He was around for the family, made all the decisions but didn't support my mother. My father just doesn't communicate all that well. He is not a real close person, but maybe I am not either.' Fabio elaborates:

I wish I had a closer relationship with my father. As a child, he was involved as a coach on my hockey team but I don't ever recall playing with him. I could never lace up a pair of skates or play baseball with him and that is what I really wanted us to do. But in any sport I played, he was always included in some way. He would either drive me to my games or be in the stands watching, so he was good in that respect. Unfortunately, he never was able to express himself to me and say 'way to go'. He just sat in the spectator stands quietly.

Fabio did not feel pressured to meet his mother's expectations. He knew for a fact that she wanted him to be the best that he could possibly be and that meant successful. He understood that he was to go to university and become a doctor. 'If I worked out that would be great and if I didn't, she did her best.' Fabio hated blood and his mother accepted his decision to become an engineer.

He did not particularly view his mother as encouraging. He explains:

I don't actually recall anything that my mother encouraged me to do but what she never did was prevent me from doing what I wanted. She let me make my own decisions and do my own thing which instilled in me a certain confidence and self-esteem.

The only occasion Fabio does remember his mother being ostensibly encouraging was when after graduating from university, she pushed him to travel through Europe for a year instead of starting work immediately. This came as a surprise to Fabio:

I guess my mother wanted me to travel and see the world because she never had that chance. She wanted me to do it for her as much as for me. I think it was the greatest thing she could have done.

Fabio considers himself to be 'self-directing' and very independent. He puts it down to the following:

Being an only child I didn't really have anyone to talk to so I was compelled into making decisions on my own. I have always been very stubborn and from an early age I knew what I wanted and I just kept doing it until I achieved my goal. I don't know if I did things which particularly pleased my mother but of course, as any child, I wanted to please her in order to get her affirmation. I know there are things I did which she disapproved of but I still did them. I still played sports even though she didn't encourage me and when I was older, took up flying although she thought it was dangerous and a waste of money. She would support me in whatever I had chosen to do and would not shoot down any of my decisions. In that respect, I was allowed to assert my independence without a struggle.

His parents' marriage, Fabio is certain, is not a happy one. He explains:

I know for a fact that my mother is not happy being married because she has told me so on many occasions. She probably realized before they married that my dad wasn't exactly the most emotional, supportive man but that was the decision she made at the time. She would probably like to divorce right now but I have told her that I don't think it is such a good idea. They are both seventy-two so what is the point of going through all that? It would be unsettling. I tell her she should just do her own thing which she does. She travels on her own with her friends and is involved in the church. My father became very close to his own mother after an accident he had at eighteen. At the age of thirty, he didn't want to leave his mother so when my parents did marry, they lived with his mother for three years. If I asked my dad if he is happily married, he would probably just shrug his shoulders and say, 'yes, things are fine.' But I know my mom is absolutely miserable.

Fabio's mother would confide in him about her relationship with his father. He reveals:

My mother used to confide a lot in her single brother but when he passed away she landed up confiding in me. She felt uncomfortable confiding in close friends because she believed that family matters should remain in the family so I was the person who had to listen. It was just a matter of her talking for about an hour or so and getting off her chest what was bothering her. I had absolutely no problem with it. I never thought about it when I was young, it was just the thing I had to do. She never had my father's support and as a result, I ended up being her emotional pillar. Given the situation she was in, I don't feel resentful towards her but I don't think that I should have been saddled with my parents' marital problems. As a child growing up, there was a lot of stuff on my shoulders that a kid really shouldn't have to bear but I think I was able to handle it.

He continues:

I resented my dad for not listening to my mom and not taking care of her as well as I thought he should have. Why couldn't he see it, why was he making my life so much more difficult when I had other things to deal with? Why did I have to tend to her needs when it was supposed to be his job, his duty? As I have gotten older, I still believe that he should have been there for my mother but I don't resent him as much. I still think though, he should have done better. But that is just how my dad is and nothing will change.

Fabio did not confide in his mother. 'I would work out my own problems,' he says, 'and I kept things to myself.'

The family communication consisted of two extremes – long periods of absolute silences or 'rip-roaring' arguments. There was very little in between, Fabio tells me. There was never any physical violence but Fabio remembers being scared 'because as a child, you don't like to hear your parents screaming, yelling and threatening each other'.

When Fabio's mother was upset with him she would demonstrate her disapproval by giving him the silent treatment:

My mother has a terrible tendency of reading into things, of thinking I am doing things behind her back. If something would displease her or if she would misinterpret something I said, she would tell me about it but it would take a while because of the way she is. I wouldn't hear about it the following hour or day but it would eventually come out after a long cooling-off period. She would be distanced, cold and only speak to me in sharp, short tones or ignore me completely. It was always the same scenario and after a couple of weeks, she would be back to her normal self.

He continues:

Her silent treatment would upset me because I know she believed that I was out to hurt her when I was doing the complete opposite. She just reads into things, the stupidest things which just makes no sense to a person who is logical. However, my mother is not a logical individual. She never was. It is her problem and she has to deal with it but I try not to antagonize her into one of her moods.

Fabio does not believe that he was given any negative messages from the fact that the topic of sex was never discussed within the family. His father was not a particularly demonstrative man and he did not show any affection towards his wife or son. Fabio's mother was only 'moderately affectionate' towards Fabio although he says, 'I was my mother's whole life, she turned all her attention towards me.'

As a child, Fabio was made to believe that he had to take care of his mother. He eventually realized that 'it is not my status to take care of her, she could take care of herself.' He adds:

She needed somebody to talk to and I was always there for that. I did as much as I could to help her out with items which were maybe technically complicated or with things my dad had no patience for. There was a sense of guilt on my part but I am stubborn and realized that I had done the best that I could in supporting her for as long as I could. However, the time has come for her to just stand on her own. There is a little bit of guilt but I think things are working themselves out.

Fabio lived at home until he married at the age of twenty-six. His mother's reaction to the news of his imminent marriage and leaving home was not what 'I had expected actually'. He recounts the incident:

My mother took the news that I was going to marry very badly. Instead of her being really happy for me she started to cry. She turned her back on me and said, 'What am I going to do without you? Who am I going to talk to? My little baby is leaving me.' She saw me as being pulled away from her and was concerned that she wouldn't have my support. She was only thinking of herself.

When Fabio married, he had to make a conscious shift away from his mother. He speaks of it candidly:

I made a choice, an internal choice. My wife would always be the primary woman in my life, no doubt about it. I made that decision a long time ago. It is difficult for my mother and I know that she feels left out of the picture but perhaps one day when she stops being so resentful, she will realize that the bond we share can never be stripped away. My mother hasn't lost me. There will always be that special bond between us, no matter what. My attitude is that Mum will eventually come to accept that I have my own life. She is not the only mother in the world who has gone through this. She will just have to adapt and adjust, like everyone else.

These cases are intended to serve as eye-openers, to make the reader confront the reality which exists in so many mother–son relationships. These are not isolated cases but chillingly apt examples of how the Mamma's Boy Syndrome emerges. It is not a phenomenon which is born in a vacuum: it develops primarily as the result of a mother's unconscious need to keep her son hostage, restrained from separating and becoming a self-supporting individual so that she may obtain from him her sense of worth, fulfilment and power. She is so discontented with her lot that she needs her son as her comfort and protection. He is held prisoner and must comply to her demands or meet his execution – the loss of his mother's love and approval: 'I know when she is unhappy with me ... she will ignore me'; 'My mother would threaten to take away my pocket money or refuse to buy me that something special if I dared to displease her ... '; 'If something would displease her ... she would be distanced, cold and only speak to me in sharp, short tones or ignore me completely.' The MBS is also facilitated by the father or, more aptly, the lack of a father as a positive role-model for identification. Father's absence, either physical or emotional, his hostility, aggressiveness or apathy do not lend protection or a means of escape to a son who is jailed by his mother.

What is most alarming is that the son blindly puts his trust and faith in Mother and is then blinded by her all-enveloping shadow. As a mother, she has an inherent power to influence and shape her son's development and sense of self. Mother's underlying desperation to get her needs met, at the cost of her son's healthy maturation and psychological well-being, overshadows her judgement and her ability to see clearly that what she is ultimately doing is using and abusing her son. She is afflicting him with a dysfunction which causes dire difficulties in many aspects of his life.

A son's relationship with his mother is the only reference he has for 'motherly love'. To contemplate her motives in keeping him dependent would shatter the illusion he holds of their loving relationship and he would risk losing his mother whom he so naturally needs for love, protection and, ideally, to nurture his self-esteem and facilitate his independence. The Mamma's Boy unconsciously remains unaware of the full extent of his mother's manipulation as a means of not having to deal with the pain that admitting it to himself would produce. He may have reservations about their relationship, but he cannot acknowledge fully his conflicting feelings or resentment towards Mother without explaining them away: 'I don't think she has done any damage to me'; 'I feel that I have to protect her – she is someone special'; 'I think she was a little over-protective but it is understandable since I am her only child'; 'I definitely feel that I have to be there for her because, sadly, there is no one else.'

In not admitting to himself that his needs are neglected – be it the need for privacy, friends, his father, or separation from Mother – he is ensuring that Mother will always be there to give him the scraps of conditional love he has come to yearn and depend on. He justifies Mother's behaviour and the relationship they share as a means of denying his reality which, if looked at properly, would be too horrific and shaming to accept. All he understands is that he is confronted with opposing feelings towards Mother which he must mask. So, in a learned and rewarded survival technique, the Mamma's Boy aids and abets his mother's behaviour in fear of losing her entirely.

The mother–son relationship, in the case of the MBS, is an oppressive one which warrants Mother taking responsibility for her actions. It is not, however, my intention to blame Mother for the injustices served upon her innocent son. Rather, it must be understood and acknowledged in the context that she too is a victim of her own deeply scarring experiences, which she subsequently and inadvertently passes on through the victimization of her son.

With that put forward, my hope is that a blind eye will no longer be turned to the power inherent in motherhood, with its capacity to pass on to the son a legacy of maladjustment and deprivation veiled as motherly concern. The only crime that sons imprisoned in the Mamma's Boy Syndrome have committed is instinctively to place their loving trust and belief in Mother.

CHAPTER TWO

How the Mamma's Boy Is Conceived

He is all the mother's, from the top to toe.
William Shakespeare, *The Tragedy of Richard III*,
III, i, 175

James James
Morrison Morrison
Weatherby George Dupree
Took great
Care of his Mother,
Though he was only three.
A.A. Milne, 'Disobedience'

For an infant, what is healthy and acceptable to sustain him is Mother's ability and willingness to satisfy his every emotional and physical need. He is dependent on Mother for his survival. But at some point he must be given the cues to prod and facilitate his independence. In the case of the MBS, these cues are nonexistent, unclear or laden with contradictory messages.

Why is it that some sons become Mamma's Boys while others are able to separate appropriately from Mother? Are Mamma's Boys born with an inherent psychic need or genetic disposition to hang on to Mother? Or rather, is the clue to their behaviour to be found in Mother's nursing of this role with delusions that she must continue, long after its sell-by-date, to provide for her son's needs so that he will, in turn, reciprocate by providing for hers?

There are no absolutes when it comes to answering these enigmatic questions. There are, however, underlying mechanisms at play, regardless of the severity of the MBS, which are clearly pointed to. Here, those mechanisms will be extrapolated in order to investigate the function they serve in the conception of the Mamma's Boy Syndrome.

THE BLURRING OF BOUNDARIES

Emotional incest

In becoming privy to his mother's adult world, a son will feel privileged and special. There is great power in knowing you are the sole focus in someone else's life and the son will magically perceive that he possesses a unique 'power' enabling him to make Mother happy, to please her and alleviate her distress. He is rewarded and loved for his behaviour and rightfully understands it to be a requisite for their relationship. More importantly to him, his relationship with mother is a requisite for his survival.

When a mother deliberately shares her secrets, marital and personal problems, fears and insecurities with her son, she is subtly demanding that he satisfy her needs. He unconsciously understands that in order to maintain his special status and sense of importance, he is obligated to maintain the position expected of him. To his detriment, he will unknowingly forgo his own needs and growth so as not to lose the coveted status bestowed on him by Mother. He is all too willing to listen to her problems in return for securing his privileged position. As Julius in Chapter 1 expressed, 'I saw it as a big responsibility but in some ways flattering....'

A pseudo-intimacy based on enmeshment and conditional love is fostered between mother and son. It is from this 'intimacy' that he receives messages of his self-worth. In other words, the message he receives is clear: 'I am special, loved, needed and powerful on condition that I please and make Mother happy by meeting her emotional needs.'

In demanding that her emotional needs be taken care of, she is, in effect, unconsciously seducing her son into becoming a parent to his mother. In so doing, he is being deprived of the fulfilment of his own needs and wants in lieu of his mother's, which signals to him his low value. He comes to internalize the belief that by adapting to her demands he will in turn get his own met and will not be abandoned, because he is meaningful to Mother as her caretaker. The son's role as Mother's carer is nurtured and reinforced by the approval and love he perceives to arise from gratifying her. It is in this manner that she has underpinned her son's dependence.

In the cases you have read in Chapter 1, the only source of tangible love Mother feels available to her, whether it be in a stale, lonely or abusive marriage or as a single mother, is from her son (this topic will be explored further in Chapter 3). As in incest, when a trusted grown-up uses a child to gratify adult needs, Mother in this instance, is inappropriately using her son to gratify her emotional demands.

The boundaries are blurred and the child understands that his compliance is necessary in order to gain Mother's love and approval. In effect, she is stimulating the child to gratify herself (Kramer, 1980, p. 328). This is emotional incest.

It is impossible to consider incest as a loving, healthy relationship. Nor should the emotionally incestuous mother–son relationship be considered in any other light. The mother–son bond in this instance is merely a means of manipulation which obligates her son to meet her needs and remain dependent in return for the sense of worth and acknowledgement awarded him for his compliance.

This son is victimized and hindered by his mother's wants and demands. Saddled with inappropriate adult responsibility, he is without the freedom to experience a fit and healthy childhood and is arrested from moving on to future developmental stages. Healthy adulthood becomes inaccessible, and his need for Mother and vice versa is secured.

MOTHER'S GROWN-UP BABY

Infantilization and objectification

Mother's conscious as well as unconscious infantilization of her son is yet another way in which a boy becomes prey to the Mamma's Boy Syndrome. As previously stated, when a mother meets her son's every need, she is hampering his eventual developmental growth and ability to function independently as a healthy individual. He will remain unsuited to challenge life on his own.

The son, still treated as an infant, is drawn into dependency because, according to Freud, 'the infant is hedonistic, seeks satisfaction and withdraws from "unpleasure" ' (Freud, 1923). In effect, the mother is unknowingly utilizing this premise to ensure her son's psychological and emotional dependence on her. The son fantasizes, or gathers from his experiences, that mother will indeed withdraw her love – causing him, as Freud put it, unpleasure. Therefore, the son will want to retain, at any cost, the protection and comfort Mother offers. His dependence is rewarded by his needs being met and Mother, in turn, is rewarded by his 'denial of separateness' (Welldon, 1988, p. 68).

By keeping her son an infant – after all, a helpless baby requires its mother for survival – Mother's belief that she is in fact powerful, needed and in total control of her son is supported. When he attempts to assert his independence she becomes angry, as she risks losing her identity as Mother, so often her sole source of status. Fourteen-year-old Ethan tells of his experience:

> My mother still asks me to sleep with her. She treats me like a baby and always tells me that, when I was young, I used to sit in her lap and give her cuddles. She wishes I was still at that age and tells me to pretend and act younger. She doesn't treat me like I am fourteen ... Mum shouldn't treat me like I was a baby ... If I argue a lot and tell her I am not a baby any more she gets angry at me and ignores me.

By rewarding a son with love and care and threatening him with its loss if he does not comply with her demands of passiveness and dependency, Mother is guaranteeing that her son will be unable fully, if at all, to break away from her.

A son, objectified and depersonalized, is viewed by Mother as a 'toy' or 'thing' (Granoff and Perrier, 1980), as an object whose sole purpose is to give her pleasure. He has been used by Mother since infancy and even though he is no longer an infant, he still feels powerless to assert himself for fear of her recriminations and criticism. Eventually, the son also comes to experience himself as an object without self-trust or worth, and will disown his capacity to want, feel and need. He is stripped of his intrapsychic existence and experiences himself as empty and void, with his world fixed to his mother's perceptions and judgments of it. He is depleted to the extent that he merely exists as a 'dehumanized extension of mother's body' (Kramer, 1980, p. 330).

As Mother's object, worthless and diminished, he has no choice but to submit to remaining her appendage, if he is to survive. Mother's undying devotion and commitment to her son is, therefore, not what it seems. Her hope in keeping him needy and helpless is that he will continue to respond to her desires. It is not a nurturing bond but insensible manipulation.

ADDICTED TO MOTHER

The sanctioned drug

Induced by insecurity and the fear of having to acknowledge his feelings of coping alone in a world for which he has not been prepared, the Mamma's Boy's drug is not a substance, but his all-consuming dependence on, and need to care for, Mother. Chosen without conscious deliberation or choice, his addiction to mother supplies him not only with a false sense of protection and security but, more importantly, with a false sense of self-worth. According to *The Oxford English Dictionary*, addiction, from the Latin word 'addicere', means 'to give oneself up or to devote oneself as a servant'. In this sense, the Mamma's Boy is surrendering himself exclusively to the power of his stimulus, Mother.

By making Mother into his sole focus in life, all his energies are spent serving, pleasing and fulfilling her whims and desires. In so doing, he is indirectly meeting his own need for a sense of value, which is stimulated by caring for Mother. He becomes dependent on serving Mother for his 'fix' – pleasurable feelings about himself – which perpetuate his dependence on her and his role as her caretaker.

His addiction is the mood-altering effect that the process of taking care of Mother supplies – distraction from having to admit and explore his own needs, inadequacies and existence. His addiction to Mother means that he can remain inauthentic and not risk the pain of feeling anything at all except that which is induced by his dependency. This state, familiar to him, is far more predictable and safe (even if he occasionally has a bad 'trip') than the reality which, without it, he would be forced to face. Therefore, Mother becomes his panacea which anaesthetizes him from having to make choices and explore his sense of inner suffering and loneliness. Without her, he would be confronted with pain and the anxieties of the real world (Socarides, 1978, p. 97).

Rather like a work addict (workaholic), whose sole identity and purpose is begot from his relationship with his work and achievement, the son addicted to his mother establishes a relationship with his drug based upon how well and consistently he can meet her needs and demands. In both instances, the addict is centered around one activity which is to his detriment and excludes him from addressing other internal and external aspects of his life.

In the belief that she is supplying her son with what he needs, Mother initiates and feeds his addiction by acting as his 'pusher'. She is all too willing to supply him with what he craves because her pay-off is his lifelong dependency on her. By making him feel good and seemingly taking away his real problems, she becomes his highest priority and his most important relationship. She is convinced, as is her son, that without her he will not be able to function in the world. By supplying him with a false sense of security and self-worth, she believes that her son will be unable and unwilling to find a substitute for her. Her hope is that as long as he remains hooked, he will be unable to envision clearly that there are available options for a full and independent life beyond his dependency on Mother.

As with any sanctioned drug that is prescribed and ingested in moderation, Mother is invested with properties that are beneficial and necessary for her son's well-being. However, an overdose of something even inherently good can have detrimental side-effects. *Warning*: In the case of the mother–son relationship, too much mothering may lead to the long-term effects of the Mamma's Boy Syndrome.

IDENTIFICATION WITH MOTHER

Identification with the abuser

A child's individual identity is contingent upon the gradual process of separation of the self from Mother. It is the child's dominant need to move from the complete support of his mother to a position of self-support and individuation. Keeping in mind that the general developmental theories to be discussed pertain to both girls and boys, this segment will deal with the developmental stages specifically in terms of the male child.

According to Mahler's theory of separation–individuation (Mahler *et al.*, 1975) which takes place before Freud's Oedipal stage, this phase of development occurs between the ages of 18 to 36 months when 'the infant is attempting to evolve and jealously guard his developing self-image from infringement by the mother and other important figures'. Separation–individuation is a natural and healthy attempt of the child to free himself from the earlier fusion with mother during the symbiotic phase, when he was totally helpless and dependent on her for his identity and existence.

In separating from Mother, whom he considers as part of his body while she considers him as part of hers, the child is determined to renounce his mother and the pleasure with which she provides him. This is a difficult and painful task even under optimum conditions but for the son whose mother is not sufficiently secure to encourage and affirm her son's separation, it is even more threatening and unsafe. When Mother unconsciously or consciously impedes this process, her aim is that he continue to meet her requirements by fulfilling his half of the symbiosis. Her need is to maintain the oneness that she so blissfully experienced from her son as a vicarious source of sensual gratification. With unconscious anger at the thought of him growing up and physically apart from her, she insistently continues, beyond the point that it is constructive for his psychological and intrapsychic maturation, to overindulge his every need as an attack against his separation and burgeoning wish and capacity to be alone. In so doing, not only is she trying to lure him into remaining artificially attached to her so she may benefit from the pleasure she perceived to gain during symbiosis, but she is also establishing for her son as well as herself, 'that she is all powerful, all controlling and the only one to protect his interests and insure his survival' (Socarides, 1978, p. 143).

According to Mahler and her co-workers (Mahler *et al.*, 1975, p. 215), enduring individuality rests upon the attainment of two levels of the sense of identity: the awareness of being a separate and individual entity and the awareness of a gender-defined self-identity. Without Mother's willingness to allow her son to successfully traverse the separation–individuation phase and become an autonomous being – an individual with a separate identity – he cannot develop a healthy gender-identity. Since gender-identity is at the core of self-identity and he remains fused with Mother, his gender-identity and sense of belonging to the male sex will consequently continue to be shaped by his primary object of identification, namely the mother.

For the son, then, Mother is the source by which his masculinity will be defined. She is his predominate symbol of masculinity – the all-powerful, strong and punitive 'phallic and penisless' Mother (Socarides, 1988, p. 63) who is capable of dominating not only him, but Father and all men as well (Father's role in facilitating his son's separation from Mother will be discussed in Chapter 3). In this case, the son will emulate his mother's 'masculinity', resulting in his internalization of a diluted and narrow prescription of his assigned gender. The way he views his masculinity will also be affected by the messages he receives from her about men: when Mother consistently degrades and belittles the worth of Father or men in general, by bad-mouthing and deprecating them in a sexual manner, she is revealing her disappointment and disdain for the male gender and hindering his budding identification with the gender to which he belongs.

For Mother, the development of masculine tendencies in her son signals an end to the perceived intimacy they once shared, under her control. She punishes his 'challenging' behaviour and emasculates her son by discouraging his masculine inclinations (Stoller, 1975, p. 44). In so doing, she is convinced that he will remain her captive provider, her creation, created solely to meet her demands and needs. Mahler and her co-workers wrote that the mother must be able to relinquish her son's body and 'ownership of his penis to him' (Mahler *et al.*, 1975). However, this mother is willing neither to allow her son's separation nor to acknowledge his need for masculine identification.

Instead, she sabotages his attempts to separate and castrates his emerging masculinity.

A healthy, secure mother supports her son's separation and validates his unfolding self-identity. She encourages his identification with Father or other male role models and rejoices in her son's independence and acquired self-esteem. Conversely, the mother who interferes with the formation of her son's physical and emotional leaving uses him to validate her own wavering sense of identity. She needs him to affirm her power and status as a mother and unconsciously neuters him so that he will not become a man like all the others, whom she perceives as having degraded her worth.

It is safer and less threatening to identify with Mother and become the 'male' she wants him to be than to be like Father and the other men who are at the brunt of her attacks. In essence, by aligning himself with Mother he is keeping her close and at the same time vicariously procuring her power which serves to protect him against her. By identifying with Mother, he will never have to fear her again. This mechanism of identification is referred to as 'projective identification', and it is an identification with the aggressor. The son is identifying with his abuser, his mother, and internalizes her contempt for men which he will act out against them.

Torn between the need for security and protection which identifying with mother affords him and his instinctual drive towards self and gender differentiation, he is left confused and unclear: he identifies with feelings of femininity and has a deficient sense of being masculine. The result is a son invested with the castrating mother's rendering of what a man should be: a Mamma's Boy who is ultimately effeminate and dependent on Mother for his identity and sense of self.

ASEXUALITY

My heart (and other parts) belongs to Mother

For males, Mother is the first woman with whom they 'fall in love' and for some, as they have been warned, the only woman never to break their heart. Mother is a constant in his life whom he has experienced as always there to gratify his every need and desire, who provides him with love and nurturing as well as a sense of worth, support and identity. For the Mamma's Boy who has been seductively coerced into the role of Mother's 'perfect partner', she too, as calculated, has become his.

The use of the term 'asexual' in describing a symptom of the Mamma's Boy Syndrome may seem severe and exaggerated. It is, however, used in its metaphorical sense to denote the effect that Mother has on her son in terms of his sexuality. Mother is in possession of his penis and will not let it go: it is 'tied up' and bound to her. The Mamma's Boy may not be literally asexual – not sexual, without sex – but in attempting to deny his sexuality he can ward off the eminent dangers of interference and complication to the existing relationship with Mother and secure his survival. His sexuality in a sense is split, whereby a part of him remains eternally frozen with fear and loyalty for Mother.

Relationships of any sort are an area in which the Mamma's Boy has little or no positive experience. Mother has subtly discouraged him from forming friendships, having contact with peers, and establishing a healthy, intimate relationship with Father. Mother orchestrates her son's life in such a way that he is denied contact with others; she views any relationship which her son undertakes as potentially conspiratorial and a threat against the control she wields. The only reference for relationships is the one he shares with his mother, and he accepts the confusion, conditional love and unrealistic demands she places on him with gratitude. He blames himself for his inadequacy and inability to connect with others and carries feelings of guilt, loneliness and worthlessness. It is in this manner – the distortion of his reality and self-esteem – that mother becomes his most important relationship to whom he must cling for comfort, relief and some semblance of belonging.

Mother wants to keep her son all to herself and covertly demands that he remain emotionally available only to her. She feels jealousy and abandonment at the slightest withdrawal of her son's attention and demonstrates hostility either by threatening him with her loss or, conversely, by digging her heels in deeper, activated by her engulfing, incorporative tendencies (Socarides, 1968, p. 33). Either way, the son is penalized and learns to protect himself by proving his undying love and faithfulness to Mother by unconsciously denying his sexual needs, drives and feelings. He is confirming not only that Mother will never be replaced by any other woman but, moreover, that her needs and feelings take precedence over his. For this son, acknowledgement of his sexuality is equated with betrayal of and ingratitude for his mother's love.

In order for Mother to continue her delusion that she is fused with her son, she perversely demands to know every aspect of his sexual life. In this fashion, not only is she vicariously sharing his experiences and fantasies but her belief that they share an intimacy, that they are one, is validated. The reverse may also apply, whereby the mention or demonstration of any sexuality on the son's part is ignored or denied, mirroring Mother's lack of sexuality and the barren relationship which exists between Mother and Father. In either instance, the son is victimized into confused and shameful feelings about his own sexuality.

The Mamma's Boy forgoes his sexuality in order to protect himself from acting upon his unconscious sexual desires for Mother which were never successfully worked through during the Oedipal stage. With no firm boundaries, nor any attempt on Mother's part to create them, an intense attachment between the mother and son has been perpetuated. With Mother's inappropriate seductive behaviour towards her son and the belief that he is her perfect partner and vice versa, he is left carrying covert incestuous fantasies which he fears he will act upon if he admits to any sexual desire whatsoever. He takes upon himself the blame for the sexual undertones of their relationship and the responsibility of guarding the sexual boundaries between them. Not only does his asexuality negate his guilt over his sexual desires for Mother and the fantasies of consummating their relationship, but also serves to defend him against his unconscious fear of being 'swallowed up' and reincorporated into Mother's body. Mother, capable of his destruction and at the same time necessary for his survival, is kept at a comfortable distance through her son's asexuality which serves to maintain the *status quo* of their relationship.

For the male suffering from the MBS, asexuality may mask the confusion he encounters over his sexual orientation and provide an escape from having to acknowledge his homosexual tendencies. Blatantly, Mother makes it clear to her son that she wants him all to herself and often encourages his homosexuality as a means of warding off the threat of being dethroned by another woman.

For the son, homosexuality may serve multiple functions: it strips him of Oedipal guilt by demonstrating to Mother that he does not have an interest in other women (Socarides, 1978, p. 72); it defends him from experiencing phallic rivalry and punishment from Mother's lovers (Father and other men); it allows him to flee the terror of Mother's castrated and castrating body which serves as a reminder of what could happen if he engages sexually with a woman; it defends him against incest with Mother; it permits him to find potency through his male partners (Socarides, 1978, p. 71); and it allows him to remain identified with Mother's body through being penetrated by another man (Kahr, 1994).

When Marsha, the mother of two sons was asked, 'How do you think you will feel when your sons get married?' she replied:

I am dreading it, I am dreading it, I really am! ... I think I have no great, great fear about them being homosexual because I think I would rather them go out with a nice man than some horrible awful woman ... I couldn't bear it.

Furthermore, some mothers, because of their own faulty gender defined self-identity, unknowingly encourage their sons' homo-sexuality because of the vicarious satisfaction they will obtain. For Marsha and many other mothers, homosexuality would also confirm her son's loyalty and firmly establish her position of power as the most important and influential woman in his life. It would prevent her feelings of competitiveness, envy and rivalry from surfacing, for which her son would no doubt be made to suffer.

On an unconscious level, homosexuality safeguards the son from merging with Mother and allows him to identify vicariously with the masculinity of his male partner, an identification that he was unable to make with his own father. In Chapter 1, Harold was introduced as one of the cases which exemplified the extreme Mamma's Boy Syn-drome. Harold speaks of the fear he has of his mother and the effect it has of 'quenching any sexual desire' for women. His father was never really around and was not a 'real man'.

Harold is homosexual. He believes that his subjective experience of his overbearing mother and inadequate father led him to find a sense of masculinity and personal peace in his sexual orientation. However, for many men, the MBS serves as a socially acceptable alternative to confronting and acting upon their latent homosexuality. The cessation of any form of sexual functioning keeps at bay any sexual tendencies which cannot be reconciled.

A lack of firm masculine and sexual identity, a fear of being engulfed by Mother and women in general, and a distrust of men because of being left unsupported by a weak father against his mother, all leave many a Mamma's Boy in a sexual limbo. Asexuality is the compromise he may make so that he does not have to painfully assess who he really is and struggle with the conflicts of his sexual identity. His asexuality is an undemanding role which appeases Mother and society and is 'ego-syntonic', that is, experienced by the self as acceptable (Rosen, 1979, p. 33).

Coming to terms with his sexuality actually challenges the intimacy he shares with Mother, since it is yet another indication of her son's growth which she views as a personal rejection. He has already experienced that his instinctive attempts to assert himself in other areas of his development have been thwarted and frustrated and ascertains that his sexuality, likewise, will be merely another provocation for Mother's disapproval and withdrawal of love. He is willing to sacrifice his sexuality in an attempt to maintain the closeness they share and on which he has come to be so desperately dependent for his definition and protection in the world. Mother cannot accept her son's natural need for sexuality and as punishment, will retract from him completely, or so he anticipates. Socarides (1978, p. 53) writes, 'The threat of separation from the mother is experienced as an equal if not greater danger than the loss of the penis.'

For the son who has been objectified and desexualized by his mother, the loss of his penis and what it represents in terms of his sexual power as an individual seems the easier loss for him to endure. His sexual pleasure is sublimated into the gratification he gives Mother through his love and care of her, as well as through his achievements which she takes pleasure in as her own. His sexual fulfilment is cast aside in lieu of his need to alleviate his emptiness and loss of self which Mother has proved only she could satisfy. By right, he is entitled to sexual enjoyment but forfeits it in order to secure his greater pleasure reward, Mother.

His asexual stand, which he has been forced into adopting as reciprocation for his relationship with Mother, is actually a testimony of the power Mother wields over her son. His sexual denial validates the extent of Mother's control over him: she has subtly rendered him impotent over his own instinctual needs and has succeeded in disconnecting him from his body. Her belief that he is, and always will be, an extension of her body and will is reinforced. Mother has succeeded in keeping her son all to herself.

THE OEDIPUS COMPLEX

Where three roads meet

In a letter dated 15 October 1897, to his colleague Fliess, Freud wrote,

> One single thought of general value has been revealed to me. I have found, in my own case too, falling in love with the mother and jealousy of the father, and I now regard it as a universal event of early childhood ... (Freud, 1897, Letter 71, p. 265).

Freud was referring to the instinctual impulse and universal phenomenon which is an integral part of the human condition. In 1910 he came to name it the Oedipus complex (p. 171).

Freud describes the child as going through five psycho-sexual stages of development: oral, anal, phallic, latent and genital. It is during the height of the phallic phase, between the ages of three and five, that the son becomes aware of his genitals, and the Oedipus complex develops. During this Oedipal stage the son establishes an erotic attachment to the parent of the opposite sex, his mother, and feelings of aggressive rivalry toward the parent of the same sex, his father. Not only does he unconsciously desire his mother in a literal and physical sense but he also wishes to replace his father as the object of his mother's love.

During the Oedipal stage, the son is faced with a dilemma; he does not have the capacity to gratify his genital impulses and, secondly, he is torn between fear and hatred of his father and, because he still loves him, suffers from guilt. His hatred for Father is induced by his jealous love for Mother, who is idealized. Father is attributed with all the dangerous attributes originally experienced by the son in relation to his mother, and Father is invested with the son's split-off aggressive drives (Glasser, 1979 p. 298).

As a consequence of the boy's longing to replace Father as Mother's love object, he fears that Father will retaliate in order to defend his position. Unconsciously, he expects that Father will punish him and imagines that his offending part, his penis, will be castrated. The son's terror of castration – the castration complex – is substantiated when he becomes aware that females do not have penises. The son fantasizes that his too can be removed.

The Oedipal conflict is resolved when the boy gives up his mother as an erotic object while still maintaining a love for her. His decision is influenced by his own fear of disapproval, retaliation and the hopelessness of claiming Mother's attentions. In order to ensure that any remaining sexual cravings for Mother will not be fulfilled, he represses – buries in the unconscious – his sexual striving and Oedipal wishes. At this point, he identifies with his father in the hope of one day acquiring his privilege and status.

Freud's theory of the Oedipus complex is based on Sophocles' fifth-century Greek tragedy, *Oedipus Rex*. It is the story of Oedipus, the son of Laios, king of Thebes and his wife, Jocasta. After an oracle foretold that Laios would be killed at the hands of his son, the infant Oedipus was given to a shepherd to expose on Mount Kithairon with his ankles pierced so that he could not crawl away (Oedipus means 'swollen foot'). The kindly shepherd could not abandon the child and gave him to another shepherd on the other side of the mountain, who subsequently brought him to Polybus, King of Corinth. He, being childless, was glad to raise Oedipus as his own. While growing up Oedipus was taunted by remarks that he was not Polybus's own son, although he was assured by the king that he was. Oedipus travelled to Delphi to consult the oracle, who did not reveal his true parentage but did tell him that he was destined to murder his father and marry his mother. In order to protect Polybus and his wife, he vowed never to return to Corinth while they were still alive.

Unknown to Oedipus, his real father Laios was also travelling in Delphi. At a place where three roads met, Oedipus came alongside Laios's chariot and he was ordered out of the way. Laios himself struck Oedipus with a staff and Oedipus retaliated by dragging him out of the chariot and killing him. Oedipus continued on his way, blocking out what had occurred, and arrived at Thebes. The city was being terrorized by the Sphinx, a creature part winged lion, part woman, who asked a puzzling question: 'What is it that walks upon four legs in the morning, two legs at noon and three legs in the afternoon?' The kingship and the hand of Laios's Queen Jocasta were offered to the man who could solve the riddle and free the land of the Sphinx. Oedipus was quick to identify its subject as man, who as a baby crawls upon all fours, in his prime walks upright on two legs and in old age needs the support of a third leg, a walking stick. Oedipus married Jocasta and became king.

They lived in perfect happiness and had two sons and two daughters. However, Thebes was hit by another plague which would only be lifted when the killer of Laios was brought to justice. As the play relates, Oedipus undertakes to seek out Laios's killer. He consults a blind prophet who is reluctant to reveal the identity of the killer but insinuates that Oedipus himself had something to do with the murder. Jocasta tries to persuade him to halt his investigation but he persists in his efforts until the full horror of the situation is brought home to him. Oedipus has succeeded to his father's throne and bed: he has killed his father and married his mother.

Jocasta does not wait for the verdict and goes ahead of Oedipus into the palace, where he follows her with what seems like murderous intent. He finds that she has hanged herself and, tearing the golden brooches from her dress, Oedipus plunges them into his eyes until he is blinded (Burn, 1990, pp. 67–73).

During the Oedipus phase, the son expresses his sexual interest and desire for his mother. After all, she is the only one who is capable of gratifying his instinctual needs and need for love. His interest in Mother may be regarded as being far removed from the intensity of the Sophocles play but many similarities can be extracted from the myth which is significant in explaining the underlying dynamics of the Mamma's Boy Syndrome. Although the Oedipus complex is a psychological mechanism, its complexities can be and are externally encouraged and induced by Mother's behaviour towards her son during this crucial phase of his development.

The Oedipal phase is fraught with confusion. There is an inherent breakdown in the delineation of generational roles, that of wife–child–husband, which contributes to the powerful impulses the child has to cross such boundaries. In the case of the Mamma's Boy, the mother uses this situation to actively contribute to the breakdown of the boundaries and to encourage her son to retain his desire for her. She stimulates her son's feelings for her by acting in an overly seductive manner, giving the impression that their relationship can be consummated. It is not necessarily a physical consummation of the mother–son dyad but the son's replacement of the father as Mother's love object and partner.

During the Oedipal phase, the child goes through a range of mixed emotions – love, hate, jealousy, envy – which the parents should be aware of and able to tolerate. Frustration is necessary for the son so that he can understand that he does not have the power to come between his parents. However, for the Mamma's Boy who shares identification with his mother, Oedipal frustration is negated. It is the parents who must be able to set up boundaries to protect the parental couple from the child who believes that he has the power to destroy it. However, in the case of the Mamma's Boy, the mother's own need and pathology allow the child to enter the boundaries which she uses and manipulates for her own end.

Freud postulates that the son and Father are rivals and that the son harbours the desire to kill off his father. However, for the Mamma's Boy, there is no need to murder Father in order to have Mother all to himself – she has symbolically killed off her husband through physical separation, divorce, emotional alienation or by denigrating and belittling his worth. Mother and son, as one, become Father's rival and together rework the boundaries elevating the son to the position of husband and husband to the position of child, helpless and at their mercy. Throughout, Mother remains the all-powerful Queen, and Father accepts his own destruction without struggling against her (see Chapter 3). The Mamma's Boy need not fear that Father will retaliate against him by attacking his sexuality. On the contrary, it is his phallic and powerful mother who threatens him with the same fate bestowed upon his father: she has replaced her husband and is capable of replacing her son. He accepts castration – the loss of his gender-identity – and submission to her seductive and inappropriate demands, rather than the loss of her attention.

Normally, during the Oedipal situation, the son feels frustrated by the parental dyad which he cannot penetrate. In the case of the Mamma's Boy, the mother alleviates the frustration that her son must experience (by killing off the father) and encourages the union between herself and her son. An incestuous or pseudo-incestuous dyad guarantees that the son is left to her own devices without the intrusion of the father. Since there is no male figure to identify with, or to protect him from Mother, the son identifies with her as a means of self-protection and gratification.

The Mamma's Boy, like the protagonist Oedipus, is abandoned by his parents; he is abandoned by his mother as he is not given the opportunity to learn the skills necessary to survive in the world. Like Oedipus, he is maimed at the crawling stage, which ultimately does not permit him to stray far from her. He will always come back to her because he has never been allowed to individuate. Out of a fear that his position will be usurped, Father physically and/or emotionally abandons his son. Father, whether aggressive or weak, deals with his insecurity and inability to cope by leaving his son unprotected so the son does not have a father to identify with, nor is he protected against his mother's over-investment in him. As in the play *Oedipus Rex*, the helpless infant is cast away because he is a threat to his father's existence. By disposing of his son, the father is in fact recreating the fate of being replaced by him. In an unconscious collusion between Mother and Father, both are responsible for the destructive outcome that will befall their son and the family constellation. To a lesser extent, the son is also a participant in the destruction of the family triad. It is his trust as well as fear of Mother that resigns him to participate in the ruin of his father's role. Unconsciously, he ascertains that he may befall the same fate as Father if he does not acquiesce to Mother's demands.

As a means of negating his weaknesses and looking deeply at his plight, the Mamma's Boy erroneously obtains much of his sense of self from protecting and caring for others and from the admiration and applause he receives from so doing. Although this role is empowering, it also leaves him susceptible and undefended himself. In the same vein, Oedipus is powerful and able when it comes to protecting others; he protects Polybus and his wife, he saves the city of Thebes (the family dynamics) from the Sphinx, and attempts to battle against the plagues by finding the murderer of his father, Laios. His efforts are selfless and at the same time self-destructive; he is unable to acknowledge his own need to be protected nor his need or ability to control his own fate. The Mamma's Boy, like Oedipus, represses the abuse he has undergone in order to protect the sanctity of his parents. Without acknowledging his maltreatment, the abuse becomes self-perpetrated and self-destructive as in Oedipus's blinding of himself.

In the myth of *Oedipus Rex*, only Jocasta, his mother, can know that he is her son (Oedipus even resembles his father), yet she marries him nonetheless. When he attempts to seek out Laios's murderer and find the truth, she is adamant that he halt his endeavours. Is it to protect her son, herself or the prohibited relationship *a deux* which they so blissfully share?

This scenario mirrors that of the Mamma's Boy's. He has complete trust in his mother and as a parent it is her responsibility to maintain the boundaries. Mother keeps her son all to herself and dissuades him, by the threat of her loss, from seeking out the truth and questioning the inappropriateness of their relationship, which is laden with incestuous undertones. Learning the truth would threaten their relationship and ultimately destroy Mother.

Oedipus loses Jocasta only when the true nature of their association comes to light and she kills herself. It is the son's powerful unconscious desire for Mother coupled with the satiation he experiences from her, that ignites his guilt and responsibility for their connectedness; he both enjoys and fears the incestuousness of their relationship. For a son to come to terms fully with the inadmissibility and taboo would be anxiety-provoking and implicate Mother's conscious awareness of its formation. It would be the symbolic destruction of Mother and the death of their 'perfect' relationship.

The Mamma's Boy Syndrome is a socially sanctioned version of the incestuous tale of *Oedipus Rex*. Mother, playing on the vulnerability of her son's longing for her, compromises her son's development because of her own unfulfilled perverse needs. Her son is her malleable opportunity to create a partner who will idealize her, protect her and succumb without hesitation to her demands for gratification. Like Oedipus, the Mamma's Boy is a tragic hero who embodies the human predicament of ignorance (Burn, 1990, p. 69). He lacks the understanding of who he is and is blinded from seeing his reality and destiny.

At a place where three roads meet – the family constellation – the Mamma's Boy is made Mother's king. A seemingly ideal relationship between Mother and son is fabricated and his development is stunted and entrapped. It is at this juncture, where three roads meet, that the Mamma's Boy Syndrome is paved and reinforced.

This chapter has examined some of the mechanisms which contribute to the Mamma's Boy Syndrome and the inherent contradictions contained within them. The Mamma's Boy Syndrome itself is a condition fraught with internal and external contradiction and ambivalence. This concluding segment of the chapter will examine how the confusing paradoxes of the Mamma's Boy Syndrome contribute to the maintenance of the condition.

Mother's covert and subtle threats of her son losing her, her love and her protection intimidate him into obedience and complacency. The fact that he has already been deserted and his needs forsaken remains repressed and unacknowledged. Instead, he creates an illusion of a loving mother, the mother that he needs, desires, deserves and anticipates that she will one day magically transform into, if he can only please her and care for her well enough. Unconsciously an ego defence, a 'fantasy bond', is manufactured, permitting him to deny his reality – the reality of his intolerable situation and his feelings of neglect and abandonment – and superimpose loving feelings towards Mother.

The fantasy bond deceives him with a false sense of being loved and cared for instead of the reality of his mother's insistence that he love and care for her. He is bonded to his fantasy mother, the mother who is supposed to be there to nurture his needs while preparing him to stand on his own two feet. To acknowledge that his mother is capable of harming him poses as great a threat as the harm itself and he denies both. As long as he can hold on to an image of an idealized mother, he remains protected from his reality.

The Mamma's Boy's identity and self are an extension of Mother. To admit that Mother is flawed would mean that his survival was at risk. It is less menacing for the son to believe that it is he who is flawed so that the illusion that Mother is capable of his care remains intact. The Mamma's Boy keeps his mother idealized and instead takes upon himself the responsibility and shame for her inappropriate and unpredictable behaviour. He blames himself and believes that there must be something wrong with him: if he is unloved, it is because he is unlovable. The Mamma's Boy reacts positively to his

mother's exploitations because she is defensively idealized.
him from seeing the evidence which is contrary to the love his
so adamantly proclaims.

The Mamma's Boy Syndrome has so far been discussed as a
reaction to the engulfing, over-invested mother who kills with
kindness. However, it is at this point important to mention that the
syndrome is also bred from the neglectful, indifferent mother. In this
reverse form of MBS, the son's needs are blatantly ignored and
Mother's inattentiveness cannot be misconstrued as loving; there is no
mistaking her coldness and lack of concern, yet she still covertly and
subtly demands that her son serve and obey her. This son, like the
son of the suffocating mother, creates a fantasy bond to protect
himself from the reality that his mother has a dark side, that she is
imperfect, and to negate the reality of his abandonment. Out of a
sense of weakness and vulnerability, he will ferociously cling to his
mother, hoping and longing to create the intimate closeness which he
so desperately needs in order to secure his survival (Socarides, 1978,
p. 111). Motivated by magical hope and the expectation that he can
somehow win Mother's love, he overcompensates and becomes overly
loyal, obedient and eager to please her, lavishing on her the love and
care he wants so desperately to receive from her. Paradoxically, the
more unpredictable and inadequate the mother, and the more unsure
he is of Mother's capacity to love him, the more the son's feelings of
weakness will force him to cling to her, or, more aptly, to the fantasy
of the mother he so needs and yearns for. In reality, both sons have
been neglected by their mother's inability to provide them with a
healthy balance of appropriate and consistent care. Both sons are left
clinging to Mother in order to subdue the fact that they are ultimately
unprotected and alone.

The Mamma's Boy seemingly becomes what mother wants him to
be because he clearly understands that otherwise he is unworthy of
her love. He receives the covert message that his authentic self – who
he really is – is inadequate, unlovable and 'bad'. He unconsciously
adopts a 'false self' which is consistent with Mother's expectations of
him and masks his true self as a means of self-preservation. In
essence, he has learned to secure his mother's love by being an
extension of her (Glasser, 1986, p. 14).

Without grounding as an individual, he is severely dependent and
sensitive to Mother's approval and affirmation as he has no sense of
personal value. He cannot exist without being in relation to her and
thus carries out her every command as if his life depends on it, and
for the Mamma's Boy it feels like it does. He has no sense of self as

he is fused with Mother and can only exist through her. He is surviving but not living an independent life; without a clear sense of self he has no choice or power.

His false self protects him from feeling and suffering. He is immunized from his pain, anguish and humiliation because he cannot perceive the reality of his subjective self. His false self is like an actor – he has been directed into a role and is unable to express his true self because it is not in the script. He has deluded himself into a false sense of security by losing himself in Mother, burying his true, authentic self which is left for dead. He remains unconscious of his own true feelings.

'The overprotective mother injects hostility into her love, giving blissful experiences to her son only if he pays for it by forfeiting his freedom', (Stoller, 1975, p. 53). Surely the son must have feelings of anger, resentment and hostility towards Mother but what outlet does he have to express them?

The Mamma's Boy has difficulty in acknowledging any angry feelings towards Mother because they are extremely intense. He fears being angry with her as it would no doubt bring punishment upon him; either Mother's threats will be carried through or her engulfing defences will be triggered. He also fears that if his anger is unleashed it would culminate in the physical and/or emotional destruction of his mother whom he loves and needs, yet at the same time hates. It is unsafe for the son to be angry with Mother so he represses his negative feelings and unconsciously acts in various ways which do not jeopardize him or, more importantly, their sacred relationship.

One manner in which his aggression towards Mother is unconsciously discharged is by turning it inward against himself. His unexpressed aggression is internalized, where it is manifested in depression, shame and self-loathing. Consequently, he is lonely yet further attempts to isolate himself as he believes that Mother is capable of invading his thoughts and knowing that he has contemptuous feelings towards her. It is with Mother's introjected voice that he chastises himself for entertaining any emotions other than loving ones. As a result, his guilt is turned into self-punitive behaviour, which in a sense mirrors Mother's feelings about herself that she is resistant to acknowledge, yet allows her son to carry for her. His self-directed aggression leaves him passive, resigned and powerless over his life. He has reinforced Mother's power and reacts by 'beating himself up' instead of communicating his anger, a positive and constructive strength against his condition. His self-punitive behaviour, however, leaves him at Mother's mercy.

Psychosomatic illness – feelings converted into bodily sickness – is another means unconsciously employed to vent his anger. Again, his anger is self-directed, allowing him a safe outlet for his negative emotions. Instead of hurting Mother, he physically creates the pain he wants to inflict on her. Not only are his negative feelings displaced, but in a physical state of illness, his helplessness will activate Mother's nurturing and caring of him. His psychosomatic illness not only serves to keep her near and secure her attention but also gives Mother a sense of purpose which reinforces her belief that she is, indeed, needed to sustain her son. Unconsciously, illness ensures that he is too weak to attack Mother and at the same time lets him feel literally 'sick' for even contemplating such aggressive thoughts. Illness excuses him from having to confront Mother, allows him to remain impotent and powerless, and ensures that he will not be abandoned.

His anger is deflected away from the object of his contempt, Mother, and is acted out on those less threatening to his survival. His strong identification with Mother operates to repress his experience of abuse and in turn he unconsciously recreates the role of perpetrator and takes out his rage on others, as Mother for so long has taken hers out on him. According to Guy R. Odom (1990, p. 37), 'To the degree the child is dominated by the mother, he will as a youth and as an adult exercise a similar degree of dominance over others, within the boundaries set by society. This psychological need to dominate and control others is based on the individual's childhood fear that becomes in adulthood a phobia of being dominated and controlled.'

Father and other men who did not protect him from his mother become one of the outlets for his aggression (Socarides, 1978, p. 222). Father is perceived as a weak and easy target on whom he can vent his aggression while at the same time unconsciously pleasing Mother with his demonstration of strength against her rival. He can safely denigrate Father without fearing that he will retaliate as he has witnessed Mother so often do. By taking out his anger on Father, he falsely fosters a sense of self-superiority and projects his inadequacies and self-loathing onto him. He denigrates Father as he has been denigrated by Mother.

The Mamma's Boy associates all men with being weak and ineffectual or conversely hostile, distant and indifferent. In either case, he harbours a fundamental need and desire to relate to men and a resentment that he does not. His essential lack of maleness and failure to identify with Father facilitate his distrust and sense of betrayal by all men in general. He compensates for his sense of inadequacy and inferiority by proving his 'masculinity', by raging against the very gender with which he wants and needs to identify. All men are seen as contemptible because paradoxically he wants to be accepted as one of them but has not been initiated into their club due to their lack of support against his engulfing mother.

The Mamma's Boy carries a secret yet intense anger towards his mother because of the indignation he has experienced; he is emasculated, engulfed by her power, controlled, dependent on her for survival and definition, and responsible for bestowing meaning on her life. His mother is perceived as omnipotent and godly and he bows down to her and protects her position by converting his anger towards her into a fearful respect. In this manner, he is not only colluding with Mother but also protecting himself from her wrath. Mother is elevated to a status above womanhood and is perceived not as a woman but as a giver of love (Arcana, 1983, p. 217). It is for this reason that he can carry disdain for women but not for his mother. He attributes his maltreatment at the hand of Mother to other women against whom he is able to assert his anger without dreading recrimination or feelings of guilt .

He fears all women and punishes them for his dependency on Mother (see Chapter 5). He becomes the perpetrator and women, his unjustified victims. He objectifies woman as he was objectified by Mother and treats them as debased objects whose sole purpose is to fulfil his needs. He will use women to deceive himself about his experience of being used by Mother and will ignore their feelings as his were. As learned from his experience of being the recipient of Mother's passive aggression, he may express his anger towards women indirectly by punishing them with silence and withdrawal of love.

Sons of engulfing mothers have been asked to be sensitive to Mother's needs and to please her. With other women, he deceptively empowers himself by demanding that his every need be taken care of unconditionally. If he is not satisfied, he reacts in rage, inappropriately directed towards a woman who does not pose a threat to him, rather than to his mother from whom he wants to elicit care and nurturing.

His anger towards women is a response to his vulnerability and powerlessness. He trusted Mother and was betrayed. He cannot allow himself to trust another woman in fear of being re-engulfed, swallowed up and spat out. Through verbal, emotional and all too often physical abuse, he is attempting to reclaim the power of which he was stripped. In asserting himself against other women, he is attempting to eradicate the feelings of inferiority he carries. He humiliates women as he is humiliated by Mother. He becomes powerful and controlling with women as Mother is with him. He cannot defy or stand up to Mother but he can act out his aggression on other women, thus maintaining the lie that he has only loving feelings towards his mother and that her actions are in the name of 'love'. It is so often these mother-fixated men who lash out and commit heinous crimes against women, often serial and brutal murders or rapes.

It is no wonder that the Mamma's Boy, seemingly loving, docile and sensitive to his mother's needs, actually carries beneath the surface so much aggression. The 'love' he receives from Mother is often confused and infused with hostility, leaving him unable to differentiate between the two. Mother's love for her son is actually about control. Her love wields the power to influence her son and manipulate him into subservience. What she is attempting is to use her capacity to love her son as a reward for the behaviour she deems appropriate. She attempts to create the perfect son, the son who will do everything she commands, the son who will be a testimony that she is indeed powerful and capable herself of being loved and respected.

Mother's love for her son is misguided, thoughtless and conditional. It is used as a tool to ensure that he will remain dependent. He has no choice but to acquiesce to her demands since he fears losing her and what he has come to believe is her love, which he so needs and craves. He is seen as obstinate, ungrateful and undeserving of Mother if he attempts to grow up and away from her. Any demonstration of individuality is viewed as a hostile manoeuvre against her control – grounds enough for the retraction of her love and approval. If he is permitted to grow up, Mother is no longer in control of him and, unconsciously, feels that she will be at his mercy, as with all other men. The power inherent in motherhood is of use to her only if she has a subject on which it can be implemented. Her son's dependence guarantees her power and authority.

Paradoxically, Mother is as dependent on her son as he has been encouraged to be on her. She desperately needs him to give her a sense of purpose and to secure her role. The son has the power to elicit her love and, by the same token, the ability to make her feel loved. Unconsciously, Mother is dependent on her son to bestow upon her a sense of self which she has not been able to obtain on her own or from any other man. He colludes with her not only because his reward is so gratifying – supposed nurturing, caring and loving – but because, in a sense, his role of caretaker is empowering. In being responsible and protecting of Mother, he obtains a sense of moral superiority and righteousness which deflects from his feelings of depression, emptiness and powerlessness.

Mother's treatment of her son is selfish and irresponsible. It is no wonder that it is so difficult for the Mamma's Boy to assume responsibility for his own life when Mother has the capacity to reel him in when he attempts to disentangle himself from her hook. The bait she uses is love.

The Mamma's Boy is entrenched within a double bind. His life is filled with contradictions and opposing messages which paralyse him from acting to free himself from his dilemma: he is nurtured with love that is punctuated with hostility; he is overprotected by Mother, which leaves him unprotected; he believes he is flawed in order to ignore Mother's imperfections; he is infused with Mother's shame so that she does not have to carry it; he is accountable and responsible for Mother's feelings yet he is incapable of acknowledging his own; as a child he is forced into inappropriate adult responsibility and as an adult he is as helpless as a child; he is beholden to Mother for his very life and security (Socarides, 1978, p. 224), yet he is without security or a life of his own; his acquiescence to Mother feeds her self-esteem while diminishing his; Mother's great interest in her son's welfare is actually in her own interest; Mother is over-invested in her son, stealing his life to make it her own; Mother overly cares for and loves her son because it is she who needs love and care; he is made to feel inadequate so that Mother can feel powerful and in control; his need to identify with males is discouraged so that he can be formed in Mother's image; the Mamma's Boy is enmeshed with Mother and abandoned by Father; he longs for, yet fears, Mother; he carries ambivalent feelings of love and hate towards the same object, Mother (Rosen, 1979, p. 41). However, the greatest contradiction and conflict the Mamma's Boy must endure is his instinctive need to separate from Mother and at the same time maintain the comforting illusion that they are blissfully one. Bibring (1953) wrote not only of the child's need for affection and the need to be loved, but of the opposite defensive need 'to be independent and self-supporting'.

The Mamma's Boy Syndrome is a developed strategy adopted by the son in order to survive; survive Mother's demands and emotional blackmail. The Mamma's Boy learns to withstand the massive emotional bombardment by excelling at his role which detracts from his pain – his utter dependence on Mother and subsequent inability to function in the world on his own, his social and sexual awkwardness, his guilt and shame, and his failure at being a differentiated and self-sufficient man. The Mamma's Boy Syndrome neatly bandages his true predicament so that he does not have to acknowledge and look at his infliction. To unravel the bandage and expose the damage would at first be unsightly, agonizing and anxiety-provoking, but in the long run would facilitate his healing with the minimal of scarring. The Mamma's Boy Syndrome allows for a superficial sense of relief from his intrapsychic conflict.

CHAPTER THREE

Father, Mother, Mamma's Boy

The world will not change until fathers can love their sons. I think it's inhuman to ask a woman oppressed by her husband to love and raise a boy child.

Alta, quoted in J. Arcana, *Every Mother's Son*, p. 140

The Mamma's Boy Syndrome is symptomatic not only of an overbearing, engulfing mother but of a detached and indifferent father. The syndrome also results from the disturbed marriage between these two 'adults' who unconsciously use their son to maintain the equilibrium of the family system as well as to deny their own failures, histories and unresolved conflicts. The dysfunctional family is a breeding-ground for the syndrome as the Mamma's Boy is needed to deflect from his mother's sense of unhappiness and inadequacy and from his father's inability or unwillingness to cope with the demands of the marriage, his wife and the responsibility of fatherhood.

Why does Father sacrifice his son to Mother? What role does Father play in his wife's over-investment in their son? What is necessary and crucial if Father is to facilitate his son's independence and separation from Mother? What are the unconscious needs and motivations that drive Mother to replace her husband with her son and her husband's motivations in allowing her to do so? Why is the Mamma's Boy expected to provide for his parents' overt and covert needs? How do the parents' past experiences impact themselves in the formation of the syndrome?

In order to comprehend fully the Mamma's Boy Syndrome it must be explored in relation to both the mother's and father's pathology and the unspoken complicity between them. This chapter will investigate the societal expectations, unconscious motivations, personal agendas and psychological make-up of each parent which together allow for the creation of the Mamma's Boy Syndrome.

FATHER

A catalyst for identification

It is a culturally accepted stereotype that women's mothering is a natural phenomenon which has evolved over millions of years. In contrast, a man always needs to learn how to be a father since fatherhood is not inherent in the procreative act (Jones, 1992, p. 24). It is very much a conscious decision that a man must take if he is to be a father in the praiseworthy sense of the word. However, fathering is a nebulous term without a specific definition or fixed role although, historically, the father's job was to provide food and shelter for the children, watch over their growth, protect them and assist in their acquisition of skills and knowledge. Above all, he was a figure of authority.

One of the most important functions the father must serve is in the facilitation of his son's separation from Mother. Under optimum conditions, Mother herself plays a crucial part in the separation–individuation process, but the father's role is also vital, especially when the mother is unwilling to allow her son to do so. According to Greenson (1968, p. 370), in order for the son to attain a healthy sense of maleness, he must 'dis-identify' from his primary object of identification, Mother, and counter-identify with the father.

Father's masculine presence is essential in order for the son to develop his own masculinity. He must consciously give his son motivation for wanting to give up the love, gratification and identi-fication he accrues from Mother and identify instead with him, the less accessible of the two parents. All too often, however, the father plays only a cameo role in his son's life and maturation process, which only serves to reinforce his son's prolonged attachment to Mother. It is necessary for the father to be available to his son as a role-model, as men feel their most masculine in the presence of other men (Greenson, 1968, p. 371).

As first put forward by Freud (1905) in relation to the psycho-genesis of homosexuality, the father who is emotionally or physically absent, weak, hostile or rejecting does not lend himself as an accessible or positive model with whom the son can identify. Freud's theory, I believe, holds true as a thumbnail sketch of the father of the Mamma's Boy as well. From the interviews undertaken, a pattern emerges in which the son who does not cease to break his identification with Mother perceives his father as possessing inadequate traits as a man, loving father and decent husband:

> My father used to spend his time berating my mother but didn't sleep with her. It made me feel that there was something inadequate about my father ... He was extremely aggressive, everything my mother was not. He abused me in every way – emotionally, physically and verbally – and I learned to hate him as a child of eleven. I stood up to him at eighteen when he was verbally abusing my mother and I had to leave home ...

Another son says of his father:

> He causes a lot of problems in the family ... He is intelligent but at the same time stupid. It is strange because it is almost as if he can't do normal things that everyday people can do ... I have learned from my dad that basically a man goes out and has an office job and brings money into the family while the mother stays home and brings up the children ... That's really the only thing that's rubbed across about being a man.

Fathering is what a man is supposed to give his son in the sheer masculinity of his gender. If Father is feared and disdained rather than revered and respected, the son's motivation to identify with him will be lost and he will remain identified with his idealized mother. Perhaps out of ignorance, indifference or sheer resignation to his wife, the father believes that, with the presence of the mother, it is unnecessary for him to be an active force in his son's upbringing. What is unintentionally dismissed is his son's need for a masculine role-model if he is to separate from Mother and acquire a healthy male gender-identity. To the detriment of his son, Father is available neither as a love object nor as protection against the engulfing mother.

The under-fathering phenomenon

The 'abdicating father', as coined by Socarides (1982), is the father who resigns his power, authority and rightfully held influence. When this form of under-fathering takes place in the context of a 'psychologically crushing mother', the son's task of separation from the mother is extremely difficult and leaves him developmentally arrested (Socarides, 1988 p. 265). The lack of a father figure in a boy's life is one of the main determinants, when coupled with mother's overbearing influence, that allows for the formation of the Mamma's Boy Syndrome.

One of the reasons a father may abdicate his power is because he is confronted with a domineering and powerful wife who intimidates him into subservience. He will appease his wife and avoid conflict in order to maintain the balance of the family dynamics and, in a sense, to ensure his own survival. Unfortunately, this father models a mode of interaction with his wife which is unconsciously mirrored by his son – he will take on father's attitudes and behaviours to become the same resigned figure in relation to his mother and perhaps, later, other women.

When Father is denigrated by Mother in a calculated attempt to isolate him from his son, her intention is for the son to retain identification with her. She paints father as a spineless and inconsequential man who cannot fight to retain his rightful position, and, hence, as an unworthy figure with whom to identify. The son will resent Father for not standing up to Mother and for being an inappropriate role-model, and will hate and mock him for his weakness. In order to distance himself from what his father represents and to prove to Mother that he, unlike Father, is deserving of her love and attention, he will ally with her in the denigration of Father. Spurred by her underlying frustration, disappointment and hatred of all men, Mother emasculates her husband and then her son in order to empower herself. With Father's masculinity demeaned, his authority obliterated and his virtual annihilation as an assertive force and role-model, Mother is free to use her son's identification and allegiance to render him a Mamma's Boy who has ultimately landed up as an object of denigration just like Father. The son has learned from his father's example that he too must yield to Mother in order to survive.

Father may also surrender his position out of jealousy. His son as an infant is helpless and rightfully in need of his mother's attention. After the birth, Mother's diminished interest in sex can lead to the father finding it difficult to share his wife's affections with the baby: Father can unconsciously perceive his son as an intrusion and rival for Mother's attention who will deprive and take away from him 'all the goodies from the maternal/libidinal breast' (Welldon, 1988, p. 27). Out of jealousy he retracts from both his son and wife, which only serves to reinforce and perpetuate their bond. Instead of entering into their world, his jealousy serves to isolate him from the mother–son diad. He withdraws as a father to his son (and husband to his wife) and emotionally and/or physically removes himself as a figure with whom his son can identify. By withdrawing from them both, Father is encouraging their needs be fulfilled through one another.

For a father to admit that his son needs his love, support and active participation would be for him to recognize the unfulfilled need that he had for his own father. He was not given a model of appropriate fathering and to give his son more than he had would instil in him a sense of loss too great for him to bear. In order to deny his feelings of loss and abandonment, he unconsciously recreates the same fathering with his son which denies his pain and maintains an image of his idealized father and childhood.

Alternatively, Father may have felt crushed by his own father's hostility or authoritarian ways and harbours anger and resentment towards him. In an attempt to shield himself from being experienced in the same way by his son, Father rejects the role of the powerful father and passively forgoes being any kind of a father at all. He willingly abdicates his power and position to Mother in the hope of absolving himself from the guilt and responsibility of adversely affecting his son. Father believes that he is protecting his son from experiencing the same indignation that he underwent in relation to his own father, but the reality is that he has absconded from his responsibility as a father and has left his son vulnerable and unprotected from Mother's engulfing powers. Without being a figure for identification in his son's life, he has unknowingly colluded in his son's denigration by Mother. Father's lack of authority leaves his son susceptible to Mother's will and, ultimately, to being shaped into a Mamma's Boy.

The father who projects an air of utter competence, success and extreme strength without showing any signs of vulnerability will be perceived by the son as possessing a penis size which is unobtainable (Kahr, 1994). Out of his insecurity of not being able to live up to his father's seeming perfection, he fears that he will never 'measure up' to his father. Noah Richler (1992, p. 55) poignantly expresses this point in the following excerpt from a piece about his father, the author Mordecai Richler:

> I must have been about five or six when I first took a pee with my father, or first remember it, sharing the same toilet bowl. I guess I came up to about his thigh, my scrotum barely descended, and my little penis like a pert nipple which I had to point well upwards to get the pee over the rim of the bowl; his, meanwhile, a mammoth sausage weighing heavy in his hand, the

urine falling noisily. I remember the shadow of his enormous dick to the left of my eye. I thought: I'll never be so big.

The father who has put himself forward as an unrealistic model of manhood may make his son feel inadequate and diminished. In order to compensate for his inability to emulate Father's high standards, he will remain identified with Mother since, in relation to her, he feels masculine and adequately endowed.

Father may believe that he is setting an exemplary model of masculinity for his son when he spends his time away from home succeeding in the work place or in his sporting activities. That is where he is perceived as the 'boss' or as strong and competent but unless the father is dominant and active in the family and takes a major role in the family decisions, his masculine preferences and a strong masculine identity will not emerge in his son (Archer and Lloyd, 1985, p. 222).

The hostile, abusive and authoritarian father may be hiding behind these traits as a defence against wanting to accept and acknowledge his own vulnerability and sense of weakness. In order to maintain his façade, he unconsciously projects his unwanted bits into his son, forcing him to carry his inadequacies for him. This father needs his son to be the lame, subservient Mamma's Boy so that he does not have to acknowledge his own deficiencies such as being a hen-pecked husband, coddled son or financial failure. Father takes out his self-directed anger on his son and threatens his self-esteem and burgeoning masculinity. This son is unable to identify with his father and remains clinging to Mother for comfort and support against his attacking father.

The surrogate husband

When Father consciously or unconsciously abdicates his position, there is a void in the family system which must be filled. The son will be elevated to Father's position and often Father takes on the role of child. Even a well-intentioned father can be rendered incapacitated and unconsciously abdicate his position. The following case illustrates the reworking of the family system in such circumstances:

> The husband was much older than his wife and had suffered a stroke. He was in a wheelchair and unable to speak. Their only child, a fifteen-year-old son, overweight, unathletic but strong, had become everything to his mother. He was allowed to kiss and touch her, and they slept in the same bed. The

husband/father could not take an active part in the family and needed to be cared for in the same way as a helpless child reliant on its mother for survival. The son had replaced his father in the family and became a husband to his mother and a father to his own father. Although this mother knew there was 'something wrong' and understood that she needed to make boundaries between her and her son, she also badly needed it to remain the way it was in order to compensate for the void left by her husband's illness.

In other cases of the MBS, the father will consciously sacrifice the son to his mother in order to protect himself from her. Unequipped to deal maturely with his partner, he is frightened and overwhelmed. He will selfishly and inappropriately yield his position to his son to get his wife 'off his back' and to escape what he perceives as her demands. By delegating to his son the task of looking after Mother, Father deludes himself that he is teaching his son 'responsibility' while divesting himself of his own. The son learns that his role is to take care of Mother by becoming her surrogate husband. He does not feel guilty for taking over Father's position because he is carrying out Father's instructions and at the same time is keeping Mother fulfilled. The message given to the son by Father is that it is his responsibility to keep Mother happy and maintain the 'peace': 'My father would say to me, "Just do it, it will shut your mother up!"' Another son was told by his father: 'Keep your mother happy or she will cause me problems. You know how she gets.'

Father is not only blatantly encouraging his son's acquiescence to Mother out of self-preservation, selfishness and immaturity, but is also setting the foundation for his son to become the sole purveyor of Mother's happiness.

Father uses his son as a buffer between him and his wife. He encourages his son to be sensitive to Mother's needs, listen to her problems and fill in for him so that he does not have to feel guilty for neglecting to do so. However, Father will eventually become intimidated and fearful of his son's sensitivity because his son is able to achieve a seemingly tender relationship with Mother, where he has failed. He has encouraged his son's relationship with Mother but then holds it against him and mocks him for not being a composed and 'real man' like himself. His son's sensitivity will be associated with his wife and Father will begin to perceive them as being one. His resentment towards his son will culminate with Father perceiving and treating his son with the same disdain and neglect he does his wife, which leaves his son confused. With no other choice, he will remain identified with Mother.

A bridge over troubled water

Father must be a motivating factor in his son's readiness to renounce Mother and counter-identify with the male gender if he is to become an autonomous and fully functioning male. However, the father who has under-fathered his son has, in a sense, betrayed him. Unable to trust his father, he not only rejects Father's destructive parts but also rejects his positive parts as well, making it impossible for him to acquire the necessary masculine identification he needs for healthy development. In essence, Father's betrayal of his son keeps him identified with Mother whom he perceives as the only constant and loving force on whom he can depend.

It is difficult to overstate the importance of the father–son relationship; fathers are the principal masculine role-model and all their actions and behaviours, by everyday example, are the raw sources from which their sons learn what being a man is all about. Whether present or absent, assertive or compliant, feared for his strength or hated for his weakness, Father exerts a powerful influence over his son by modelling a view of maleness. Whether or not a father has succeeded in facilitating his son's identification with the male gender will determine the extent of his son's self-esteem, confidence and power as an individuated and independent man. What is necessary for the son's dis-identification with Mother and counter-identification with Father is an available, loving father who does not frustrate his son's desire to identify with him. Father is an important link between his son's dis-identification from Mother and his achieving individuation, a sense of self and gender-identity. The son can only master this feat if Father is a healthy, balanced and mature role-model who demonstrates a love towards his son which is needed to bridge his son's fear of losing his primary love object, Mother.

MOTHER

Mother's preference for a son

In order to understand the existence of the Mamma's Boy Syndrome, an historical and sociological exploration of the denigration of girls and the idealization of boys is essential.

Although women become mothers for a myriad reasons, what is apparent is the approval and praise bestowed upon the mother who bears a son. In traditional societies, and still today in many parts of the world, a woman's ability to bear children and particularly sons was considered very important; it was often judged by the number of brothers she had (Safilios-Rothschild, 1977, p. 28). Sons were widely needed as a source of family income, as labour for the fields, and were viewed as a financial asset. This Chinese proverb sums up the value placed on boys:

> Show me a rich man without any sons, and I'll show you a man who won't be rich very long. Show me a poor man with many sons, and I'll show you a man who won't be poor very long.

The son was viewed as an extension of his father, the one to take over the family business, title, respect or wealth. In effect, a son was wanted and needed to pass on the family name so that the father and his family could be assured immortality. A son is the patriarch's system of assuring that extinction of the family line will not occur. Even today, in the case of the British Royal family, there was great pressure on the Princess of Wales to produce an heir to the throne. She was greatly praised and thought of as the 'perfect' wife and breeding-stock for producing, as coined in the tabloid press, 'an heir and a spare'.

Throughout history, girls were considered to be of lesser value than their male counterparts (Kahr, 1994, p. 49) and the systematic infanticide of children and especially of girls led to a large imbalance of males over females. During antiquity infanticide was an accepted, commonplace occurrence. The first-born was usually allowed to live, especially if it was a boy: 'If, as may well happen, you give birth to a child, if it is a boy let it live; if it is a girl, expose it,' Alis was instructed by her husband Hilarion in 1 BC (deMause, 1974, p. 26). Not far removed from the acts of infanticide of that period, in today's China where parents are officially permitted to have only one child, couples will abandon babies – particularly girls – in their determination that their only child will be a healthy boy, who will grow up to support them in their old age (Franchetti, 1995, p. 23). Girls are left to die of starvation and neglect in the state-run orphanages and it is estimated that 15 million baby girls have disappeared since 1979 when the communist leader, Deng Xiaoping, declared that people were to use whatever means necessary to achieve the country's goal of controlling its spiralling birth rate (Franchetti, 1995, p. 23).

In traditional societies, a daughter is viewed as a monetary liability for whom a dowry was, and still is, paid. She is perceived as an expensive 'object' which must be maintained and the father is expected to subsidize the husband-to-be in order to persuade him to undertake the responsibility of her upkeep (Safilios-Rothschild, 1977, p. 34). Therefore, women have learned that they are objects which are traded from one owner to another and whose worth is calculated by the amount of dowry offered for them.

According to Anti-Slavery International, even today there are examples where marriage is still tied to an exchange of goods. In parts of Pakistan, if a woman is raped, a female member of the rapist's family is married into the victim's family as 'compensation' (Abdela, 1995, p. 67). There are also cases which exist of parents taking their daughters back to their native country – Africa or Asia – where they are forcibly married when they arrive. These marriages mean the girl must live with her husband's family, to whom she has to prove her worth by working hard and producing children (Abdela, 1995, p. 67).

Religious beliefs have also served to impose restrictions on women and expectations for them to bear sons so that the religious obligations, which can only be carried out by men, are fulfilled. In Judaism, the 'Tsena', a version of the Torah (Bible) for women and ignorant men, reminds women of their subordinate role and encourages her, if she is pious, to pray 'to give birth to a Torah student', a boy (Shepherd, 1993, p. 29).

Through religion, be it Christianity, Islam or Judaism, women are placated by being given a sense of pseudo-value. A woman is taught that she is the backbone of religion in that it is she who cares for the family and instils in them integrity, morals and values. In one of the weekly general audiences at the Vatican the Pope criticized women who choose to work rather than to fulfil their 'innate vocation to be a mother'. In some cases, the Pope said, 'the need for women to work to provide for the growing demands of the family, and an erroneous concept of freedom, which sees in the bringing up of children an obstacle to autonomy and the possibility for a woman to affirm herself, have clouded the meaning of motherhood for the development of the feminine personality' (7 December 1995). The reality of the Pope's words and religions' concept of women is, however, very different – women are far from equal and are viewed as a source of evil, a curse which must be tamed and managed by men:

> All women are viewed as 'bad', since they are seen as objects of temptation and cannot control themselves sexually. This is why women must be protected and restricted by fathers, brothers, husbands, and sons —they are ideally kept far from men so that they can remain pure and 'good'. (Mernissi, 1973).

Women were viewed as inferiors who needed to be protected, yet served to protect men from other women, 'to suppress man's deep fear of his own libido' (Shepherd, 1993, p. 29). They were objects whose value depended on their attractiveness and ability to serve men. In China, small feet were considered an attribute for women and the practice of foot-binding, despite the pain and mutilation to the girl, was carried out for the sexual pleasure it gave to the man (deMause, 1991).

Girls learn to fulfil the needs of others and to emulate their mothers by cradling and taking care of their dolls. Characteristics such as warmth, expressiveness, compliance and sensitivity to others are encouraged while they are socialized into believing that 'masculine' characteristics such as competence, independence and assertiveness should be minimized (Lemkau and Landau, 1986, p. 227). What do these messages convey to a girl, woman, mother? Covertly, the internalized message states that it is advantageous and culturally rewarded to produce a son – the male is competent, independent and assertive. From a very young age, men are approved and liked when they achieve, but women can be liked regardless of achievement, if they are willing to conform to what others want them to do (Safilios-Rothschild, 1977, p. 22). According to Stoll's five stages of female development (1978), the primary focus for women is other people – their husbands, their children, their grandchildren, and finally, in widowhood, another partner.

Women's dreams of mothering begin long before there is a foetus in the womb. By bearing a child, a woman can experience herself as a creator and delude herself with a sense of grandeur and power (Lemoine-Luccioni, 1987 p. 25) which is not afforded her in other avenues, merely because of her gender. We live in a patriarchal society in which culture is made and governed by men. The bearing of a son is universally viewed as obtaining status and merit not only for the mother but for the family and society at large, as it is through the male, the son, that society perpetuates its power.

Through motherhood, and specifically through the bearing of a son, a woman can mark her presence on the world albeit once removed: Plotina, whose husband Trajan had been Emperor of Rome until his death, was not permitted to rule. She, however, secured the throne for her favourite son, Hadrian, and subsequently continued to be active in government through him until her death in 120AD (Arcana, 1983, p. 65); Diana will never become Queen but through her son, Prince William, she may rule and direct royal policy by ruling and directing him. Her position as the mother of the future king will always secure her presence and power in the world.

Woman's low self-image, worth and esteem, as well as her sense of inability to achieve, is an intergenerational handicap passed, for the most part unknowingly, from mother to daughter and prescribed by the fathers, husbands and men who regulate the patriarchal society. When a woman hopes for a son, one of the many points she is revealing is that she does not want to repeat consciously the patterns of instilling a daughter with the same damaged sense of self as was ingrained in her. In one manner, to bear a son enables a woman to break the learned pattern she would no doubt perpetuate. To bear a son means that her child will not be in her image: inferior, worthless and secondary.

By the hand of society and its institutions, women have experienced a deep sense of limited worth and achievement. It is only through the act of motherhood that a woman can achieve a sense of praise and power; and it is only through the birth of a son that she is given the opportunity to wield that power either against him, or through him, while fulfilling her unconscious pleasure.

The penis

According to traditional psychoanalytic theory, a son represents the mother's missing phallus, a metaphor for the power and domination that is 'hung on men, visible for all to envy' (Rich, 1977, p. 198). The mother–son relationship can be regarded as invested with an unconscious quality; the son is not only a baby, but the penis Mother has always craved. Therefore, the birth of a son resolves Mother's penis envy as she has finally created a penis of her own. Mother's unconscious fantasy on giving birth to a son is that she feels herself 'anatomically more complete' (Stoller, 1975, p. 48). Hence, through the birth of a son, her castrated penis is replaced along with her feelings of inferiority. It follows then, that Mother's wish to bear a son is so that she can live a powerful life through him: 'women who feel in an inferior position try in a vicarious but vigorous way to achieve their own fantasies of power through their own reproductive organs, and furthermore, to act them out' (Welldon, 1988, p. 46)

In many respects, bearing a male – the gender mother unconsciously wanted to be – feeds Mother's need to express herself and her ambitions. Simply, a son becomes not only the penis – the power mother desires for herself – but an extension of her capabilities and identity. Her son (and his penis) represents the male position of dominance which allows the mother to transfer the ambition she has been forced to suppress in herself onto her son (Roith, 1988). He becomes the vehicle by which she can drive her ambitions forward and achieve vicariously.

The mother of the Mamma's Boy is a seemingly selfless and, no doubt, insecure woman who bears a son whom she unconsciously uses as an instrument through which she lives her life. Her son is used to live out her yet unlived life in order to achieve what she could only ever dream of as a woman with perceived and real limitations. Linda Wildmare in her article 'Raising a Male Child' illustrates this notion in the following:

> When I was pregnant, I wanted a boy child. Now I know that that was because I saw women, I saw myself, as powerless. A male child could do all the things I'd only dreamed of doing and never felt I could.

It follows, then, that the mother would not allow her son to become a separate and independent entity. By securing her son as a Mamma's Boy, she is cementing her claim on the advantages of his gender. Through him, she is entitled as his mother to achieve vicariously and to reap the rewards of his achievements and, more generally, those of the male gender. She cannot separate her female body and identity from that of her son's body and identity because she needs the illusion that as an extension of herself, his achievements are hers and that her dreams and aspirations can finally be realized. Her son has made her complete by complementing her own gender with that of the male – allowing him to separate would once again render her powerless and without a penis; it would be equated with her once again feeling castrated and impotent. Her identity and sense of worth as a woman and a 'good' mother is bound to her son and his success.

The mother of the Mamma's Boy exhibits many of the characteristics consistent with what is termed 'narcissistic-personality disorder' (DSM III). Her excessive love for her son, who is after all an extension of herself, can be interpreted as self-love. Her preoccupation with her son allows her to become grandiose and self-important as she commands admiration and attention for his talents and achievements. She gains power and vicarious sexual fulfilment through him. Her humiliation, rage and emptiness, indifference and defeat, her feelings of entitlement to her son's favours and her inability to empathize with his feelings are also indicative of the pattern of the narcissistic personality (Goldenson, 1984, p. 483). It is Mother's narcissism that compels her to turn her son into a Mamma's

Boy who is used and loved as the idealized image of herself. He has become Mother's narcissistic supply and is forced into losing himself in her, while being deluded that their oneness will ensure his approval and survival, at the expense of his own separate being. In effect, Mother can only love her son as an extension of herself and not as a separate and independent object.

It is especially important to the mother of the Mamma's Boy that her son achieve, so that his glory will be reflected back on her and give a glimmer of life to her deadened existence. Her son is covertly expected to bestow a certain cachet onto her through his achievements and he is expected to please her as such. Through her son's monetary success, she is unconsciously able to share the virile strength and power of the male. Mother may not have her son in the sexual sense, but with his financial success he is overtly expected to lavish her with gifts as a demonstration of his love and care for her. In this way she is able to share in his potency and is made to feel an object of his desire. Her son's financial gain also assures her that she no longer needs her husband for financial security.

The Mamma's Boy is over-burdened with his mother's unrealistic hopes and expectations. It is through her son that her existence in the world is legitimized and made known. It is through her son that she is – in her own mind at least – elevated, given status, respect and a sense that her life has not been wasted. It is through her son's achievements that her sense of power, identity and self-worth is ultimately created. With only the role of motherhood to give her an identity, her purpose lies in bearing and bringing up a son who will validate her. If her son achieves then it is to her credit. If he becomes a doctor – which is the will of the so-called Jewish mother – then the sacrifices she has undergone because of her gender have not been in vain. Her son (the doctor) has succeeded for her failings and she can now live with a sense of pride that her martyrdom and selflessness were not to benefit herself but were for the good of her son and society. As a woman, she could not accomplish on her own; as a mother, she has succeeded in moulding her son into that from which she could experience accomplishment and a sense of purpose.

Mother takes more pleasure in her son's achievements than the Mamma's Boy himself because he perceives himself as an objectified 'trophy' which will always belong to mother. Although he is seemingly able to function adequately in the world, he is ingrained with the belief that his success is due to the strength and power he accrues from mother, when in reality it is the reverse. Thus he can never leave her lest he be shorn of his power, like the cutting of Samson's hair.

Conversely, the Mamma's Boy will act out mother's prophecy – that he cannot survive without her – by remaining incompetent and forgoing any attempts at reaching out into the world. This, I believe, is due to the son's self-punitive behaviour and low self-esteem. He fears surpassing Mother's own achievements and meeting her anger, disapproval and abandonment, which is worse than the inevitable guilt he feels for not living up to her expectations. The Mamma's Boy's success in the world would signal to both mother and son that he is capable of forging a life of his own and this would ultimately endanger their seemingly peaceful co-existence. Mother's message to her son is ambiguous; he is expected to achieve, but not to the extent that he is able to live without the life-line she throws him. Woody Allen, in the episode 'Oedipus Wrecks' from his film *New York Stories* (1989), puts this point forward and illustrates the opposing feelings of love and murderous wishes a son entertains towards his mother:

SHELDON: I'm fifty years old. I'm a partner in a big law firm, you know. I'm very successful and I still haven't resolved my relationship with my mother.

DOCTOR: You still react to her like a small boy. You really have to have some sense of humor about it.

SHELDON: I can't. I try, but I can't. You know, I, she just gives me a hard time. She's always telling me I look terrible and she's critical. You know, listen, what can I say? I love her but I wish she would disappear.

Mother's jealousy of her son is often disguised under an umbrella of motherly guidance by which she can undermine, criticize and belittle him in order to build herself up and become seemingly self-sufficient.

Mother's sense of castration leaves her lacking – she must hold on to and possess her son, her 'treasured phallus' (Stoller, 1975, p. 42) in order to feel complete and fulfilled. She uses motherhood to reap the advantages associated with her son's member and sacrifices her son's masculinity in order to resurrect in herself the power of which she adamantly believes she has been robbed. Through her son, she is transformed into a man because she possesses and controls her son's phallus and is also a woman because she is a mother (Lemoine-Luccioni, 1987, p. 45). She is finally made complete at the expense of her son's mutilation: he has been forced into handing over his power, will and penis to Mother, to only carry her feelings of degradation and hopelessness. She has become the self-appointed custodian of her son's penis.

Mother's rebirth

Every woman brings into her role of motherhood her own childhood experiences. The mother of a Mamma's Boy is no doubt carrying the scars of her own childhood – a sense of weakness, inadequacy, female inferiority and a need for love – which can be remedied through bearing a son, or so she unconsciously presumes. The Mamma's Boy is selfishly nourished so that in turn he will feed Mother with what was unavailable to her through her own mothering. Through her son she is able to secure the love, respect and complete admiration that was lacking from her own childhood experience.

The need Mother had for her own mother is, therefore, converted into the need for her son through whom she could finally and fully be gratified; the Mamma's Boy fulfils her underlying fantasy that she finally has created an object that will look after her and all her needs. By ensuring that her son remains dependent, she is guaranteeing that her needs will never be abandoned as they were by her mother. He is the only object that can give her a sense of love and purpose, that never before was she able to experience, from either of her parents, or for that matter, from her siblings, a daughter or husband.

With the birth of her child, and with each developmental level that he meets, the mother's same developmental needs are triggered, making her aware of what she has missed in her own childhood. Pregnancy merges her with her own mother and brings to light the ambivalence of their bond (Lemoine-Luccioni, 1987, p. 38). The birth of a child sparks a reassessment of the new mother's relationship with her own mother; it may bring to a head her feelings of hopelessness and result in post-natal depression (Raphael-Leff, 1991; Kiverstein, 1993 p. ix). The birth of the child also leaves her feeling void and empty where the baby once was (Pines, 1993, p. 68) and her later inability to allow her son to separate and individuate is an attempt to maintain the fantasy that he can fill her emptiness, that he is an intimate part of her body and life.

Through her son she attempts to recapture her lost childhood by selfishly demanding that her son furnish her needs at the expense of his own. Mother converts the need she had for appropriate parenting into the demand for her son to become her loving parent. He becomes not only the mother, but the father with whom she was unable to make an attachment. The birth of a child also proves to her own father that his rejection of her femininity has not hindered her ability to be a woman and, in a sense, create a man of her own who loves and accepts her.

The mother of the Mamma's Boy projects her needs onto her son and lavishes him with what she herself wants. Her son (the penis) becomes the breast which she never was given by her own mother, and her expectation is that he will nourish and feed her to satiation. He is needed to complete her and becomes the ideal baby-self that had never been mothered by her own mother (Pines, 1993, p. 86).

Through motherhood, a woman is given a sense of power and control which she can wield as long as her child remains dependent. Her power is used to manipulate her son into meeting her needs, and serves as evidence to her own mother that she has finally succeeded in obtaining the eternal love and devotion that was unobtainable to her as a child. The son who is a Mamma's Boy is confirmation that she has created something of worth and that she is an exemplary mother, unlike her own, who has secured her son's devotion where her mother has been unable to secure hers.

In the belief that she is unlike her mother, and in an attempt to give her son the mothering she never had, she becomes overly absorbed in her son's life to the extent that he is unable or permitted to separate from her. Her desire to disinherit her mother's ways comes full circle when her son is unconsciously suffocated with her compensatory over-mothering. Her son is laden with his mother's childish magical belief that if she loves him enough, he will reciprocate that love and never leave her. Unconsciously, she expects her childhood needs to be fulfilled by her son; through him, she is reborn and invested with the love and protection, power and sense of purpose she could not obtain as a child or as an adult. Her son may seemingly gratify her but is denied adequate mothering, since he has become a parent to his own mother.

The mother who is compelled to transform her son into a dependent and developmentally disabled Mamma's Boy is exhibiting 'perverse' attitudes of motherhood or the deviation of maternal instinct (Welldon, 1988, p. 64). 'Normal' maternal instincts would allow for the spontaneous and instinctive capacity of the mother to facilitate and encourage her son's growing up and apart from her rather than hinder it. Maternal power affords her the opportunity to procure from her son what she could not secure from her mother. Through her son, who is in her total control, unable to survive without her, unable to escape or abandon her, she is able to manipulate and eke out the love and respect she was so desperate for as a developing child. According to Stoller (1975, p. 4), 'perversion serves to convert childhood trauma into adult triumph'. The Mamma's Boy is her triumph, her living proof that she has seemingly shed her insecurity and inability to be loved. She has broken her son – his spirit and independence – and has triumphed over her son (and mother) by proving her power.

Mother's action toward her son is perverse. According to Welldon (1988, p. 8), 'The main difference between a male and female perverse action lies in the aim. Whereas in men the act is aimed at an outside part-object, in women it is usually against themselves, either against their bodies or against objects which they see as their own creations: their babies.' In creating a Mamma's Boy, Mother is overtly practising her perversion behind a veil of maternal dedication without her actions being diagnosed or acknowledged as such.

Mother uses the Mamma's Boy as a 'depersonalized' thing which becomes a penis substitute as well as a substitute for her father, mother and husband. I put forward that the Mamma's Boy becomes both Mother's transitional object (Winnicott, 1953) and her fetish.

A transitional object is an object selectively acquired because of its anxiety-reducing value. As a transitional object, the Mamma's Boy is something comforting and serves as a substitute for Mother's diminished sense of self and body. Unconsciously, the birth of an infant fills a gap between mother's legs and serves as her penis (Lemoine-Luccioni, 1987, p. 41), which she unconsciously needs to make her feel complete and powerful. As her transitional object, the Mamma's Boy can be enjoyed, played with and manipulated for her own pleasure and gain. He is used to ensure good feelings, protect her against loneliness and to ease her inability to cope due to her own immaturity and inadequate individuation (Greenacre, 1979, p. 96).

A fetish is 'a symbol for something regarded with peculiar veneration and awe which the fetish serves to embody' (Schindler, 1982 p. 375). It is characteristically something which suggests the male genitals but has some female attributes as well (Greenacre, 1979, p. 97), which explains Mother's need to feminize her son. According to Greenacre (1979, p. 106) the central core of fetishism as a perversion seems to lie in a severe castration complex which results in an illusion of some actual impairment of the genitals; this is consistent with Mother's feelings of inferiority and impotence about her own life. Her son becomes the symbol for the penis from which she receives vicarious sexual satisfaction and power.

Metaphorically, the Mamma's Boy is a substitute or addition used to reinforce Mother's body parts which she considers inadequate. In the case of this mother, her son becomes her object choice to soothe and comfort her. As such, the use of her son as a transitional object and fetish are indistinguishable as both are objects related to the own-body as well as to that of the other (Greenacre, 1979, p. 96). Mother never relinquishes the need for her transitional object, her Mamma's Boy, and, therefore, he can be regarded as a fetish without which she cannot function. She suffers a permanent need for her son whom she cannot give up spontaneously; he serves as her eternal security blanket to cover and protect her against her real or imagined fear of inadequacy.

The Mamma's Boy unconsciously serves as a substitute from whom Mother can be guaranteed that her needs are met. However, her perverse tactics for securing that love are camouflaged by motherhood; she has the power to make her son love and perform for her, filling her with elation and a sense of strength in finally being able to obtain gratification and self-esteem.

Mother's longing to find all that she has been forced to do without is realized in the Mamma's Boy. With possession and control of his male organ, she is reborn.

Revenge

Mother welcomes with great pride, relief and achievement the fact that she has borne a son. According to research undertaken by Moss (1970), mothers held their male three-week-old babies almost one half-hour longer in each eight-hour period than their girl babies. Bearing a son not only pleases Mother; Father's desired choice is also a son. According to Rebelsky and Hanks (1971, p. 65), fathers' preferences for male children has been shown in their greater involvement through talking and playing more with their infant sons than with their daughters. So, then, what is Mother's misguided motivation for converting her son into an emasculated Mamma's Boy? It is not an overwhelming desire, conscious or otherwise, for a female child but rather it is due to her deep-seated need for revenge.

In creating a Mamma's Boy, Mother is unconsciously avenging those men – her father, brother, lover, husband – who have denigrated her worth. She harbours a deep resentment towards men and, according to Stoller, her son becomes the culmination of her lifelong hatred and envy of males (1975, p. 49). In effect, Mother has aligned herself with those men who have devalued her and unconsciously she punishes and emasculates her son by discouraging any of his masculine tendencies to develop (Stoller, 1975, p. 44). She has claimed her son's penis and its power as her own, and utilizes it to control her son, and symbolically all men.

Her deep-rooted feelings of being consistently devalued by men play upon her treatment of her son. Mother carries ambivalent feelings towards him; she both loves and hates, fears and desires her son, as she does all men. Unconsciously though, her hatred of her son is somewhat placated by the hope that, through him, she will be invested with male power and opportunities which are not afforded to her as a female; he is dehumanized and put up with because he is attached to a penis (Lemoine-Luccioni, 1987, p. 27). However, by keeping him emasculated, under her control and unsuited to the demands of being an independent and self-reliant man, she believes that she has succeeded in extracting his masculine power and can now claim it as her own to become a 'phallic woman' (Stoller, 1975, p. 42), cold and powerful. By denying her son the full potential of his masculinity, she is assuming that his power will not be used against her to denigrate or abandon her. By creating a Mamma's Boy, she is guaranteed that she will always possess his penis, albeit vicariously, and that it will bestow upon her the advantages of the male gender.

The Mamma's Boy is used as retaliation for the contempt Mother feels towards her own father. She was unable to acquire her father's love, so unconsciously her son is moulded into her 'idealized father' who is forced to give her the love and attention she demands. This woman has not reconciled her Oedipal desires to secure her father as her love object whom she turns to in order to regain the lost penis (Archer and Lloyd, 1985, p. 110); the Mamma's Boy, however, is her assurance that she will always be loved as she wished her father had loved her and is the source by which she can replace her missing penis and feelings of inferiority.

Mother's unconscious and sometimes conscious hatred of her husband manifests itself in her behaviour towards her son. She takes revenge upon her husband for his failure to provide her with vicarious self-fulfilment and after impregnating her with 'her lucky charm' – a son – he is rejected as a punishment. Her son, who is an extension of the sexual partner, is treated with disdain because the father is not accepted as a 'man' (Pines, 1993, p. 61). Mother further emasculates her son by making him an extension of herself, thereby avenging and insulting her husband's masculinity by not allowing her son to identify with him.

Mother's hunger for the 'perfect' husband is fed by elevating her son to the role of husband so that he can love, protect and ultimately fulfil all her needs. By creating this perfect spouse, she is declaring that she does not need her husband, a man, because she has the ultimate companion, her son. By creating a surrogate husband, the perfect partner, Mother has total control over her son and symbolically over all men. Her belief is supported that she is, in fact, all-powerful, needed and in total control of her son, who is, after all, a male. Furthermore, her fantasy is that her son is the penis stolen from her husband (Lemoine-Luccioni, 1987, p. 12), who is now left rejected, redundant and lacking. Mother now possess vicariously, through her son, the power which once belonged to her husband. The son has replaced her husband and is invested with the unrealistic expectation and responsibility of fulfilling her and making her complete.

Mother's fantasy is that her son is invested with the magical quality of bonding the husband–wife relationship and cementing her husband's love. This notion of pleasing one's husband by bearing him a son is rooted as far back as Biblical times: 'And Leah conceived, and bore a son, and she called his name Reuben: for she said, "Because the Lord hath looked upon my affliction; for now my husband will love me"' (Genesis 29:32).

On one level, Mother perceives her son as a 'gift' to her husband (she is giving him a gift which is really benefiting her) and when her husband fails to reciprocate by responding as she had hoped, she feels jilted and abandoned and uses her son to get even with him. Like Medea, the protagonist of Euripides' drama, who murders her two sons in order to take revenge on her husband Jason (who has left her for a more powerful woman), Mother uses her son, the Mamma's Boy, to punish her husband. Mother has given the gift of life to her son and now attacks his emerging self with her overwhelming love (Orgel and Shengold, 1968, p. 382). By destroying her son's masculinity, she is unconsciously taking vengeance on her husband by making him suffer the loss of his extension, his son, who is a reminder to Mother of the humiliation her husband has caused her. The Mamma's Boy becomes the only source of power available to her by which she could disarm her husband while at the same time arming herself.

The mother of the Mamma's Boy does not find contentment and recognition in the role of wife and, therefore, seeks to achieve it through her son. In many instances, the son replaces Mother's need for sexual intercourse with her husband, as her libido is sublimated into the energy she puts into grooming her son into the perfect, obedient and loving Mamma's Boy. Breast-feeding her son for a prolonged period of time is one way in which she garners vicarious sexual pleasure under the maternal pretext of nurturing her offspring. In essence, this *alma mater* – nourishing mother – is nourishing and gratifying her own needs. As an extension of herself her excessive love, concern and interest towards her son is self-enhancing and, therefore, of a narcissistic nature. Through her son, she obtains gratification and the Mamma's Boy becomes Mother's narcissistic object choice upon whom her libido is invested.

Mother is often unconscious of her seductive attitude towards her son and, conversely, the spurning of her husband's sexual needs, which serves to create a father–son rivalry for her attention. This gives her a sense of power over them both and allows her to relish the delusion that she is loved and pursued by two men. She manipulates and controls them by withholding what they really need and want from her, and only gives them her 'gifts' when it is she who will take pleasure and reward in the giving.

Mother believes that her life has been sacrificed to those men who have eradicated her potential to achieve her ambitions and ultimate contentment. She now symbolically sacrifices her son by slaughtering the very qualities in him that she resents not having been able to develop in herself. Without just cause, she has been treated as the under-sex and therefore, feels vindicated in her treatment of her son: Mother now demands servitude from her defenceless son in order to establish a semblance of power over all men, and as retribution for her diminished sense of power and self-worth. In essence, the Mamma's Boy is made to pay for man's domination of women.

The selfless woman

The Mamma's Boy Syndrome is the result of Mother's over-investment of herself in her son's life. When the treatment of her son and his subsequent condition as a Mamma's Boy is examined in the context of the prescriptions she follows as part of her routine socialization as a woman and a mother – her ability to serve others while denying her own needs and aspirations – her behaviour can be understood as a response to her unhappiness, hopelessness and subordination. As a result of her internalized belief that through her demonstration of selflessness she is playing out her social role to perfection, her son becomes an acceptable and sanctioned outlet by which she can unconsciously accrue self-fulfilment, power and control over her otherwise restricted and lonely life. She is perceived as a loving mother who gratifies, serves and cares for her son to the point of martyrdom. However, her selflessness is self-serving and becomes unconsciously selfish in intent. What is perceived as her maternal involvement becomes an unconscious smothering of her son's development and an effective tool to gain his love, gratitude and loyalty.

Women have been forced into a position of self-effacement and denial in order to be honoured and revered. This psychological deprecation which they are expected to assume often, and understandably, results in depression, loneliness, irritability, anxiety and self-doubt (Lemkau and Landau, 1986, pp. 227–32). Through Mother's 'concern' for her son, her predicament can be apparently remedied or forgotten; over-involvement in her son's life allows her to avoid her own depression and seemingly overcome her feelings of emptiness and powerlessness. By keeping her son as a permanent rumination in her life, her focus need not be on herself. The son who is nurtured into the role of a Mamma's Boy becomes not only a source by which she can deny her own life issues but the only outlet by which she can demonstrate that she is capable of control and power.

Maternal altruism is supported in women and in adhering to this edict she is inadvertently playing into the males' socialized entitlement of being gratified by women. Fanatically carrying out society's expectations of motherhood, she is unconsciously able to release her frustration by smothering her son with excessive and inappropriate care under the pretext of carrying out her motherly duties. She is absolved from guilt and feels justified, as her actions are consonant with her female socialization. Mother is given little support or encouragement to achieve separation from her son, as her sole source of identity is bound to her role as mother. If she allows her son to separate and become independent, she will lose her status and *raison d'être*: the Mamma's Boy gives her appreciation where there was none, fulfils her hopes and dreams, reflects her undying dedication, loves and cares for her and bestows upon her a sense of worth and achievement, all the while staying at her heels. Most importantly, he is her cure for loneliness (Stoller, 1975, p. 48).

Mother copes with her lot by deceiving herself that her son is a part of herself and a perpetual infant who needs her protection. She ensures that he remains attached and dependent so she can retain the sense of purpose that the role of mother affords her. As a mother her identity is fixed; if she allowed her son to grow up and leave home she would lose that security and become redundant. If her son slips away from her grip and manages to become independent, she will lose her identity and control over him. He is a constant source of human contact, warmth, appreciation and support. If she loses him, she will be abandoned to the starkness and emptiness of her existence. She is unconsciously protecting herself by creating a Mamma's Boy who will never leave her, and she clings to him as if he were her saviour from feeling neglected, humiliated, inadequate and lonely. Her all-encompassing interest in her son has been misconstrued as selfless, maternal concern when in actuality it is a defence against feelings of intense despair about being left all alone.

Mother is dependent on her son and, as a result, dominates his emotional and psychological life, engulfing and refusing to let him go. She is detached from her own life yet takes control of her son's, demanding that he bestow upon her meaning and purpose. She does not take charge of her own happiness, yet attempts to claim it through becoming the master of her son who is forced to be her loyal and loving subject. Without her son, she is lifeless and impotent: because Mother does not live out her own life, the Mamma's Boy carries the pain and towering responsibility of remaining dependent in order to protect and fulfil her. He is the pillar of support that shields her from the weight of her heavy and tiresome reality.

Esther Harding so aptly writes (1971), 'lifelong mothering is a denial of her wholeness ... A continuing maternal protectiveness is an unwillingness to face the harshness of life, for herself as much as for her child.'

This chapter has examined the emergence of the MBS from the perspective of the boy's mother and father. The Mamma's Boy Syndrome is regularly formed within a marriage where there is discord and dysfunction, divorce or separation, or when the mother has decided to be a single parent. It goes without saying that in any circumstance where the mother is unfulfilled, she will unconsciously look to her son for the comfort and support that is ordinarily supplied by an adult partner within a relationship.

The dynamics of the family are instrumental in the development of the MBS as the son learns to adapt to the system in order to ensure his survival. A strong marital foundation to a great extent guarantees that the parents' needs will be met through one another as well as from their own psychological well-being. A son who is the product of mature parents in a healthy relationship will be treated as a child and not be expected to take on inappropriate responsibilities, thereby freeing him to experience his childhood and its developmental stages. Mother will not fear that her son's separation will mean that she is left powerless and alone and Father will not need to rely on his son to play interference for him; a sound marriage allows both Mother and Father to be there for their son. Conversely, in the case of the Mamma's Boy, his needs go unnoticed and his voice unheard. He is expected, and covertly demanded, to become a parent to his parents so that their needs can be satisfied. Mother is incapable of allowing her son to separate as she herself is not an independent and self-actualized woman. Father cannot assist in his son's separation from Mother, nor act as a model for identification, because he too is unable to accept his adult role as a father and carry it through maturely.

The role of the Mamma's Boy into which a son becomes socialized serves to keep the status quo of his parents' relationship by allowing his father's indifference to be tolerated by Mother. With her son by her side, she can bear the lack of communication and support of which she is deprived by her husband. The Mamma's Boy fulfils the needs that have been neglected by her husband and gives Mother a sense of accomplishment which she cannot get from her role as wife. Furthermore, the Mamma's Boy fills a void and serves as a distraction from his mother's lack of control over her own life and the bleakness of the marital bond. As a Mamma's Boy, he is used by his parents to fill the vacuum of their marriage and he quickly adapts to this role in order to safeguard his survival.

The dynamics of the family into which the Mamma's Boy is bred works like a domino effect: Father's behaviour impacts on Mother, who then responds by needing to cling to her son for support. In declining his responsibility as a husband to his wife, he is also declining his responsibility as a father to his son. It is not enough for a father merely to be present. He must contribute to the family structure by being a 'good enough' father, a positive male model with whom his son will want to identify, and a supportive husband to his wife so that the task of separation from her son and vice versa is eased. Otherwise, Father has betrayed and abandoned both Mother and son, who will remain comfortably and eternally fused in a symbiotic lull.

Father's lack of participation in his son's upbringing contributes, albeit passively, to his son's ultimate predicament, for which the father must also be made accountable. Not only is he withdrawing from his duties as a father, but he is also abandoning his wife by not being able to support her emotionally. Consequently, Mother turns to her son, whom she is left to reign over and on whom she desperately remains attached. With her confidence and self-esteem destroyed, which she attributes to her husband, her resentment is manifested by turning her son against him. If her husband does not love her, then at least she can make her son understand what a despicable man he is and destroy the possibility of her son ever identifying with his father, and in her mind, eventually treating her in the same manner. According to Greenson (1968, p. 373), the son's motivation to identify with the father stems from the mother's love and respect for the father. I contend that without mutual love and respect between husband and wife, the son will feel instinctively obligated, let alone encouraged, to protect and side with Mother, as she is his primary source of security and love. His unwillingness to identify with his cold and distant father, who is scorned by Mother, further ensures his trusted position alongside her. The Mamma's Boy becomes Mother's comfort against her unhappiness and his insurance against the threat of being abandoned.

The manner in which the parents interact with one another serves as a model of replication for the son. There are covert and conflicting messages, no sense of consistency or stability, no problem-solving measures, a denial of existing problems and a lack of communication between husband and wife, all of which transcend into the relationship that each maintains with their son. What is understood to be intimacy between the husband and wife is merely a means of smoothing over and denying conflict so that issues are not dealt with in a constructive manner. What is considered to be intimacy is, in reality, a pseudo-intimacy which propagates the belief that the family system is healthy and adjusted. Like the Mamma's Boy, who outwardly appears to be the epitome of perfection, the family structure outwardly appears functional and sturdy while inwardly it is distorted and disturbed. It is for this reason that the Mamma's Boy does not view his role as inappropriate: he has adopted a passive attitude towards the events of his life because he is covertly taught through example not to question it lest he upset the balance of dynamics. He merely fuses with the family rhythm and denies that there is any apparent conflict or incongruity. Just as it is inevitable that resentment is built up between husband and wife, and the son is unconsciously made to bear it, so unleashed resentment is built up in the son which has implications for the way he will relate to himself as well as to others.

The parents' marriage does not mirror any sexuality either by outward demonstration of affection or by open discussion of the topic.

The lack of sexuality between the parents leads to Mother's unconscious seduction of her son; Father does not intervene as he is pleased to be relieved of the pressure to perform as a sexual partner to his wife and as a father to his son. Unknowingly, the son's sexual development will be thwarted by the crossed boundaries and the denial of sexuality as a normal and healthy function.

Mother's gender and her sense of castration leave her feeling powerless. She finds her apparent masculinity and equality, if not superiority, by marrying a man who has strong feminine traits which serve to lessen the difference between the sexes (de Saussure, 1929, p. 554). With a weak, emasculated husband, she can become the powerful, phallic woman and unconsciously legitimize her desire to be a man. Likewise, through the Mamma's Boy who is identified with her, she is able to invest in him her unwanted femininity so that she will always remain, in comparison to him, the more dominant and controlling 'masculine' figure.

The Mamma's Boy is used by both his parents as a 'receptacle'. Lloyd deMause in his article 'The history of child assault' (1990) explains that children are used as 'poison containers' into which the parents project the disowned parts of their psyches so that these feelings can be controlled in another body without danger to themselves. As a Mamma's Boy, he is made to carry the disowned parts of his parents – their anxieties, negative feelings, insecurities and unresolved issues – so that they seem free and cleansed of them. As such, the Mamma's Boy is selfishly weighed down with the responsibilities and attributes which rightfully belong to his parents, forcing him to grow up much too quickly yet paradoxically remain a 'Peter Pan', so that his parents need not look at their own lack of maturity and individuation. As adults, his parents are incomplete and do not have the capacity or skills to promote their son's independence.

It is through the complementary actions of under-fathering and over-mothering that the Mamma's Boy Syndrome is cemented.

CHAPTER FOUR

Mamma's Boys – The Research Study

Milk is the symbol of the first aspect of love, that of care and affirmation. Honey symbolises the sweetness of life, the love for it and the happiness in being alive. Most mothers are capable of giving 'milk', but only a minority of giving 'honey' too. In order to be able to give honey, a mother must not only be a 'good mother', but a happy person – and this aim is not achieved by many. The effect on the child can hardly be exaggerated. Mother's love for life is as infectious as her anxiety is. Both attitudes have a deep effect on the child's whole personality; one can distinguish indeed, among children – and adults – those who got only 'milk' and those who got 'milk and honey'.

Erich Fromm, *The Art of Loving*, p.46

In risking to research a little-understood phenomenon which had not been labelled or discussed in psychological terms, my intention was to give credence to the plight of the Mamma's Boy and name it as a male dysfunction caused by an intrusive and abusive form of mothering. I did not know whether research findings would corroborate my hunch, nor whether, in fact, the basis for a concise theory would emerge. Nevertheless, with only a tentative hypothesis and no other preconceived notions of what I would discover, I undertook research through interviewing mothers, sons and mother-and-son 'couples'. It was not presumed that my subjects would fulfil the aims of my work.

In total, 100 interviews were carried out. Due to the constraints of space, only thirty-two of the interviews appear, including the six cited in Chapter 1. Eleven interviews are with sons, six with mothers and six with mothers and their sons. The mother–son interviews can be further broken down into the following: three interviews consisting of mothers and their one son (interview thirteen, Louise, is the mother of Mark presented in Chapter 1) and three interviews with mothers and their two sons. The sons' ages range from twelve to sixty-four. The mothers' ages range from thirty-nine to fifty-two. The participants are of differing backgrounds, cultures and social strata.

The method of research took the form of prepared questions in a semi-structured interview. The questions (see Appendix) evolved as I collected data and they were not used as an attempt to test my hypothesis. The questions were used as a guideline only, and often took spontaneous form. At other times, questions were omitted entirely or phrased in age-appropriate language in the case of the young sons interviewed. Subjects were not shown the questions nor asked to fill out any information.

As the research progressed, the questions were continually being modified to learn more about the topic and the participants. The subjects themselves very much set the pace of the interviews, which allowed for a flow of narrative. In several instances, at the close of the interview, subjects commented that the nature of the questions had brought to awareness issues they had never considered before. I had the trust of those I interviewed and no doubt they felt safe enough to divulge their personal experiences and insights in such minute detail. I was fortunate to have had subjects who were articulate and open to share of themselves. Their responses allowed for their attitudes, values and feelings to come through. They were assured of confidentiality.

I did not go out to seek the 'type' of subject that I wanted to interview nor did I have the expectation or proof that he/she existed. My interview population was initially drawn from students, who were approached through a letter. The response was overwhelming. An advertisement was also placed in the British Jewish monthly magazine, *New Moon*. Through word of mouth, other subjects contacted me and agreed to take part in the study.

The lengths of the interviews varied; the average interview lasted approximately one and a half hours and each subject was interviewed only once. Mother-and-son 'couples' were interviewed individually and their responses were not made available to the other. For the most part, the interviews took place in a consulting room. Only four interviews were conducted in the participants' homes, at their request.

The interviews were taped with the participants' consent and were then transcribed in full. The presentation of the cases are abridged versions of the original transcripts with only the names and identifying details modified. I could not include all the details of each interview, but, within limitations, an attempt has been made to put forward as many points as possible (in the subject's own words) in order to get the 'feel' of the subject.

The personal interviews have the advantage of putting forward life stories in a way which needed to be said. The method freed each interviewee to speak in his own way and gives the reader the chance to learn from it and find some elements of identification. Respondents brought up what was relevant in whatever way they chose.

As the process of interviewing progressed, patterns, notions and assumptions were born and new theories constantly developed. I was conscious of this and endeavoured to 'bracket' my biases until the data collection was completed in order not to sway the participants in any way.

The interviews which appear suggest that certain assumptions can be formulated. My observations reinforce the view that there is a Mamma's Boy Syndrome which is contingent upon the mother's way of being with her son and which is determined by her past and present experiences. With the last of the interviews completed, I was free to consider and formulate certain hypotheses, which appear at the end of this chapter.

What follows is a glimpse of human behaviour and the realities of those subjects interviewed.

SONS

Interview one: Barry

Forty-five-year-old Barry is the third of five children born to Irish parents. They were not happily married but 'they accepted each other'. There was no open communication and a lot of arguing in the family.

Barry married at the age of twenty-seven and remained so for six years until the marriage was annulled because he 'came out as being homosexual'. He and his wife did not have children.

As a child his mother did not work outside the home and Barry 'fell in with his mother's routine'. He would spend time walking and swimming with his mother. He slept in her bed 'for quite a period' as he was an ill child.

Barry 'doubts that he was breast-fed' and describes his relationship with his mother as excellent. She was happy in her role as mother and was quite happy with her children. She has always been supportive 'even when I came out as gay. She has been there if I have needed her.'

Although his mother was upset when she learned that Barry was gay:

> She was happy that I found myself, as she called it. Mother is quite progressive for a Catholic and she didn't go into torrents of temper, frustration or crying when I told her. She just asked me what it meant and I tried to explain to her as best as possible without really upsetting her. All she said is, if I have to sleep with men, be careful. She was quite good.

Barry feels a duty towards his mother:

> I think a lot about her and go home two or three times a year to see her and help out. I send her things and call her long distance during the week if she is feeling lonely – it is a sense of guilt in some respects, that she is on her own.

It is out of a sense of duty that Barry feels that 'he owes her, as her son. She was there when I needed her and she made herself available to us five children and as a child of hers I have a duty to look after her in her old age.' Barry takes this sense of duty quite seriously: 'It is out of a sense of duty besides the fact that I love her dearly. I don't know how I would cope if she passes away.' Barry said he is 'not close to his mother, we are family'.

Barry's mother had a close relationship with her own mother. She grew up a very strong Catholic and had a typical mother–daughter relationship. She was very dutiful to her mother and they were very close: 'I think they shared a lot together.'

Barry's mother did not confide in him as a child but she did in recent years and 'certainly since I have come out as being gay'. She was close to his partner as well, and would tell them things she wouldn't tell the rest of the family. She would say, 'You understand, don't you' and tell him her problems. Barry's mother would laugh a lot with him and would love to go on holidays with her son: 'I would bring her to gay bars and she would never know if the men were looking at her or me!'

His mother would also confide in him about his father who died fifteen years ago: 'She was terribly bitter about my father, angry for years. I think she is still angry because she has never accepted that he died and left her.' Barry hated his father but nonetheless, tried to get her to talk it through. From the time Barry was twenty, his mother waited until her husband died before she could talk about him to Barry. She would tell him 'very few good things about Father but a lot of terrible things'.

Barry does not have nice memories of being a child because of his father with whom he had a 'terrible relationship'. He still suffers from his experience of his father: 'I have nightmares of him and to this day I still look over my shoulder occasionally. For some years, I used to change my jobs frequently because any time someone would get on to me I sensed my father ... it was like he was there.' Barry suffers from inadequacy, guilt, lack of confidence, grinds his teeth, bites his nails, and can't lose weight. Barry told me that his father 'wasn't good but he probably had some good points as well'.

His mother was dominated by a very powerful man 'so she is not powerful but she can be quite scheming if she is let to get away with it'. Barry identifies with his mother and likes to get his own way: 'I am sensitive and caring, that is what I have inherited from my mother.'

She instilled self-esteem in Barry by all the pride she took in his achievements, which gave him the confidence to move on. His father, on the other hand, would always knock him down. However, Barry believes that he disappointed his mother by not living up to her expectations: 'She would have liked me to have stayed with my old profession of banking and I know that she was let down because I didn't stay married. It was more because of what the neighbours would think than how she felt.'

As a child, Barry tried to please his mother: 'Every week my mother would dish out work and I always did the domestics. I always did the things like cleaning the kitchen, baking and cooking, which I enjoyed. I felt it was good being near my mother and I felt very safe with her.' His mother believes 'it is the reason I am gay'.

When his mother was aggravated with Barry, she would slap him but 'she never sent me to bed without supper or anything like that'. She would stop his comics or sweets or she wouldn't take him places. 'When I believed in Santa Claus as a child, she threatened that I wouldn't get anything for Christmas and I was always sure that she meant it but she always relented in the end! Basically', Barry told me, 'I tried to placate both my mother and father at all times.'

The topic of sexuality was never discussed: 'It was ask your mother and she would then say ask your father.' His parents couldn't cope with sexuality; they did not show any sexuality between them and slept in separate beds. Barry's father was from the old school: 'mention the word sex and you would get a belt in the face.' Anything to do with sex or sexual feeling was taboo in his family.

Barry does not believe that his emotional needs were met as a child. He grew up with a terrible sense of guilt and despair:

From the age of twelve, I fancied my brother's friends, not sexually, I only wanted to be physically held by them. I missed that as a child. I couldn't understand how other children could have parents that loved them and held them and hugged them. My father didn't believe in that.

Barry knew he was gay before he got married but hoped that he would change. In his twenties he would go out with men twenty or thirty years older than himself because 'it was this father image'.

His first day at school was traumatic. He was taken by his mother and 'I felt a sense of abandonment, I felt on my own.' He cried the whole day and was sitting between two girls and a nun. On the second day of school he peed over a wall and wet a nun who badly slapped him: 'It was my first real hatred of women.'

Barry was not encouraged by his mother to have friends or bring any one home because 'my mother was terrified of Father'. He did not enjoy playing sports because 'I was terrified of undressing in front of the other boys'.

Barry sees his mother's inability to stand up to his father as her most negative quality. For years his mother wanted to work outside the home but his father wouldn't let her. Barry believes that his mother should have stood up to his father so 'that she could have found herself'.

Interview two: Laurence

British-born Laurence, age forty-six, is the younger of two sons. His parents have been married for fifty years although they do not 'radiate marital bliss'. Their marriage is 'a par for the course one'.

He describes his mother as feminine, who 'tended towards the fluffy feminine type without going the whole hog. She is very quiet, and not particularly emotionally demonstrative.' She did not work outside the home and was Laurence's sole carer. He was not breast-fed.

His mother adheres to 'old-fashioned Christian values with the emphasis on doing good rather than being good'. Laurence's mother never spoke about her family or her relationship with her mother. All he knew was that her mother had to work to support the family because her father was often out of work.

Laurence does not remember playing with his mother and 'just followed her routine around the house'. His father was the more likely of his parents to play with him and when he had nightmares he would go into his father's bed rather than his mother's.

Laurence's mother had academic aspirations for him and would have wanted him to become a university lecturer, 'my son the professor and that sort of thing'. His mother's brother was academically gifted and won a school scholarship but the family couldn't afford the incidental costs. He continues:

> When my mother realized that, unlike my older brother, I was academically gifted, there was the ambition for me which was unfulfilled in her brother. I was encouraged by both my parents and they even gave up the television so that I could study in the lounge.

Laurence feels that he disappointed his mother by not fulfilling her hopes. Laurence tries to please his mother more now than when he was younger:

> In a way, it is rather like in marriage when you are there to some extent, in an ideal sense, to please your partner. I don't have a partner and if you are the type of person that likes to be liked, then everybody that you are dealing with is there to please. I agonize over my mother's Christmas and birthday presents because at eighty-five, she doesn't get out very much and I don't want to just get her something token.

Laurence was married from the age of twenty-five for five years but had no children. His divorce was a huge disappointment to his mother although she had definite ideas about the type of person she wanted him to marry:

> I think my mother thought my wife was unsuited for me and when we did divorce there was an element of 'I told you so'. She wanted me to marry someone like herself, a nice, tame and timid, respectable English, Christian girl. My wife was flamboyant, Italian, and rebelling against Catholicism. She was masculine, a captain's daughter, who took more after her father than her mother.

Laurence looks at things in terms of 'not wanting to rock the boat' while his mother is still alive:

> By this time next year she can be gone. I would not marry another flamboyant woman because it would upset her. I want to give her a reasonably quiet time. Perhaps as I am getting older, I am getting more like my mother, wanting a quiet life.

The women Laurence is attracted to 'seem to be at least on the surface, temperamentally very different than my mother'. His mother was not demonstrative and there was no sexual awareness in the family. 'I have more friends that are women than men. My emotional relationships are completely divorced from my sexuality and I have been celibate since the end of my marriage.'

It is Laurence that maintains the relationship with his mother because 'I am a single person and I feel it is down to me to do the running if I value the relationship. My role is the court jester. I bring the outside world to my mother by bringing her a blow-by-blow description of my events.' His parents don't ask a lot of him – they like to know that he is all right and vice versa. 'When push comes to shove, if my father dies before my mother there is no question that I would go and live with her,' Laurence states.

As a child, Laurence believes that he might have been his mother's favourite but is now convinced that it is his brother because he can do whatever he wants and Mother will defend him: 'I am expected to behave in order to compensate for my brother.'

Laurence lacks self-confidence and never felt that his mother instilled him with a sense of self-esteem 'besides the platitudes that Christians dole out to their children about self-respect'. Laurence, however, believes that his father was more visibly proud of his achievements and always praised him unconditionally.

Laurence describes his relationship with his mother as 'friendly rather than intimate'. His monthly visits to his parents' home, four hours from where he lives, reflect the pattern of how things were when he was younger: 'When I arrive, my father will join in the conversation for about ten minutes and then disappear to do whatever it is that he does and I am left talking to my mother about what I have been doing.'

Laurence describes his relationship with his father as 'a male conspiracy against Mother because we both have a dark sense of humour which she doesn't like'. He puts his relationship with his father down to being 'the dutiful son who listens to all of his father's same old stories and jokes year after year'. His father was present while Laurence was growing-up and was not the type to go to the pub. When at home, his father would work in the garden or walk the dog.

His father has always tried to do things for himself because of his loss of an arm during World War II. Laurence was not very athletic and not actively encouraged by either of his parents. His lack of athletic interest is due to his father 'not being a role-model in that sense'.

Laurence respects his father but cannot emulate him: 'My father was a professional soldier and I am a pacifist. His idea of masculinity was shaped by being in the army although in later life he was not one of the lads.' Laurence felt that he had to define masculinity for himself which to him means 'something I am deeply suspicious of'.

Laurence did not have a lot of friends but 'was not a loner'. He was not encouraged to bring friends home because 'my parents were embarrassed to have my friends in the house'. He was taken to school until the age of seven by his mother. On his first day, he did not cry but he remembers that 'the little girl sitting next to me was crying and I put my arm around her'.

Laurence was the 'good one' and his brother was the 'naughty one' in the family. His brother was a negative role model for him and Laurence was 'everything his brother was not'. The only time he achieved any credibility with his brother was when he divorced and 'I was made human'. His brother suspected that 'I was duped to go through life as nothing more than a goody-goody, that I had never drank from the cup of bitterness.'

Laurence was the incapable son who on occasion could 'deliver the goods' as it was his brother who would usually do things around the house. 'My brother has taken care of my mother's expectations as far as grandchildren. I feel it is my responsibility to take care of my mother in her old age. It is a trade-off.'

The communication in the family was not particularly open. There was a certain amount of arguing but nothing out of the ordinary. His mother was not authoritarian but when she was angry or disappointed with him she would withdraw: 'There was a stick that she would chase me around the house with but never used on me.' His mother did not confide in him anything she would not say in front of his father. Laurence was not certain, but had a hunch that it was his mother that made the decisions in the family.

Laurence wishes that he had had a more open and honest relationship with his mother, that she had been more tolerant and more open and able to laugh at herself. On the whole, she was unemotional and undemonstrative. He says of his mother, 'I don't suppose I could have expected anything more from her than what she was able to give me.'

Interview three: Chris

Thirty-nine-year-old Chris, the youngest of four children and the only son, was born in Wales eight weeks after the accidental death of his father: 'I think that I have a special place in people's hearts because I was born after my father died.' His mother remarried when he was twelve years old.

Chris had a very good relationship with his mother, who died when he was seventeen: 'My mother was a good friend, she was someone I could count on and talk to. She was there whenever I needed her.' He described his mother as having an open attitude and appreciative of all things spiritual. She worked outside the home. He was not breast-fed.

Chris does not think that he become a substitute husband to his mother: 'I think we all filled some of that loneliness for Mother. I am the nearest thing to my father you can get as a substitute, and I did take over something because of the idea of succession in the family. She saw me as my father's successor.' Until the age of seven, Chris would go into his mother's bed at night. The next day she would say to him, 'You don't really need to sleep with me, do you?'

His mother would consult him on matters after 'she had worked them out a bit on her own'. In his mid-teens, when she had a 'blow-out' with her second husband:

> she sort of talked to me about the options that would be open to her if she did decide to leave him. The next morning when it blew over she said, 'Hey, what am I talking about? I have a good deal here' but she didn't confide in me what the good deal was. I don't think she ever loaded me with her problems.

His mother never wanted to disappoint him; 'She wanted to make sure things would work out before she told me.'

Culturally, it was expected that he go out and presumably do well for himself. This was basically coupled with 'my mother's expectation that I get an education and go out and find a serious job, a career. Other than that, my mother did not load me with her expectations.'

Chris never knew his real father and learned 'how to be a man' from school friends and neighbours. For Chris, masculinity means 'being who I am. It includes going out towards a goal and not being overly aggressive.'

What Chris knows of his father is 'probably filtered':

> My mother could not really talk about the marriage. She would talk about their courting and tell me that she was really lonely

when I would ask her about him. My sister tells me that Father was always laughing and playing jokes. The pictures I have seen of my parents together look like they were very happy and having a good time. My father was never a concrete person in my life because I never knew him.

Chris confides:

I like feminine, colourful women that have some element of mystery attached to them. When I think of feminine, I think of sexy and I am having a hard time seeing my mother in feminine terms because I can't see her as sexy. My mother was colourful enough and mysterious in the sense that there was a lot of things I didn't know about my mother and father's relationship.

Chris sees several similarities between his mother and his partner:

My mother was very much interested in what was going on in the world and my girlfriend, likewise, has an open attitude. That is actually my attitude now and maybe I picked it up from my mother. My mother used to enjoy talking to people, not just chit-chat, and I used to talk a lot to her. My partner tends to be the same way.

Chris was 'the only man about the house'. He was the only son in a patriarchal family and it was up to him to make the family decisions. He was consulted about such matters as inheritances and whether his uncle should be buried in the family grave: 'It was me who had the say so and I was only nine.' Chris told me, 'It gave me a sense of responsibility. I don't feel that I grew up before my time.' He doesn't think it made a difference that he was the only son and says his biggest responsibility was that 'he was expected to make the most of things'.

Interview four: Conrad

Fifty-seven-year-old Conrad is the youngest of three children. He is English and was breast-fed for a brief period. His father died when Conrad was seventeen and his mother is ninety-five years old.

His mother was not his sole carer. He had a nanny but his 'mother was there for the occasional rounds'. Conrad described his nanny as 'reasonably warm' but he couldn't remember much about her except that 'I began to resent her, not because she had replaced my mother, but in the respect that someone was telling me what to do.'

Conrad's mother did unpaid work as a magistrate, volunteered her time for charities and did 'all the right things for someone of her position'. Conrad does not have memories of actually playing with his mother but has recollections of her 'being around when playful things were happening'. Neither did Conrad play with his nanny. His childhood was happy, 'a kind of benign neglect'.

His mother came across as a very attractive woman but asexual. Conrad is attracted to more earthy women although he sees some similarities between his mother and his wife: 'They share a certain physical resemblance and a certain coolness. My wife has strict concepts of what is permissible and what isn't in terms of acceptable good form. My wife would be shocked at the similarities between them.' Conrad's ideal mother would be someone he could talk and be open with as 'my son now talks to my wife'.

Conrad described his mother as 'fundamentally shallow, narrow in outlook and upbringing, spoiled, intelligent, with a tremendous sense of duty. She was remote and cool, certainly with her relations with my Father. My father was the affectionate one.' Conrad recalls climbing into his mother's bed and 'I was welcomed but I think she was more like a cat than a kitten.'

His mother had a strong sense of family and she loved her children in a 'mild sort of way for what we did rather than for who we were'. Conrad was not sure how she envisioned her role as a mother but thinks 'she probably brought us up partly because it was what she was supposed to do. We fell within the pattern of being appropriate children for that class of background.' His mother saw herself more as a 'manageress' of the household than a mother: 'She was fulfilling the function for which she had been bred.'

Her own relationship with her mother was characterized as 'efficient' and cold. At the age of twenty-six her mother told her, 'You may get married this year if you wish,' and so she did.

It was understood that Conrad had to please Mother:

I had to keep Mother happy and please her because, if not, she got bad-tempered and difficult. If she was the centre of attention, if I did what she wanted, she was far more witty, bright and lively. That was the central theme of her life, to be the centre of attention.

If Conrad did not please her, she would cry or take to her bed although it 'didn't happen very often because she chose not to see things that she didn't like'. His mother was not intrusive but had very rigid standards of what she expected him to do and achieve. However, Conrad did not perceive a lack of closeness between them.

His mother encouraged him to take an interest in the law and to read. She also took pride in his athletic achievements, which she took part in as a spectator. His mother instilled in him self-esteem by encouraging him to take part in various things and 'I wasn't afraid to do things right.' As the 'little one', Conrad was the rebel but nevertheless felt valued. His mother 'always stuck up for me probably because being her son, I had to be good by definition. I was a trophy child and she would fight fiercely on my behalf if she thought I was being ill done by.'

Conrad believes that his mother saw him as a reflection of her mothering: 'If I was bad than she was a bad mother.' Her expectations for Conrad was that he would be successful in terms of material success, position and rank: 'Mother wanted me to achieve for her benefit. She perceives me as having achieved success even though she doesn't have the faintest concept of what I do. She didn't acknowledge me as a person so much as a position.'

His mother was glad to have both sons and a daughter:

> There were things that sons did and things which daughters did. Sons grew up tall, clever and handsome and wore well-cut dinner jackets and got decent jobs. Daughters married chaps like that and produced the next generation, which my sister obligingly did.

Conrad's mother did not confide in him nor was there any semblance of communication in the family although 'it was a natural thing to see one's parents in order to be given money. It didn't imply a lack of love or respect, it was automatic.' There was not much quarrelling in the family except from Conrad who 'struggled and fought. I sensed early on that this strict performance was not for me. As soon as I could, I escaped and lived my life abroad.' He left home at eighteen.

Sexual matters were never discussed although Conrad has a gut feeling that his mother never achieved orgasm 'because she had no concept of sexual matters – sex was wicked. I could remember that Father was quite demonstrative towards her and she wouldn't be interested.'

Conrad believes that his parents' marriage was a 'moderately happy one'. Decisions were made together and 'they were a good partnership'. His mother would make small decisions and his father would make most of the big decisions.

Conrad's father was warm but 'there wasn't enough of it because he was a very busy man. He was very caring and calm and I loved him very much.' He was always present in spirit and 'occasionally present in the flesh. He was strong, clever and hard-working.' He encouraged Conrad to be athletic and played cricket with him. Conrad thinks his father was 'an excellent role-model'. From his father, Conrad learned that it is all right to be warm, loving and demonstrative and that those born privileged 'have a duty to repay our debt to the world'.

Conrad described his relationship with his mother as 'improving':

> I desperately want to get it right for her because basically, I am all she's got in this country and she is ninety-five years old. I love her and protect her, the old bitch that she is, and I need to help her. I know her pretty well and she knows me not at all. I would like our relationship to be warm.

Interview five: Gregory

Fifty-one-year-old Gregory is the eldest of one brother and two sisters. He was born to English parents. He was not breast-fed.

He feels a great closeness to his mother, which goes hand in hand with 'great hatred that operates at all times without me being aware of it'. He sees his mother as his most formative relationship, which gave him a measure of the quality of love. She did not place demands on him and 'she was really very good at not being too caring'.

He believes that 'because I was the first child, I had a significance which the other children in the family never quite had. It wasn't so much an expectation as a significance. I was proof of their potency.' Nonetheless, he doesn't think that he lived up to his mother's expectations.

When Gregory was born, there were many people who lived with them; his mother's parents and an aunt and uncle, so he feels that he had many carers including his mother who did not work outside the home. His father, however, was away in the army.

His mother idealized her own mother. She died when Gregory was eight but 'everything I heard about her was that she was a wonderful person and they had a wonderful relationship.'

On Gregory's first day of school at the age of four, he was taken by his mother and 'left at the gate like a parcel. I screamed and shouted. The doors were locked to keep me in and I was furious that I was locked in a place that I didn't want to be.' It took him some time to adapt but he was not angry at his mother: 'After all, no amount of preparation or sweet-talking can get around that actual "leaving the child" and both parties know that in the end.' He resented his mother for making him go to school at such an early age but can't remember any other time that she wasn't 'good-enough'.

Gregory came to see school as the provider of his intellectual needs. 'I wouldn't have needed to have done that if my mother had been more intellectual.' Gregory formed an attachment to school 'which was almost maternal in the sense of really needing it. My emotional needs were met from my teachers' interest in me and they became the first adults to whom I felt close.' He received 'a kind of emotional satisfaction which my mother couldn't provide me because she wasn't in any way learned'. He saw his mother as 'a protector, a good companion in play and adequate at looking after my physical needs. Apart from my needs that could be channelled through intellect, I would say my mother took care of my needs.'

His father was not there for several years after he was born but after that period, he was very much present: 'He was the most directly forceful member of the family.' His father was a powerful man and 'one was aware of his status. It was derived from him having to go out and tackle the real world and from doing all those horrible things children and wives don't do, like dealing with the monstrous world.' Things had to be done his father's way and Gregory was 'bribed and cajoled' into doing so. Gregory does not remember playing with his father but is sure that he did.

His parents' marriage veered from 'very happy to very unhappy but they wouldn't have wanted it any other way'. His mother did not confide in him and neither of his parents leaned on him or used him 'as a football tossed between them'. His parents had hourly 'episodes' rather than daily ones and 'I just had to wait till things got back to normal.' Decisions were made by his father although 'I think Mother was subtle at manipulating things to get her own way.'

Gregory left home for university. Although he went back at holidays, visits become more infrequent:

At eighteen, I was ready to go and I didn't really relish going back home. My mother was always really good at just letting me do what I really wanted. If I went back I could, and if I didn't want to go, there were no recriminations, no upsets. It is still very much the same today.

Gregory's ideal mother is like his own: 'She is herself and doesn't act at being a mother – she is a mother.' His mother did not fulfill his needs but 'which mother does? No mother can ever not fail to let the baby down. It is a matter of whether it is dropped or put gently down onto the floor,' Gregory told me. 'I was gently put down on the floor.'

Interview six: Tom

Twenty-nine-year-old Tom is the youngest of three children, with a sister of forty-five and a brother of thirty-five. He is the only one of them who was adopted by his British mother and American father.

He describes his relationship with his mother as a 'constant exploration in a dark room'. He has very little idea of who she is 'besides the fact that she is a perfectionist who leads a superlative life'. He feels that he has learned more about her from newspaper articles than from her as his mother.

His mother did not work outside the home but was not his primary carer:

> There were nannies, male governesses and a lot of staff. My mother would delegate the warmth of the hour to others but wished to arrive as the queen bee and make the ultimate decisions. When the toys came off the shelf Mother was not down on her knees with us. I call it hands-off parenting and I wouldn't advise it.

Tom describes his mother as 'dependent on her husband and hostile because she wants to create a "snow-white" environment. She would like to be self-directing but has never been released from her gilded cage. She is an appendage of my father and a weak running mate at that.' His family was, as he put it, 'parent-centered and, moreover, socially centered. First came my mother, second the staff, third came Father and then the kids, who were an extension of the art on the wall, little trophies.' His mother's concern was, 'How can I keep the guests happy who are coming to dinner in three nights' time, and where am I going for lunch today? It was really about her life.'

His mother's energies were put into keeping a pleasant house within the community. Tom describes his mother as 'externally focused': 'She did not muck in with us, she didn't eat the food we ate, she didn't sleep the hours we slept and she didn't play with us.'

Tom's upbringing was 'quite rigid, regimented and destructive. It was a situation where the child was never brought into the solution. I was not allowed in because she was never there and I felt indifferent to the fact because I didn't know any different.'

Tom remembers going into his mother's bed (his parents had separate bedrooms) only once when he was five but 'my mother didn't really like it'. He went to look for some comfort, because as a child he was often constipated, and his mother 'rammed a suppository up my ass and I hated it. After that experience I would never go to her again.' He sees this experience as indicative 'of my situation at the time – I was lost in a sea of servants who were marching around and Mother was the drill instructor. It's funny because my brother could never find a loo, and he was always shitting in his pants. It is very sad actually.'

Tom believes that his mother did not play the role of mother at all: 'Her role was in loving Father and he had such a good mother that the way he chose his wife did not include the mother element. He did not need to find a mother substitute.'

Tom was expected to succeed 'but not too well as to make my brother look bad. My mother basically asked me to "ground my aircraft" so that my brother could fly higher.' He has lived up to his mother's expectations 'by not destroying the family image'.

His self-esteem was gained by default:

> I learned to survive because of my mother's rejection. My mother's wisdom is not about the clothes in her closest or about the size of her bank account – she would tell me to stand on my own two feet and as a result I am strong. My self-esteem has come from beating my mother at her own game.

Tom tries to please his mother and if she told him to 'jump off a cliff I would, but guess what? I would spring back up as if I was attached to a bungee!' He has tried to 'please Mother for all the wrong reasons and I have realized that it is pointless because my self-respect is always being shattered'.

Tom does not know anything about his mother's relationship with her own mother and doesn't even know his grandmother's name. However, he believes that his mother had a 'bruised' childhood and a traumatic relationship with her father, who married her off at eighteen 'because it was a business merger'. Tom's mother was given a second change when she remarried, to Tom's father.

Of his parents' marriage Tom said that his mother found her scripts for life from Sydney Sheldon novels: 'She has actualized the dreams of women who buy the books for that romantic passionate drama. The drama has to end – my parents are still in the passionate romantic stage. I think it is time they wind down a bit.'

Tom's relationship with his father was controlled by his mother: 'She was the gate-keeper who allowed me though the door to my father.' His father gives him a whole lot more respect than his mother does but 'no matter how good I am, she will not allow me to get close to him'.

His father was present and did all that he could but 'was not the father that would help with homework or toss a ball with me. That just wasn't him. My mother would always tell me, "your father could only help you so much and the rest is up to you."' Tom's father would give him money instead of love.

It is Tom who maintains the closeness with his father, which is welcomed: 'I do the same with my mother but she only rejects me.' His mother very rarely calls him and she jokes that the 'mountain must come to Mohammed'.

Tom has learned from his father to be ethical and giving. His father would always say, 'The price of being a man is expensive. I must keep your mother happy.' Tom respects his father and views him as a success who has 'conquered the world'.

The facts of life were explained to Tom by his mother. However, she believes 'that my sex life is a ball that belongs to her. She says that if she is to accept someone else into the family she wants to have the say in who I choose. As a result, I am dick-unhappy.'

His childhood was about a lack of hugs and warmth and he never felt that he had an identity in the family. When Tom was six, his mother called him into the study and told him that if he didn't like the family or if he didn't live up to the family standards, he would be 'sent back':

> My mother raised me as if I was from another family, which I am. She raised me in the belief that my brother would take over the power from my father and that I would get the second-best alternative. My brother was raised in the image of my father, whereas I have never been my father's son according to my mother.

Tom believes that he has 'a basic people problem because my social skills have been rejected by the very people who were supposed to teach them to me. I feel that I have gotten the short end of the deal but I am trying to learn to celebrate who I am.' He often feels that he is a social misfit, even though he knows that he is not:

> I am learning to survive and would like to believe that I am going to win. There is grieving to be done but I must accept that what is gone is gone. I have survived by shutting off and being a robot. I have survived by putting on the clothes my mother

needed me to be seen in. I am really an extension of my mother rather than an evolution of me.

MOTHERS

Interview seven: Julie

Julie, the mother of an eight-year-old son and an adopted six-year-old daughter, is British and the second of three sisters. She is forty-four years old.

When Julie was pregnant she really wanted a son because 'I came from a family of females and I was aware that my father wanted a son and never had one. If I had a son, I thought it would be the son he always wanted.' Her father probably wanted 'one of us to be a boy, so maybe I would have fulfilled his expectations more if I had a son'. Julie was a tomboy as a child and 'it helped that I developed late'. She wasn't eager for the onset of puberty and loved the tomboy period in her life.

Julie had a difficult time conceiving and although her husband didn't care what sex the baby was, 'I thought that if this baby would be a one-off, I wanted a son to carry on the family line even though it is not my line. There was that kind of old-fashioned thinking.' Julie's marriage is a happy one with 'healthy tensions'.

Julie's relationship with her mother has been 'up and down'. As a child, she was very close to her mother, who was very feminine and very 'mumsy'. Her mother's sole ambition was to get married and have children so 'I think she was very fulfilled by her children and home.' In her teens, Julie went in the opposite direction to spite her mother and accepts her mother now, although she doesn't want to be like her and 'I'm not'. Her mother is pleased that her daughters turned out to be different from her.

Julie had a happy childhood and was a 'good little girl'. Her mother was loving and nurturing and her parents' marriage was a contented one. Her father was very much present and she was aware that she was his favourite: 'I would go fishing with him and I did all the things a boy would have done.'

Julie described her son as very outgoing, 'a real extrovert' and she thinks it is wonderful that he doesn't have a problem approaching people. She sees her son as going into the world and carving a space for himself. He has an inner self-confidence which she doesn't see herself as having: 'He has an inner sense of feeling right wherever he is and it is something his father has. Maybe he sees it in his father and sees that that is how men are in the world.' Julie's only expectation for her son was that he would be bright: 'It would have been a disappointment if he were really thick!'

Julie and her son are close and 'we are a physical family, a lot of hugging, kissing and touching'. His father is the same with him. On an emotional level, Julie is closer with her son than he is with his father and 'that is because I am a "feeling" person and I like to know what he is feeling. My husband is more of a thinking person.'

Julie believes that 'it is always difficult for a mother to allow her child to separate and the issue arises from day one and is an issue till he leaves home. My son is going through the stage of testing out how he can organize his own life. It makes me ask myself, "Is that the right thing to be doing now?"' She hopes she is giving him the message that 'I am here and I love you no matter what happens' rather than the message 'You can't leave me!' 'He is not mine, he is a little person in his own right and he doesn't belong to me.'

Until her son was nine months old, Julie was home with him exclusively. He was breast-fed for five months and that time was total bliss: 'I was on cloud nine and then it became boring and I started to go potty.' Her son demanded a lot of attention and was given it non-stop. Julie played with him all the time, he spent a lot of time on her body and she carried him a lot. She felt a real 'guilt trip' because he was a wanted child whom they had waited a long time to have. By the time he was three, Julie had help in the house and worked part-time.

Julie could not understand how parents could push their children to achieve and gain so much satisfaction from it:

> I always believed you must do things for yourself. I am proud of my son's achievements but I don't fulfil myself through him. I have no sense of wanting him to do things because I haven't achieved them and I don't expect or want him to give me something I haven't got out of my relationship with my husband.

Interview eight: Barbara

German-born Barbara, fifty-two years old, was convinced that her first child would be a girl and her second a boy: 'It wasn't a fantasy it was an absolute certainty! I never had any doubts. I have always had flashes of insight about events that would happen.' Her first child, a daughter, is seventeen and her son is eleven. Both children were very sleepless which was 'very stressful for both me and them'.

When her daughter was born, she was unmarried. When she eventually married, on some level she believed that her husband would actually prefer to have a son. Her son was initially breast-fed but continuing proved impossible because of medical reasons: 'I suffered from post-natal depression when he was born so he was removed from me when he was a few weeks old.' Barbara's marriage broke up soon after his birth.

Described as 'one-dimensional', her husband equates happiness with material comfort. She sees him as an 'OK' role model to her son and they share a close, father–son relationship. Although they were separated when their son was young, her husband was very much present.

Barbara spent the first seven and a half years of her son's life at home with him. Time was spent 'mixing and mingling' with other kids. They would go to parks, the zoo and on different outings in the push chair: 'We were always moving around and doing things.' She had no expectations for her son: 'It is entirely up to what God and nature intend.'

Barbara was not raised by her mother. She was handed over to foster parents at birth although she maintained a 'fractious' relationship with her birth mother: 'She would come and go when I was a child. She is a "sphinx-like individual" who maintained a distance. She is quite cruel and nasty with me if I allow her.' Barbara really didn't know her father except when he was drinking. Her natural parents' marriage was always troubled, yet they remained married until her father died of alcoholism seven years ago.

Barbara considers her foster parents to be her 'real' parents. Her foster mother was feminine but very strict: 'She looked feminine but she was the one that ruled.' Her foster mother worked while she was growing-up. Barbara says she comes from a long line of dictatorial, domineering women who were very strong. Both her birth mother and foster mother were strong-willed and strong-minded.

Her foster father was very 'spiritual' but was overshadowed by his wife. They were married for over fifty years and had a good marriage. They were demonstrative and loving towards each other and towards her.

Barbara was a tomboy up until her twenties. She always felt more comfortable in the company of men 'because there was a boy next door who was like a big brother to me. He was an only child and so was I, so I always felt comfortable with him.'

She describes her relationship with her son as 'sensitive, intuitive and very close'. He lives with his father but she gets him in 'chunks' and there is a continual communication through the post. Barbara describes her son as 'very impish, beautiful and big for his age'. He is athletic and Barbara supports that in him.

Barbara confides in her son 'as much as he can take on board. He is extremely intuitive and clued in – a tremendously good reader of people. He is always right about them.' She shares with him all her intimate feelings and also discusses in detail the break-up of her marriage: 'My son takes the lead in these talks and I follow. He has a major capacity for insight.'

Interview nine: Mary

Mary, aged forty-five, has been happily married for twenty years. Her eldest child, a son, is sixteen and she has two younger daughters. She is British and has one sister six years her senior.

Mary and her husband both wanted a son for the first child. She believes she wanted a boy because 'I didn't have any brothers.' With her son, she has always had the expectation that he would go to university: 'I don't really know if he has much of a say in the matter. The pressure is on him.' She also had the expectation that he would be an all-around kid. Mary does not believe that children should be controlled but 'a certain amount of control is necessary in the form of discipline'.

Mary thinks that her son does things to please her, and that he knows exactly what does and does not do so. Mary, however, is unaware of any expectations she has of him. When she is displeased with him, she will withdraw and he will 'come and find me out and want to talk about it'.

There is open communication in the family and a lot of it:

> There is a lot of shouting, anger, and lots of screaming. Reasoning has gone out the window a bit since the children have gotten older. As a family we all sit down to dinner together and we might talk openly then. I wouldn't say to my son, 'Oh, you know I have big sexual problems' or something of that sort but I would say to him, 'Your dad is getting on my nerves!'

Mary works outside the home, although she did not when her son was an infant. She was the sole carer of her son and her husband was 'always around and a big help'. She played a lot with her son and carried him most of the time in a sling on her body. Mary describes the early years of motherhood with her son as 'a time I muddled through from meal to meal and from nappy to nappy. It was difficult learning to be a mother and having the responsibility of a small baby. It wasn't easy.' Mary had mixed feelings about that period of her life and she was 'very up one minute and very down the next'.

Mary's husband is 'very masculine, yet very feeling'. Her son looks like a man but 'he is really a sensitive child. He kisses me goodbye every morning when he goes off to school and he kisses both me and his father good-night when he goes off to bed.' His relationship with his father is very good and there is a 'real father–son bond'.

Her relationship with her son is 'OK':

> At the moment, our relationship is that he is separating and I have very strong feelings about what is going on. I almost want to hold on a bit so that he won't go. I don't have very good feelings about separation – both my parents died when I was a child and I want this separation to be all right. Even though I know it isn't a death thing, it still frightens me a bit.

Interview ten: Laura

Divorced, Laura has one twenty-six-year-old son. She is the youngest of one sister and three brothers. She is fifty years old and British.

Laura was anxious about becoming a mother and didn't think that she would be any good at it: 'I was shocked that I had allowed myself to become a mother. I didn't believe that I could give birth to a healthy child and I was really surprised when he had ten fingers and ten toes!' She judged herself as a good mother in terms of her son's behaviour: 'My son was not a good baby and cried a lot, didn't sleep and went rigid if I tried to cuddle him. My feeling of being a bad mother was fortified.' Her belief that she was not an able mother pushed her to allow her son to take on too much responsibility. She let him make his own decisions because she did not want to be accountable in case she made a mistake.

Laura wanted a son because she had the idea that boys were better than girls. Her expectations of her son was that he should be the best at everything. He had some problems with learning and 'It came to me then, that he didn't have to be a doctor or a lawyer.'

At an early age, her son was having difficulties:

> A child psychologist was consulted who made me hear that my attitude toward parenting was that of ownership of my son. I expected him to fill my needs and views. I then realized that he was separate from me and that I would have to let go and I just wanted him to be happy.

This was a freeing idea for Laura as she realized that she was not totally responsible for 'this other human being'. However, she is still aware that consciously there are a lot of things that would please her if her son complied with her demands.

Laura's relationship with her son is 'good, contained':

> My son sees me as someone who doesn't need his support or help. He sees me as a mother who it is perfectly safe to be away from, and he knows that he could always come back and I won't be resentful.

Her son lives with his father and Laura is angry about it. She is concerned for her son and feels that his father fosters the belief that he needs him to look after him. Her son gets very emotional about his father being on his own. In contrast, her son sees her as very strong and independent, 'someone who can stand on my own two feet. I don't need him to lean on.'

Laura is very open with her son and she freely talks to him about how she sees their relationship and how she sees him. They also discuss how his childhood has contributed towards his growing difficulties.

Her son has a drug problem and Laura believes that this is due to the fact that he does not have any self-esteem. She feels responsible for not enabling him to be confident in himself and sees his drug problem as a symptom of his lack of self-esteem, because he 'has turned to drugs rather than people. He hasn't had a normal social development.'

Laura worked outside the home when her son was an infant and would take him to a child-minder in the morning. She didn't play with him as 'I didn't have time for that. I expected him to very much get on with things on his own. There was very little shared time.' Laura was very unhappy at that time in her life and her son's needs were a real burden to her: 'I had done a lot of rejecting and pushing away. It was two-sided because when he came home from school he wouldn't want to talk to me. When I was engaged in something, he would then want my attention.' Her son was breast-fed for a brief period of time.

Laura did not have a good relationship with her own mother, whom she was separated from 'on and off' since she was a small baby. She died when Laura was seven. Her mother was not a particularly feminine woman and Laura says, 'My own femininity is a mysterious thing and occasionally I am aware of feeling good about being a woman.' Laura was a tomboy when growing up and thinks, 'I am still a bit of a tomboy now.'

Her relationship with her father was 'bad'. He was emotionally withdrawn and he 'did not value women, girls'.

Laura's relationship with her husband was very poor. He was not particularly involved in family matters and it was she who made all the decisions. He was a 'weak, dependent person' who was emotionally distant like her father.

On her son's first day of nursery school at the age of three, he was disturbed about being away from his mother. She felt very cruel. He was not an athletic child and had a very small circle of friends which never changed.

When her son was nine, Laura felt panicked that she had never spoken to him about 'the facts of life'. She went to the extreme and told him everything: 'I think I knocked him out a bit.' She did not feel comfortable with it but she thought, 'It was something I ought to do.' Sexuality does not mean a great deal to Laura and she thinks that came across to her son: 'When he was very young he would want my husband and me to kiss and cuddle and he would nag us to do it.' As a child, he never slept in bed with her and her husband.

Laura would be relieved if her son marries providing he 'doesn't marry someone like me'. She sees her son as putting her on a pedestal and she finds it a terrible responsibility. Laura's fantasy is that if he would marry, he would have somebody else to share his life with, and she could stand back: 'My life would finally be undisturbed.'

She believes that even though she was a poor source of nurture 'there must have been something there because otherwise we wouldn't have the relationship we have'.

Interview eleven: Lucy

Forty-four-year-old Lucy was never married. She is the mother of two sons aged twenty-two and twenty, both from the same father. She is British.

Lucy's fantasy was to have a very cute little boy: 'It was like a little girl wanting a boy doll wearing a little duffel coat and red wellingtons.' She wanted a son for the first child and a daughter for the second and was disappointed that her second was not that daughter she had hoped for.

She never had any expectations for her sons. She wanted to be a 'friend' to her children and wanted them to feel that they were understood. She never imagined that she would have to enforce discipline or structure: 'I wanted them to have freedom. That is how I felt when I was a young mother. I feel that I have lived up to that.'

Lucy worked when her children were infants and her mother helped out with them until they were twelve and ten. Lucy spent a lot of time doing everything with her children 'almost overdoing it. All the kids would be over at my house, which was children-centered.' She felt resentful because she did not have an adult life but on the other hand, wanted to do it for them. Both her sons were breast-fed for a year and she spent a lot of time carrying them. Her youngest 'practically lived on my back. He was very clingy, clinging because of panic and a need to hang on. I guess I clung to him as well.'

Her sons slept with her until they were ten or eleven. She stopped because she thought, 'What would happen when I would have a boyfriend?' She doesn't think she has been good at setting boundaries and did what she thought 'ought' to be done.

Lucy's relationship with her older son is good and 'we are friends'. However, she feels a bit of guilt because of being a single parent: 'He had to do a lot of parenting and I always feel guilty that he had to support me, that he had to take on a role before his time'. It started very early on, from the time that he was a baby. He had a 'compassion' and an 'empathy' for Lucy that she never experienced before in her life; 'He had a quality, a love that was concern and care.'

Her relationship with her second son is 'problematic and extreme'; 'I feel that we are similar and that we clung together. We were alike … two peas in a pod. He is a part of me because we are the same type and look alike. My older son was more delicate and softer. I saw him as independent from me.' Lucy explained that it was as if she and her younger son were clinging together 'in the face of something quite dangerous, which at the time was their father who was quite unhinged'.

Lucy feels that she grew up with her children and did not take on the role of adult. She is concerned that she may have confided too much in them and hopes that she has not confused being 'open and honest' with saying too much.

Lucy's parents had an unhappy marriage. Her mother was very domineering and always complaining. She had all kinds of expectations for her which she did not live up to. Her mother was 'not very feminine but I would see her soften up and become sexual around my father'. Lucy was a tomboy and 'I don't think that has ever stopped.' Towards the end of her mother's life they had become good friends. Lucy never really knew her father but has a masculine image of him.

Lucy doesn't really understand the relationship she had with her sons' father and believes she was much too young to have children: 'I was repressed and unable to express my needs to my partner and didn't have a clue about having a relationship.' Her partner was alcoholic, irresponsible, aggressive and 'just not there in an emotional sense'. As a result, her sons had no constant father figure in their lives.

Her younger son was very fearful being around his father and 'became unmanageable and highly strung and, consequently, became a drug addict'. It has been difficult for Lucy and there have been a lot of arguments. Lucy feels tired and has rationalized that 'He is a very male boy and really needed a father. His father was useless to him and caused a lot of chaos.' Lucy feels guilty but has always tried 'her best to be his friend. It is hard, very hard.'

Lucy feels guilty because she was promiscuous when her sons were young:

I don't know that they picked it up but neither of them are particularly promiscuous. On the good side, we talked a lot about sexuality and I am pleased the way they have formed relationships. It seems the 'mess' they received from me has not affected their healthy relationships.

She would feel good about them getting married if she thought the relationship was not a destructive one.

Her sons moved out when they were twenty-one and nineteen and live together within walking distance of their mother. She was relieved when they moved and 'felt really good about it. It was a great achievement because I made them move out and set it all up.'

Lucy says of her sons:

They are both wonderful people, handsome and loving. Having my sons was my first experience of unconditional love. That is why having a child is such a big thing ... because there is this helpless thing that you love and is yours. You love him and they absolutely adore you and it is very simple and very private.

Interview twelve: Gloria

Happily married for thirty years, fifty-two-year-old Gloria has two daughters and a son who is the youngest.

Gloria couldn't imagine that after two girls, she would have anything else but another daughter and was extremely excited to have a son: 'I thought it was a miracle.' Her daughters were breast-fed for a short period of time but her son, not at all.

She believes that her children respond differently towards her according to their sex; 'My daughters and I have a lack of trust whereas I never experienced that with my son. I think he has always trusted me and he is not looking for trouble. It feels more fun and easier to be with him than with my daughters.' Her son is twenty-three years old.

Gloria has the expectation that her son will be able to support a family one day but 'I don't know if he has that same expectation for himself.' She is disturbed because he is more interested in a 'quality of life which means he does not like to work too hard'. Her son has not established himself as a professional person and 'I don't think that he has intentions of doing so.'

Gloria worries because 'I was not a very pushy mother.' She hopes that her son will be able to 'bring home the bread in a responsible way' but concedes that he is still young and single. She expected her son to be educated and 'he chose that for himself'. Her hope is also that he would support himself and live independently which he has achieved.

Gloria did not work outside the home when her son was an infant. She spent time with her son playing with him and making sure his needs were met; 'I was an old-fashioned type of mother.'

Her relationship with her son is very good and she respects him. She has always allowed him to be independent and tried to instil confidence in him by being encouraging and supportive of whatever he wanted to do, 'even if I disagreed with his choices'.

She describes their family life as 'rather boring, and typical, without any seeming problems'. There is open communication and her husband has always been a 'good and involved father'. Her son and husband have a particularly strong relationship although 'he has not chosen to emulate his father and become a doctor, much to my chagrin'.

Gloria was not a tomboy growing up but 'neither was I feminine'. She was independent and took every opportunity to get away from home. She moved to England from Canada when she was eighteen.

Gloria's mother was 'very angry most of the time so I tried to stay out of her way'. Gloria's role was to 'make things OK, to keep the peace in the house' because her only sister, six years her senior, had a stormy relationship with their mother. Her mother is 'intellectual and a powerful influence on me although she is actually a very vulnerable person'. Gloria always found it easier to talk to other peoples' mothers.

Her relationship with her father was 'terrific'. He was more fun than her mother and when she was young, he was always there when she needed him: 'My father was very much involved in youth groups and everybody knew him as "Uncle Joe". I felt that I had to compete for his attention, which was irritating.'

When she was growing up, Gloria's grandmother on her mother's side would come and stay for the summer:

> She was always suffering from headaches and never seemed to be well. She loved to cook and did all the things my mother didn't really like to do. Grandma was a nice influence. However, Mother would get really angry with her and would go into fits of anger when she was around. Grandma had a big effect on my mother.

Gloria has tried to create a family situation 'devoid of stress and arguments' and hopes that she achieved open communications with her children. Sex was discussed with each of her children 'when they were ready and came and asked me about it'.

She hopes that she has been a good mother to her son. She looks forward to the day that he will come to her and tell her that he is getting married and only hopes that 'whoever my son chooses, she will love him as much as I do and make him very happy.'

Interview thirteen: Louise

Louise is the mother of Mark who is cited in Chapter 1 as an example of a moderate Mamma's Boy. She is fifty-two years old, British and has been 'happily' married for thirty-four years. She also has a son eight years older than Mark. Neither of her sons was breast-fed.

With each of her pregnancies Louise wanted a girl because 'I was used to girls and felt more comfortable with them.' She also grew up with one younger sister whom she often looked after, and she thinks that had a bearing on her desire for a daughter.

Her only expectation for her sons was that 'they wouldn't waste the talent they were born with'. She has tried to teach them 'that if you have an opportunity to further yourself, to make life more appealing, go for it. It might not work out but at least you have tried.' Louise believes that that is how her sons have been instilled with self-esteem, 'by grabbing every opportunity'.

Louise wanted to be kind, loving and 'there' for her sons and believes that she has achieved that. She respects both her sons for what they have done in their lives and she loves them both as individuals. Her relationship with her sons is 'loving and warm'.

Louise remained at home with each of her sons when they were infants. She would play with them, take them on outings and talk to them: 'Every Monday and Friday I had housework to do and they would follow me around the house when I did my routine. My older child was more of an adventurer. Mark, however, loved to be there even if I went to the toilet. If I had a bath, he was there.' Louise enjoyed spending time with her children and does not believe that she exerted control over them.

Louise does not expect her children to please her 'or at least not all the time. I guess as a parent I have hopes and aspirations but I pray that I am not one of those parents that demand things from their children, but I am sure at times I do.' She shows her disappointment towards them by holding back and then exploding.

In her mind, 'We are all pals. It is a nice, friendly, robust atmosphere and they show me a lot of affection.' Louise describes her relationship with Mark as friendly, loving and honest: 'I think we listen to each other. He is a confident person and I respect him for that.' She describes him as noisy, 'a big gush of wind blowing in, which makes me come alive. Mark is intelligent and everything about him is alive. He was a fighter from the minute he was born.' Her older son is quieter and more reserved: 'He is also very loving. He is extremely bright and more analytical and more serious than Mark.'

Louise thinks that 'maybe I confide in Mark more than I should, especially about his father'. She says her sons have been easy to talk to and 'I have been easy to talk to as well. I think unconsciously I look to my sons, especially Mark, to fulfil the things in my life that my husband does not fulfil for me.'

Louise's mother confided in her about everything and 'It was too much at times. I felt that things she should be confiding she didn't, and what she did was inappropriate.' From this experience, Louise learned that 'children should never be underestimated because they are very knowledgeable and aware of what is going on'. Louise is fully aware of what it was like for her to be brought up in that situation and has 'tried to the best of my ability not to be like my mother'.

Her mother placed heavy expectations on her and made comparisons between her and her sister. She never felt that she could please her mother. Her mother was feminine and Louise identifies with her mother in that she was a good role-model for housekeeping, personal hygiene, feeding and looking after the children wonderfully; 'but on the emotional side, not at all'. Louise was very feminine growing up – 'a nice girl, a pretty girl, a good girl' – and wanted to be a housekeeper. She was a virgin when she married. Louise believes, 'It is easier to be a woman because men have the responsibility of being the bread winner.'

Louise's mother was pregnant with her before marriage. Because of the war, her father was away for five years and her parents became strangers. Her parents' marriage was 'horrible' and it had an overwhelming effect on the household: 'It was a house full of battles. My mother wanted us to take sides and she used to play my sister and me up against my father.' Louise did not know her father and he did not know her: 'We were like strangers and my mother kept it like that. When my sister came along, Father took a liking to her because he could get to know her.' Louise did not like her father but recognized that he was 'a very nice person and a gentleman' but 'I could never relate to him and could never have a proper conversation with him.'

By contrast, Louise's husband and family have open communications and hardly ever argue. Big decisions in the family are made jointly between her and her husband, although 'he likes to think that it is him that makes the decisions'. Her husband is involved in the family with respect to finances and with their sons' education but 'he is not as involved as me'. The family is affectionate and her sons' relationship with their father 'is on the whole, good. They do love their father and I think my eldest son has in the past been intimidated by his father but Mark has never been.'

Louise offered to discuss sex with her sons but 'I don't think they felt comfortable with the idea.' She hopes the message they have received from her is that 'they shouldn't have hang-ups'.

Mark's first day at school was quite emotional for Louise: 'It was another hurdle and I couldn't wait for him to get home to find out what it was like for him. I think I was relieved in one way that they were both off at school and I had some spare time to myself.' Her older son's first day at school was even worse because he was the first to go and the separation was very hard on her: 'With each development they make, it is another hurdle. I guess I cried inside.'

According to Louise, Mark slept with her and her husband until the age of three: 'He used to creep into our bed in the middle of the night and we let him ... we put up with it because he wasn't well. Once he was operated on and he was better, he never came into our bed again.'

Her older son was nineteen when he went off to university. He wanted to move out so Louise said:

'Do whatever you want to do.' I was quite hard on him because he wanted to bring home his laundry and I told him that if he was going, then he was going, and that if he lived on his own he would have to do things for himself. He turned out to be a very capable man. Initially, it made me feel sad and then very relieved. The relief was because my workload was cut down. Again it was another hurdle and I missed him for a few months until I adjusted. It was a whole new experience for me.

When Mark left, 'I really missed him because he makes me laugh. Again, I got used to not having him around.'

When Louise's older son married, she was not very happy with whom he married because of the type of relationship they had and the type of girl she is:

My disappointment probably showed. On one occasion my son threw his arms around me and was kissing and cuddling me and she literally pulled him off and said, 'Your mother doesn't like it' and my son said, 'Yes, she does. My mother loves it.' Since then, she doesn't want to be in my company ... I think she is jealous.

Louise wanted to clear the air with her daughter-in-law and explained to her that they are not in competition with each other and that, as her son's wife, 'she is number one and that the love he has for me is different'. Louise told her that, if 'we want to make him happy, we must try to get on together.' Since her son married, 'He lost the ability to communicate with the family and it has been a general disappointment.' She hopes that when Mark gets married, things will be a lot better.

Louise believes that on the whole, 'I have given my sons the respect and privacy that they deserve.'

MOTHERS AND SONS

Interview fourteen: Marsha

Marsha, the mother of Terrence, age sixteen, Alex, age twelve, and a daughter of fourteen, is thirty-nine years old and married. She is British.

She wanted a son and couldn't see herself as the mother of a daughter: 'It was a cultural, social and media thing. I picked up this idea that it would be really good to have a little boy. I could picture myself with him and that is the little boy that I had.'

Marsha had a lot of expectations for Terrence that she did not have for the others: 'He was going to be the cleverest and the best and the prettiest. It was all very competitive as my friends all started to have children and I got caught up in it.' Now, 'I dare not have any expectations for him because who would it be for, him or me? I think my only expectation is that he should survive, really live.'

Marsha went out to work part-time when Terrence was six months old. When her children were infants she did a lot of things with them like painting and gluing and 'all that ghastly stuff'. She found being stuck at home with a baby very difficult and boring.

Terrence was not a particularly easy or happy baby because of 'the problem with the breast-feeding'. She had tried to breast-feed him but had to abandon the idea at four weeks:

> I had called in the services of a nurse who was from the old school and had very strict ideas of how you treated children. She put him down at such and such a time and she tied him up in a certain way and if he cried, he was left in his cot. The nurse did not encourage demand feeding or taking him into bed with me. It was very regimented and I did this to his detriment and mine.

Marsha did not have the courage or the knowledge to do what she wanted because she felt Terrence might break if she listened to her maternal instincts: 'I really thought that I had ruined him at the time by doing what I was told to do, and neither he nor I was very happy.' Marsha thinks that she had slight post-natal depression after Terrence was born and wonders how much that affected him.

Marsha went her own way with her other children – they were put to the breast and took to it immediately and it 'was wonderful':

> My younger son was treated very differently because he had a hearing problem and besides, I wasn't as worried being a mother as I was with Terrence. Alex just came along and fitted in. Somehow with Alex there wasn't the same expectation and I realized that whatever I do, he is going to grow up no matter how much I worry.

Marsha remembers taking Terrence to school on his first day and being told, 'just leave him and go. I felt terrible, bereft, and quite deserted by the experience.' With Alex, she felt worried because of his hearing problem and wondered how he would cope: 'I am very protective of him and worry immensely.'

Marsha describes her relationship with Terrence as enjoyable and caring: 'I understand him, where he's at, what he's up to, his need to have his own privacy and to do his own thing. Our relationship gets very tarnished when the others are around and there is a lot of jealousy.'

With Alex, the relationship is 'not as much fun as with Terrence. He just sort of tags along with me and I still see him as being my baby.' Alex is not a very open child and he keeps his 'little private affairs' very much to himself: 'He will only let me in when it suits him. He is sweet and so caring but he can be an absolute nuisance and drive me to distraction – he is so manipulative.' Her relationship with Alex is good 'when the others are not around to contaminate it'.

She finds the relationship with her sons easier than with her daughter who is 'strong willed, stubborn and difficult. She also has an eating problem.' Her sons are 'easier, more open and straightforward and I know where I stand with them'.

Marsha trusts both her sons to get on with their school work and she doesn't like to nag or hound them. She does not believe in controlling her children and believes that there is 'invisible' control and discipline: 'They have got to learn to take responsibility for themselves and to cope with things.'

Independence has been instilled in her sons, Marsha says:

through my own laziness because I can't be bothered. It is my own failings which has let them be independent because I don't really want to drive them places, and I don't really want to sit through another lousy film, so they have to go on their own.

Marsha has made conscious efforts to instil her sons with self-esteem: 'When they have done good, I encourage them but I would rather they see that they have done well themselves. I try to make them appreciate their own talents rather than me saying "you are wonderful".'

Marsha confides in her sons: 'I don't like to keep secrets. I will discuss my relationship with my husband with them, and they do as well.' She will not discuss financial matters with her children.

She wants to allow her children privacy and is not eager to know everything that goes on in their lives: 'When I do learn things after the fact, I would rather not know because I don't know how quite to deal with it.'

Marsha does not expect her sons to please her but 'I also don't expect them to antagonize me. If they want to play the distance game then it is fine by me but for them to be absolutely hostile, I don't accept that. Terrence has moments of being hostile which is a new phenomenon.'

When her sons are distant with her she becomes quite distant as well: 'There is no point in fighting back. When Alex is revolting, I just tend to ignore him and that tends to work. They don't like being ignored. If they are going to act badly they are not going to get my attention.'

Marsha's parents have been married a very long time and 'they make the best of a bad job. They are completely mismatched and a lot of their marriage is based on companionship.' Marsha's relationship with her mother is 'sound', but Marsha is very critical of her because 'We can be frank with each other. I tell her what I think and it causes a lot of trouble. I think if I had more respect for her and just backed off, I would have a much easier time of it.' In contrast, 'my husband's relationship with his parents is respectful because he doesn't want to offend them'.

Her relationship with her father was 'fine as a child' but as she grew older, she grew away from him and there was very little understanding between them: 'He is not a great communicator and it is not easy to talk to a man like him.' Marsha identifies with her mother except 'that my father is a much more practical man and I am more like him in that respect'.

Marsha is 'reasonably' happy in her marriage, although 'my husband makes me despair: he is very difficult to live with and an impossible man. But he is a good man and I couldn't be happier with someone else. I find it very difficult being married although we share common interests.' Decisions are made jointly.

Her husband is involved with the children although he would like to do more with them. They don't feel the same way: 'My husband can't stand that the children are who they are. He wants them to be vivacious and have lots of interests and he wants to do things with them.'

There is open communication in her family but 'we don't get involved in each others' problems. It is not that we don't share, it is that we each have our own thing to do.' There is a lot of yelling and Marsha says that 'I yell because no one takes any notice of me. When my husband yells, he means it.' Her sons are very honest with her and will highlight parts of her that she didn't realize existed: 'I don't mind it most of the time although there are moments when they are very critical and it is usually justified. When it isn't, I get cross but on the whole, their perceptions are excellent.' They are an affectionate family and there is open affection between husband and wife.

The children get embarrassed by their parents' affection and when Marsha and her husband discuss sex openly, Marsha can see that they do not want to discuss it. The messages she has hoped her sons have received about sexuality is that it is all right to be homosexual: 'If any of them were, it wouldn't break my heart but it would break their father's. I know he couldn't accept it in his sons.' Terrence has all of a sudden become vehemently homophobic and Marsha doesn't like it and finds it offensive:

> I don't know where he picked it up from, his friends or his father, and I don't know if it a stage but I find it quite worrying. I wonder if it is covering up his own homosexual feelings. I have not talked to him about it yet because I think he would be so upset and embarrassed by it.

Marsha's definition of femininity is 'helplessness'. She considers her mother to be feminine and helpless. Marsha does not see herself as feminine and considers her looks to be 'butch'. Marsha thinks that people are either feminine or masculine and she thinks of her husband as being very masculine in the non-complimentary sense: 'He is boorish, slovenly and domestically incapable although he is fairly helpless … I am married to my mother!' In Marsha's opinion, neither of her sons are particularly masculine:

> When Terrence was a baby, I actually joked that he was a 'poof in the making' because he was very pretty. My husband almost killed me. And Alex, he has always loved pretty things like flowers and nature and he loves cooking. He is not a sporty child, rough nor macho.

Marsha is dreading the idea of her sons getting married:

> I honestly don't want them to get married. I have a fear of a typical, grabby, nasty bit of work and I don't know if I could bear that. I really don't want them to marry conventional people and that is why I have no great, great fear about them being homosexual because I think I would rather them go out with a nice man than some horrible awful woman. I couldn't bear it.

Marsha believes that she has been a good role-model for the type of woman she wants her sons to marry:

> I am not perfect and I have a lot of failings but generally I don't see myself as a typical Jewish, middle-class housewife, I really don't, and neither does my husband. In that respect I feel that I

have done my sons proud although it embarrasses them to some extent.

Interview fifteen: Terrence

Sixteen-year-old Terrence, Marsha's elder son, describes his relationship with her as 'most of the time very good. She is the closest person in the family to me. We get on best with each other and agree on most issues. We think the same way and from an early age, people would tell me that I am so much like her.' His mother can be a bit snappy at times and her moods fluctuate.

His mother is very clever, funny but can be 'cold':

My father's side of the family say she is cold-hearted and not very warm but when you get under her skin she is very soft and I can detect emotion there. If I say hello to her I get this angry stare and I think, 'What have I done?' but I know that she is just in a bad mood that day.

Terrence's mother 'gets on' with her own mother 'but she is always criticizing her. They have a very open relationship.' His father, however:

can't say anything to his parents which would be in the least bit offending. He has the utmost respect for his parents whereas my mother can be rude to hers. I would rather be like my mother and I have that kind of relationship with her. I have to be one person to my father, respectful, and another person with my mother, honest.

Terrence can't remember playing with his mother. She did not work outside the home and they had a nanny. He slept in his parents' bed if he was ill, scared or if his father was ill and sleeping in another room. Every Sunday, all the children would sit on their parents' bed. Terrence doesn't know if his mother is happy being a mother. If she is screaming at them, he will ask her why she had three children and she will answer, 'God only knows.'

Terrence feels that he has to please his mother because 'I feel better if I do because then there is no awkwardness between us. If I am going out I will do something to please her so she will be more understanding and she won't be obstructive. It makes my life easier if I please her.'

He feels that his mother has the expectation that he should be a really cultured, rounded, intelligent person who enjoys doing everything. He continues:

I try to live up to that but it is really hard when you are sixteen. I don't feel that I have lived up to her expectations and it makes me feel stupid and if I haven't read something that they are discussing she will call me an 'uncultured moron' and she'll be angry with me. On one occasion she swore at me because she was disappointed in my academic results and I was a bit shocked and went up to my room. It hurts me because I feel that I have let her down. I feel really empty and there is nothing I can do to make it better. I have let her down and she is disappointed.

Terrence believes that it is him that maintains the closeness with his mother: 'If I am chirpy and friendly to her, then she will be chirpy and friendly back. If I am in a bad mood then she will snap at me. If she is already in a bad mood I can sometimes get a smile out of her and then she'll calm down and become happy.'

On his first day of school, his mother took him and he did not cry. He only wanted to go because he had a friend with him; 'If I were on my own I wouldn't have liked it. I really don't like doing things on my own and it is only recently that I have realized that I have got to do things by myself.'

Terrence is athletic and it is his father who encourages him:

My father is slightly obsessive about tennis and he always wants to play with me and it gets on my mother's nerves. Every Saturday he wants to play tennis and she screams at him not to. The reason I haven't played for a while with my father is because Mother is so bothered by it. I think it is better for her if we don't play. It is just something my father has to sacrifice.

Terrence also has sacrificed things for his mother like staying in to babysit when he had plans to meet his friends; 'I felt really good about it because Mum was really happy and it pleased her.'

Terrence describes his relationship with his father as 'not as good as with my mother because he is quite old-fashioned, narrow-sighted and he doesn't appreciate anyone else's view. He causes a lot of problems in the family.' Terrence doesn't get on with his father because there are not many things they have in common:

He is very intelligent – I am not stupid but I'll never be as clever as him. He is intelligent but at the same time stupid. It is strange because it is almost as if he can't do normal things that everyday people can do like fix a plug or change a light bulb. I think it is probably because his mother did everything for him and he just never had to do it.

Terrence doesn't remember playing with his father as a child but remembers having baths with him. He also remembers going swimming with him and coming home and having to have his hair washed: 'I hated having my hair washed and my father would say to me, "Just do it, it will shut your mother up!"'

What he has learned from his father about being a man is that 'basically a man goes out and has an office job and brings money into the family while the mother stays home and brings up the children. He has always made it important to go out and earn the money and come home.' His father is always home by six-thirty and he is always around on weekends; 'He is always wanting to do things as a family which we are not interested in doing.'

Terrence is not as masculine as his father:

My father has nothing feminine about him. He is one of those men that doesn't like homosexual people. I really have nothing against them but if I were homosexual he would probably disown me. It is important to him to be a masculine person and it doesn't really bother me. He is old-fashioned and if I were to cry, he would tell me to stop ... but nowadays it is fine for a man to cry.

Terrence is more like his mother and enjoys artistic things and working with his hands.

Terrence's mother doesn't do everything for him like some of his friends' mothers: 'If I have to go to a friend's house she doesn't take me and I get there myself. I prefer it like that because it makes me more independent.' He believes he has self-esteem because 'my mother has always had self-esteem herself, so I guess basically it has rubbed off on me. She has never done anything to make sure that I am confident, it just rubs off.'

His parents are happily married although they have arguments 'but nothing serious', Terrence explains. 'There was one incident a couple of years ago where Dad was thinking of moving out but I think he was trying to scare us. We all sat down and talked it out.' Terrence felt that he had to protect his parents' marriage: 'When they had this argument I just thought, well, I have to sort this out ... they always sort out the arguments between me and my brother and sister, so I'll just do the same for them.'

His mother respects his privacy and doesn't want to know everything that goes on in his life: 'She is allowed to keep things to herself and so am I.' She did not tell him about sex but gave him a book about 'making babies'. 'I learned about sex from my friends and watching movies.' His mother does not confide in him and does not tell him anything: 'I didn't even know about this interview until this morning and she just told me that I am doing it without asking me if I wanted to.' There is always a lot of screaming and yelling in the house.

He believes that his mother wants him to be happy: 'On many occasions she has told me that she wants me to marry a nice, non-Jewish girl and my dad would say, don't you dare.' His mother tells him not to go out with girls who will rule his life and that she wouldn't mind if he were homosexual. Terrence chooses 'girls that are like my mother but they have to be like me as well. I'll never find anyone exactly like my mum.' He believes his mother 'is a good role-model for the woman of the nineties'.

Terrence's ideal mother would be 'my mother without a temper and someone not so strict. I love her very much.'

Interview sixteen: Alex

Twelve-year-old Alex, Marsha's younger son, describes his relationship with her as quite close: 'I love my mother and she is a good friend. I can always count on her and she helps me out with things.' He does not remember playing with her and 'she is often too busy to do things with me'.

His mother is kind and helping but 'sometimes she yells a lot for no reason'. Alex believes that his mother is overprotective of him and wants him to 'stick up for myself'. If he has a problem, his mother is always there to sort things out.

Alex does not believe that his mother has expectations of him: 'She is happy with me the way I am.' His mother doesn't want him to please her, 'she just wants me to do the best that I can'. Often his mother will be in a bad mood and Alex will stay out of her way. When she gets angry at him 'for no reason, I feel very angry at her and I get upset'.

Alex's self-confidence comes from his mother talking and explaining things to him: 'If I am nervous about something she is nice to me and tells me how I can get it done. If it seems that I can't do it on my own, she will do it for me, but I will feel stupid.'

Alex feels that he has privacy 'and if my mother asks me something and I don't want to tell her, she may get upset but she leaves me alone.' He does not always tell his mother his 'secrets' and she does not tell him her secrets but 'when she is angry at Dad she'll tell me things about him. Well, it is not directly to me, but to all the children.' There is open communication in the home and 'either there is a lot of yelling or none at all'.

His relationship with his father 'could be better'. 'I get along with my mother better because my father is a little bit too pushy. He always wants me to do things his way and my mother tells me not to listen to him. She says that I don't have to do what he asks if I don't want to.'

Of his parents' marriage Alex says, 'they argue a lot but in the end they make up'. He doesn't like when they argue and most of the time he will go to his room to block out the noise.

Alex believes that he is his father's favourite 'because he gives me more attention than he does my brother and sister because I am the youngest. My mother doesn't have a favourite.'

He identifies more with his mother because 'I could talk to her more. She is more comforting and she is closer to me.'

Alex would not want his mother to be any different but 'she would be the perfect mother if she didn't have a temper'.

Interview seventeen: Liz

The mother of four children – two daughters aged seventeen and thirteen and two sons, Martin fifteen, and her youngest, nine – Liz is forty-one years old and has been married for twenty-one years. She is British and has two younger sisters.

Since the age of fourteen, Liz had the fantasy that she was going to have two sons. She believes it was because her mother always wanted a son. When she was pregnant she actually denied that she wanted a boy as a reaction against everyone's comments; 'I was very angry, and actually felt for my daughter that she was looked upon as second-best.'

She loved the time when Martin was an infant: 'It was very rhythmic ... coffee mornings, play groups. I felt very strongly about keeping him with me at all times. He was always with me in my arms or in a sling.' She felt that it was a very warm time. Her only regret was that she left Martin when he was thirteen months old to go to summer school for a week and when she returned, he did not want to take to her breast. She loved giving birth and felt fully feminine.

Liz felt that Martin was an extension of her when he was a small baby 'especially at the breast-feeding stage. I think it was important that I felt that way.' She still feels a connection and 'if he would be threatened by someone, I think I would kill for him'. She does not believe that their relationship is maintained, 'it just happens'.

The relationship she had with her sons was very different from that with her daughters and it created a bit of jealousy with her elder daughter. Her relationship with both her daughters was very hard. Martin is her favourite son 'and my other son too. It is interesting because the girls picked it up from a very early age. Everything went smooth with my sons, and with my daughters it has always been strained.' Martin's older sister really resented him because he slept in their parents' bed; 'My daughter screamed for the first year of her life and it is my biggest regret that I did not allow her into our bed.'

The only expectation Liz had for Martin was that he would be healthy and emotionally happy and that he would feel good about himself. She wanted that for all her children. Martin tells his mother that 'he wants to be a breast surgeon so that he can be very rich and have the big boobs at the same time! He wants to be able to afford to look after me when I am old and says he would put me in the most expensive old folks' home.'

Liz describes Martin as very affectionate and charming: 'He could wrap the little girls around his finger and he tries it with me.' He is very intelligent, good-looking and strong. She hopes that he will turn out like his father, 'very loving and gentle'. Liz does not believe in controlling him, although she would often like to. She guides him and gives him information. She does not expect her son to please her but 'I think I try to get him to do what I want by using baby words with him. I will say things like "come on and be a good boy".'

She deliberately tries to instil self-esteem in her son by making him think about things for himself: 'If I don't like something I will tell him but the decision is his. I only got small amounts of praise at certain times from my parents so I try to give him more than praise because I want him to feel good about himself. I do not use labels or put him down.'

Liz was worried about Martin on his first day of school:

It was in America and it is a different system. I really grieved. The thing that terrified me the most was the school busing because he was alone and I remember him walking down the street and I thought how the hell is he going to cope. I was afraid for him and I really worried but he got on really well. He didn't cry but I did.

Liz's parents were not happily married: 'They had an awful relationship and I won't cry about it any more. I can't remember when it was ever good between them.' As a child she was terrified of her father's violence and the fights between her parents. Liz was never accepted as a separate person. She had no sense of 'being OK with myself'.

She describes her father 'as a violent, lonely and sad man. He had affairs and "psychotic" fantasies. When I got older he would introduce me to his girlfriends. He is so untrustworthy that I don't want the children around him.'

Her mother would confide in her and 'I landed up looking after her. At one point my father was having an affair with a seventeen-year-old and my mother told me. I then was made to go to Sunday school where she played the organ.' Liz's mother was feminine and very helpless, 'a victim'. Neither of her parents was 'there' for her. She identifies more with her father but 'I don't like to admit it'.

Liz did not have friends as a child and was never allowed to bring anyone home. She wanted to be different from her mother and wanted to be accepting of her children's friendships: 'I want my children to be allowed to have their friends at home and sometimes it is to my detriment! I love it because I never had that.'

Liz was a tomboy: 'I didn't want to be a girl at all until I was eighteen and became sexually aware and very interested in men.' Her husband was the first man who 'was ever kind to me. He was very gentle and he believed in me.'

Liz is happily married:

> We have been together twenty-one years and that is a hell of a long time. There are times that I think I could walk out the door. It has been a tough two years and I have had to readjust my life style because my husband was made redundant and he is very depressed but won't admit it. So what is happily married? I have never been interested in another man and wouldn't want to be. I think my husband is a terrific father but not a terrific husband, although I think he is a good, supportive man.

Liz believes that her husband is a great father to their sons and that he is very concerned about being a good parent.

There is open communication in the family and also a lot of arguing. She doesn't confide in Martin about herself and if 'he sees things going on, that is one thing, but I don't go to him with my problems. He will come to me and say "I see the way Dad is treating you and it is not right" but I don't want him to get involved because my parents used to make me pick sides.' Family decisions are discussed and if it affects the children they will be involved. Her husband makes the financial decisions.

Sexuality is openly discussed:

> I hope that the message my children have received is that it is OK to enjoy your body and someone else's, as long as it is agreed upon. We have tried to tell them that homosexuality is fine too. My husband and I have talked about it and we would accept it if our sons were gay but we worry about how others would react to it and the fact that there might not be grandchildren.

Her children speak openly about sex and sometimes 'I don't even know what they are talking about!'

Liz doesn't feel good enough to consider herself a good role-model for the type of woman she would want Martin to marry: 'I hope that he will find someone who feels good in herself and is confident.' The thought of her son Martin getting married fills her with emotion:

> It makes me feel warm and tingly, a mixture of joy and sadness. It is joy for him and sadness for me. Martin is warm and loving and I hope that whoever he marries – if he gets married because I don't have the assumption that he will – I hope that he will be very, very happy.

Interview eighteen: Martin

Fifteen-year-old Martin, Liz's second child, describes his relationship with her as quite close 'although she is more of a mum than a friend. She nags me about my friends, about getting into trouble and things like that.' He describes his mother as affectionate and says 'She works really hard to achieve whatever it is that she wants for herself. She is quiet but can be quite forward if she is comfortable with the people she is with.' He considers his mother to be feminine.

Martin remembers playing with his mother and remembers 'her getting down and dirty with me'. He thinks that she 'loves being a mother because she loves her children, although 'she prefers sons because she gets along better with the boys than with my sisters.

There are no arguments with us.' He believes that his younger brother is her favourite.

His mother does not have expectations of him: 'I think she wants me to be happy no matter what I do. She doesn't tell me what I should be. I want to be a doctor. I think I live up to my mother's expectations ... most of the time.' Martin tries to please his mother but does not always succeed: 'When she is disappointed in me she will tell me what she thinks and we will discuss it.'

Martin remembers his first day at school: 'I was really excited to go but I felt sad because my mother was crying. She was really worried about me.'

Martin says that his mother 'does not confide in me that much'. He believes that he maintains the closeness with his mother. The family is very affectionate.

Martin is very athletic and is encouraged by his father. His mother comes to his games and 'encourages me with whatever I feel comfortable with'. His mother 'makes me feel good about myself. She'll say, "well done" and even when I have done badly she makes me feel good. She never puts me down and she accepts me for who I am.'

His mother is close to her mother but not with her father: 'He is an alcoholic and she won't have anything to do with him. My mother allows me to see him if I want, and I go to visit him because I feel that he is getting old and is trying to change.'

He considers his parents' marriage to be a happy one 'but sometimes my father will say something and my mother will take it the wrong way. Both of them make the family decisions.'

Martin's relationship with his father is excellent. His father is caring and masculine, he is a good role-model, and Martin identifies with him.

Martin likes girls that are intelligent like his Mother: 'I do try and choose intelligent girls so I can talk to them and they will understand.'

Martin believes that 'if my mother thought the girl I wanted to marry was the right girl, then she would be happy. If Mother didn't think she was, and I did, I would marry her anyway.'

Martin's perfect mother would be 'caring and easy to talk to. If I could change my mother it would be her nagging. She will tell me to do something and repeat it about five times. She makes me want to scream!'

Interview nineteen: Judith

Forty-four years old and American, Judith is the mother of four children – David, age seventeen, Simon, age thirteen, and two daughters, ages sixteen and nine. They were all breast-fed. Judith has been widowed for the last five years and her marriage was a very happy one. She has one older sister.

Judith was surprised to have a son because her family is predominantly female: 'I think the male psyche is very different and I don't understand it. Funnily though, my relationship with my sons is much easier than with my daughters.' She had no expectations for her sons nor of motherhood and 'just let it unfold'.

She doesn't expect her sons to please her. She believes that 'I am not judgmental. Whatever they do within the bounds is OK. I am not going to control or try to run their lives.' Judith believes that she has instilled self-esteem in them by encouraging them in things they want to do and by giving them 'good positive feedback'.

Judith's relationship with her sons is 'really good'. She spent their infancies at home with them and enjoyed it but 'at the end of the day I always needed space so I would go to bed early and spend time with my husband.' She would play with her sons but also gave them the space to do things on their own; 'they were quite self-sufficient.' She had help in the home but was the principal carer of her children. None of them slept in bed with her and her husband.

After the death of her husband, Judith 'went back to work full-time but I work from home so I am always around for the children. It is important for me to know that I am there for them when they need me.'

Judith remembers her eldest child David's first day at school but not Simon's: 'I took David to school and when I asked him what he did and he couldn't remember, I felt like there was a whole day I couldn't share with him. It was a feeling of betrayal.' David did not cry but Judith did: 'It was a terrible day and I was very sad that he was moving on to his next part of his life. I was very conscious that I wouldn't be there to share it with him, to protect him. It was a betrayal that I wouldn't be there to fight his battles.'

Of David she says: 'He is on the verge of taking off and it makes me feel very excited for him and very sad for myself. The sadness is the same sadness as when he started school. ... It is another phase of his life and I won't be involved and sharing it with him.'

Of Simon she says:

He just merged and followed on from his eldest brother. Simon, more or less, brought himself up ... he went to the same school as David, did the same things, he just followed in David's footsteps. It is a shame, but he doesn't really have a lot of room to be himself. He is in David's shadow.

Judith does not believe that it is appropriate to confide in her sons although they have a very open and communicative relationship. There is often arguing but she sees it as healthy friction which allows 'steam to be let off instead of harbouring resentment'. Everyone has a part in the family decision-making. She has been open with her children about sexuality but waited for them to come to her when they were ready. She sees sexuality as 'an enriching part of life' and hopes that she has given that positive message to her sons.

The loss of her husband had an 'enormous effect" on her sons. However, Judith is more conscious 'that there is no father around for my daughters'. She does not think that her eldest son has taken the place of the 'father' except in 'religious matters'.

'The fact that I survived my parents is a tribute to me,' Judith said of her relationship with them. She was not close to her mother and her nanny was her primary carer. Her mother was 'subservient to my father. She was busy running around cooking for him and all the things women did. Mother is very proud that my father doesn't know where the kitchen is. My mother is this really typical Jewish bag.' Her mother was not happy in her role of mother: 'She wasn't a mother at all, she is incapable of loving. My nanny was my mother.'

Judith's relationship with her father was always difficult: 'He is not a man who shares. He is very defended and he never delivered straight messages nor was he ever there for long enough. He would start off being there but lost his attention very quickly to Mother.' Judith identifies with her father's business sense.

Judith was a tomboy until the age of eighteen, when she discovered 'her hormones and boys!' She would rather be a woman 'as men have a raw deal. I think they are on a mouse wheel from very early on. They can't stop work to have babies and they are always paying the mortgage. Men have a very rough deal.' Her definition of masculinity is 'empathy, being self-aware, and being well grounded'. She considers her sons to be masculine as was her husband. She has always 'aimed to produce sons who face the world squarely'.

Judith will be very happy when 'my sons get married because it won't be a shock to me as I am involved in their friendships anyway. It will be quite a natural progression and I will feel that I am gaining.'

Interview twenty: David

Seventeen-year-old David describes his relationship with his mother 'as not the archetypal mother–son relationship in which the son treats his mother as superior. I seek guidance from her. She is a friend. I don't visualize her as a mother, which I think is better. She is someone who is there for me and cares.' David thinks his mother is strong in a feminine way and 'she knows what she wants and does it'. Their relationship is a 'two way street – there is not one holding on to the other'.

Their relationship is very warm, loving, and very friendly: 'It is not maternalistic in the way that she is a strong backbone that I have to rely on, that's not her at all. I tend to rely on my friends more than I do on Mom.'

David believes that his mother is happy in her role as mother because 'women who are unhappy being mothers generally take it out on their children but it isn't the case with us'. His mother does not confide in him and he 'wouldn't expect her to because it is adult problems. She does confide in me about family things and I confide in her as well.'

David likes to make his mother happy but 'won't go out of my way. I also don't do things that would upset her. She doesn't get disappointed with me. She is there for me and wants to guide me through it. I don't need to get good marks to make her proud.' David's ambition is to become a barrister.

His mother expects him to be normal 'like honest and kind – those types of things – but she doesn't expect me to be a super brain or super athlete or whatever'. David sees his self-esteem 'coming from the way I was brought up' and not necessarily from his mother.

There is open communication in the family and a lot of arguing as well, mainly about petty things. David remembers having one serious argument with his mother: 'It was about her relationship with her boyfriend and at the time, I wasn't too happy about it. It was discussed and then it blew over.' David finds it difficult to discuss sex in the family situation. He believes sexuality is 'a private thing between two people in a relationship'.

Religion plays a very big part in David's life and is more important to him than it is to the rest of the family:

It doesn't interfere with their lives. It infringes on my life but that is the route I have chosen to go. I think I have chosen to be religious because subconsciously, my father became religious when his father passed away and maybe I want to keep the flame burning. If I gave it up, I would feel guilty not because of my father, but because I would think that I was doing myself a great disservice.

David's father wasn't 'this massive macho person'. He didn't learn very much about being a man from his father,

because when you are twelve, you haven't yet started, except superficially, to work out what is masculine and feminine. In some senses, I have grown much quicker because I became the head of the family, well, the oldest male in the family, which is an added responsibility. Whenever there is something that has to be done, like a caring thing, it is up to me. I have a great responsibility to my brother as his older brother.

David believes that his mother is a very good role-model of tying in family responsibility with having an outside life: 'She always has time for us, the whole family, my grandma and friends. She works full-time yet has the knack of giving as much time as she can to everything, and that is how I hope to be.'

His mother's relationship with her own mother was 'very strained at times and I know that she felt squashed and suffocated by her. She was not over-pampered or anything. I think her parents tried to control and hassle her a lot but now they are very close.'

In a fantasy world, David's ideal mother would be:

someone who is there all the time, I would want everything all the time. Obviously it is very difficult for my mother being a single parent and having a job. Occasionally she goes out with her boyfriend and she isn't about at all. It isn't like she is never about, but I would like her to be here all the time so I could have her on tap.

David thinks his mother will be sad when he gets married 'because she will have one less in the roost but she will be happy because she will know that I made the right decision'. Marriage is a dodgy point for his mother 'because she was married once before my father for three years and it was a big mistake for her. She was under heavy parental pressure to get married.' David thinks that his mother will have pleasure knowing that she didn't pressure him into marriage: 'I don't think she will be upset when I marry but she will feel that it is the final step in her tuition of me, the final step of her guidance of me, and now the rest I will have to learn on my own.'

Interview twenty-one: Simon

Thirteen-year-old Simon describes his mother, Judith, as 'really annoying. I am always nice to her and she throws it back in my face. It is normally pretty good between us but she could be too strict and not let me do what I want. Apart from that, our relationship is all right. I can live with it.'

Simon has privacy. He has his own room and 'I stay in there and do my homework and stuff. She is annoying, like if I have a friend around she is always coming into my room asking if we want a cup of tea or a biscuit. Sometimes she doesn't leave.'

His mother doesn't tell him that she has expectations of him but,

I know that she does. She expects me to be as smart as my brother. She expects me to get good marks. She will tell me to just do my best but at the end of the day, I know that she expects me to do well. If I don't get such good marks, I don't think she will be that annoyed. She won't show it, but I know that she is. I don't think that I have lived up to her expectations.

His mother shows her annoyance because, as Simon told me:

She is always shouting. She is moody and shouts at everyone but mostly at me. I am the only child that talks back to Mum and sometimes I think she wants someone to answer back to her. It is very strange because everyone else just takes it. I think she has a go at me because she wants me to answer back. She would like me to have respect for her.

Simon is glad that he shows his point of view: 'I think I am the better for it.' He does not believe that his mother has given him confidence or self-esteem because 'she hassles me so much about school work and she is always so damn patronizing. It annoys me so much. She basically tries to run my life. She does it to all four of us.'

Simon likes sports, especially contact sports:

I get aggressive and it lets me get out some of my steam. My mother doesn't like that I play rugby but she can't stop me because she knows that I want to do it. She is always scared that I am going to hurt myself – she is such a Jewish mother!

'I am not my own person', he believes, 'because my mother bosses me around. She doesn't let me be my own person and she runs my life. She is always telling me what to do and I don't want to do the stuff she wants me to do, like cooking and cleaning. I want to be playing football and tennis.'

Simon was taken to school on his first day by his mother:

When I was four it was nothing special being away from my mother because I didn't appreciate what it was all about back then. I remember it was quite good and that I was happy to go and get away from my mum a bit. If I knew then what I know now, I would have been thrilled to be away from her.

There is 'quite a bit of arguing at home. I don't really think there is open communication. I talk to my friends rather than my mum and my family. I don't feel really close to them to talk about my personal affairs and relationships but sometimes I talk to my mum.'

His mother's good qualities are that 'she can cook actually quite well and her boyfriend is really nice'. His ideal mother 'wouldn't be so strict. I would like my mum to win the pools so she would give me more stuff. She doesn't really give me any allowance and I would like to have some pocket money. Even though she annoys me sometimes, my mum is all right.'

Interview twenty-two: Thelma

Thelma, the mother of two sons, Stuart, twenty-one and Ethan, fourteen, is fifty years old. She was born in Morocco and has been married for twenty-seven years to an Englishman.

Thelma always entertained the idea that she would have girls because 'girls are always with you, that is a belief my mother gave me. A son will always belong to his wife so I thought having sons would be a bad investment.' Stuart was not breast-fed and Ethan was 'semi-breast-fed' because 'I did not respond successfully to breast-feeding'.

Until the age of fourteen, her son Stuart was very good friends with her and then 'he dropped me like a ton of bricks. He wanted to assert himself and to move away from me. The relationship now is that he doesn't go out with me very much and I couldn't even dream of going shopping with him so we don't really socialize.' With Ethan, her relationship is different; 'He is more affectionate, and he shows his feelings more. Even now he kisses me and his father and puts his arms around us, but I think he is moving away as well, even though he still calls me "Princess".'

Thelma thinks that the way she feels about her sons 'moving away' depends on whether she is busy or not: 'When I have a lot of things to do, it is not so bad but I could just imagine myself with nothing to do and becoming very touchy if they don't eat the meal I have prepared. I would take it personally, that they don't appreciate me.' Her sons haven't grown up yet:

> They are partly dependent and I have not yet seen the part of them which is independent. They have their own style of dressing and they don't ask me when to have their hair cut, but I think emotionally, they are very much dependent on both my husband and me.

Thelma has always worked outside the home and when Stuart was an infant she 'encouraged him to talk to himself and I used to ask him what he was saying. I found myself drawn to his monologues and the games he played when his friends came over.'

Thelma was their sole carer in terms of emotional input and love. 'Of course my husband gave them love but in the way of chauffeuring them and pocket money. I would stroke, kiss and cuddle them.' Thelma was too busy to play a lot with her children but 'I think that I used that as an excuse. I did things with them that interested me.'

Thelma recalls that on Stuart's first day of school, she took him with her mother and he 'just wanted us to leave – he enjoyed it so much. I was really proud that he was so independent and part of me, well, I am reluctant to remember. My mother was really angry that he wanted us to leave and felt insulted.' Thelma remembers taking Ethan to school on his first day but does not remember what it was like. Her sons slept with her until they were of the age of twelve: 'The little one would come and read in bed with me.'

Both her sons are sporty and 'I think they get that from me. They are naturals at it, no matter what game they play. I don't push them but I encourage them to enjoy whatever they are doing.' Thelma believes that she encourages them to be independent by allowing them to be curious and by answering their questions. She would only lose her temper when they were deliberately being angry or bored.

Her expectations for her sons are quite explicit:

> I want them to be very good businessmen. No doctors, no lawyers, no academic qualifications – just position and wealth. I have instilled in my sons self-esteem through example and I never ask them to achieve things because of social pressure. I think I have instilled the little one with more self-esteem than Stuart.

Thelma thought that she would rather be friends with her sons than a mother:

Half of me thinks that I am going the same way that my mother did. I sound like her, that is, she had very high demands of me but I don't think I am as bad as her. Yes, I do have a set of demands that my sons should meet, like being serious, not wasting money and thinking of the future. There are a lot of shoulds.

With Stuart, she expected him to meet her needs and reacted by 'putting him down'. She would say, 'You haven't got it, what is going to become of you?' She knows now how important it is to give them validation. She hardly puts Stuart down anymore and does not do it at all with the 'little one'. Thelma knows that she has made mistakes but thinks that she has been trained by Stuart so she hasn't done the same with Ethan.

Thelma confides in her sons. She continues:

But I don't do it so much because my father died when I was very little and my mother used me as a support and I became a partner to her rather than a daughter. I don't want my sons to grow up too quickly and start acting like partners instead of children so I try not to tell them too much. However, when I argue with my husband and erupt, the whole house hears and very often I want my sons' approval and will say to them, 'Did you see what your father did?' I try not to do it with the little one though. I think the older one had to experience my mistakes.

Thelma views her children as extensions of herself: 'When there is a "lovey-dovey" moment, a mutual thought, or when we react the same way, I think they are an extension of me. When they do something I don't like, I feel totally alone and they are like strangers.' She believes that many of the things she has done for them 'is really for myself. It is security to know that they will achieve but I don't push them.'

Thelma describes her sons:

They are very stylish boys and quite nice-looking. They are show-offish like me. I don't think of them as very strong nor are they totally independent because the older one has his lazy bits. I don't think either of them is capable of finishing something they start, which is something I admire about my husband. When he puts his mind to something, he can do anything from start to finish in one sitting.

Thelma could not say if she is happily married but put it this way: 'I would rather be with this family than without it. I wouldn't like another husband in any way, shape or form, and it is not because I think my husband is perfect.' She trusts her husband and respects him. He is involved in the home because 'I make him, but I could easily see him not being involved. Just give him a few of his toys and he is satisfied.' It is Thelma that makes the decisions in the family.

The relationship between father and sons is good:

> He responds to them because the younger one is so affectionate with him and I think they have a special bond. The older one is similar to my husband so they talk about computers and that is what their relationship is based on. They can be boys together and relate on the same unemotional level.

As for open communications in the family, Thelma and her younger son are open and Stuart and the father are 'men of few words'. It is usually Thelma that argues as she needs to get a reaction from them. She believes that it is she who maintains the relationship with her sons because 'they can take me or leave me. Ethan thinks I am perfect and he really loves me. I think he has got it right!'

Sexuality is openly discussed 'although they don't discuss it with me'. Her children have never asked her, nor has she told them about the facts of life, but they are free to use 'whatever' language and to talk about gays and lesbians.

Thelma's relationship with her mother consists of a lot of arguing: 'She is very possessive of me and holds a lot of expectations. Nothing is up to her standards and she will always find fault.' When Thelma's father died, her uncle became her 'father'. 'I never idolized anyone like I did him [her uncle] because he knew how to command respect. When I was a small child, he would just give me a look of disappointment and I would dissolve. He was so caring as well. I loved him.'

She was a tomboy until the age of twenty-two and would still like to be a 'hell-raiser' if she could. She is very strong and opinionated and likes those qualities in herself. Her mother is very strong, yet needy.

Stuart moved out of the family home a few months ago 'but I don't know if you call it leaving home … he lives a block away in an apartment we own, and he comes home to eat and to get his laundry done.' When Stuart left, she did not feel happy about it:

It feels like rejection. There is an anxiety, an emptiness, a void. I don't like it that he left home but part of me says yes, it is good in a way, semi-independence. I have the desire to recapture the time when he was little and I feel guilty that I was not a perfect mother.

Thelma thinks that when her sons do marry the way she will feel will depend on whether her life is occupied and 'whether I approve of the girls they marry. If I don't approve, I would imagine it would be quite difficult.' If there is one thing that she hopes her sons will do for their wives it is to 'remind them that they love her and to be emotional and share their feelings rather than just being a good bread-winner. I would really like them to be open with their wives because my husband has never been that way with me.'

Thelma thinks that if she is happy with herself and her needs are met, then 'I don't nag and I accept my children as they are. But when I am unhappy inside, and I experience emptiness, I demand it from my sons and of course, I land up blaming them.' When they do not live up to her expectations, Thelma takes it personally:

> Very often I don't show it but I am sure they know that I am disappointed because I can't totally hide it – I show a look, hiss or storm, and it is never dignified.

Deep down Thelma knows that both her sons are proud of her because 'they tell me so'.

Interview twenty-three: Stuart

Twenty-one-year-old Stuart, Thelma's elder son, describes the relationship with his mother as 'good-ish and sometimes bad. We are very close. If I want to tell her anything I could go to her but I don't very often. At least I know she is always there if I really need her.' His mother is powerful and feminine and happy in her role as mother.

When Stuart was a child, his mother took care of him while she was doing her work 'but I wouldn't be doing any social activity or playing. She didn't have much time for me.' Stuart remembers playing with his mother:

> When I was three years old I had a friend and we are still friends to this day. We were just talking about how when we were small, my mother would play games with us and she would give us medals for honour and bravery and things like that. She taught me to be good to myself through playing those games.

Stuart is very athletic. His mother encouraged him and she is very proud: 'Anything I do she encourages me as long as she thinks it is OK. I play the guitar and she encouraged me to do that. If she feels that there is something I should do she will approach me with the idea.'

His mother confides in him:

> She is always asking my opinion about everything and she takes my word. If I say something is not right, she will listen to me, like a dress for example. If she asks me if I like it, and I say no, then she will never wear it. She reads me her work and wants my opinion on it. Anything she does she involves me in it.

His mother always wants to know everything about him,

> but I don't tell her unless I feel I need to. She asks me about my social life and who my friends and girlfriends are, and what they do for work. Sometimes I feel that I have no privacy. All mothers are the same, they just want the best for their children so they interfere.

Stuart feels that his mother meddles in his life: 'For instance, she saw a good job opportunity advertised and she filled out the application and sent it off for me. At the time, I was pissed off but sometimes it works out OK.'

Stuart believes that his mother expects a lot from him: 'She expects more of someone like me at my age. She expected me to have a steady job. What she wants for me is a balance – on one side, a good social life and on the other, a good work life.' He does not feel that he has lived up to her expectations and she has reacted with disappointment: 'It doesn't really bother me. If I want to do something I will do it, it is up to me. It's nice to please her but I come first.' He describes himself as 'outgoing, athletic, quite clever with good common sense'. He is good at everything and he always tries his best.

Stuart's relationship with his father is 'different' from the one he shares with his mother; 'I have always been her little boy.' His father is 'very technical, quiet and clever'. Their relationship is 'just there'. He did not play much with his father when he was growing up because 'he was always too busy working. They both were.' He has learned 'self-control and patience' from his father and considers him to be very masculine. His father is 'kind of' a good role-model, 'there is better but … there are good qualities I see in him and other qualities that he doesn't have. In the end, I wouldn't change him. We are close.'

Stuart considers his parents' marriage to be happy. His mother makes all the decisions and 'she even decided that I was doing this interview!' There is open communication and a lot of arguing but they are an affectionate family. The topic of sex was never discussed: 'I don't think they needed to.' He did not get any messages about sexuality from his parents.

Stuart considers himself to be his mother's favourite because 'I am the first-born'. He does not think that his brother has the same experience of the family as he does because 'now my parents have more time than when they brought me up and they have more experience with children. I wonder if my brother got the better deal.' Stuart identifies with his mother.

Of his mother's relationship with her own mother, Stuart says:

I think they have a good relationship. My mother had a rough childhood. Her father died when she was three and my grandmother didn't remarry so my mother was doing a lot of work at an early age to bring in money. My mother has a lot of respect for her and I have a lot of respect for my grandmother too.

Stuart equates respect with love.

He recently moved out of his parents' home and now lives down the road; 'It just worked out like that. It's quite far actually, it's all the way down the road. The further away the better!' He still goes 'home' for dinner all the time and 'I bring home laundry because I don't have a washing machine.' Stuart has always been independent, 'my mother has always told me so'.

Stuart's mother has taught him 'a lot of stuff' about respecting women; 'How you treat your mother is the same as how you treat any other woman. My mother has taught me to respect women and to have sensitivity. I am masculine and sensitive.'

His ideal mother would be someone that just stayed at home all day but 'if my mother had done that, I wouldn't be as self-reliant as I am now.' Also she would be the 'perfect mother who cooks and cleans and still has time for other things. I am happy that my mother works, but sometimes I envy the mothers who cook and so on. I would like a mother who took care of everything.' Stuart's mother has not taken care of all of his needs, 'no one can, it is an impossible job'. His mother shows him love 'by kissing me all the time. It's good to know that she cares about me but sometimes, on the spot, when she is right there in front of me, I feel like getting away from her.'

Interview twenty-four: Ethan

Fourteen-year-old Ethan, Thelma's 'little one', describes his mother as a 'strong character and quite clever'. They are 'quite close' and their relationship is 'all right, nothing great'. It is his mother who maintains the closeness between them.

His mother took care of him as an infant and she played with him. Ethan thinks his mother is 'very happy as a mother and she is glad that she has sons because she is used to us'.

Ethan remembers sleeping with his mother:

> She still asks me to. She treats me like a baby and she always tells me that when I was young, I used to sit in her lap. She wishes I was still young and tells me to pretend and act younger. She treats me now, like I am more grown up, but not the way I should be treated. I should get more money and my mum shouldn't treat me like I was still a baby.

His first day of school was very 'exciting' and he looked forward to it. His mother took him and did not want to leave him. Ethan did not cry 'but my mother kept wiping the tears from her eyes'.

Ethan does not think that his mother keeps any secrets from him but 'she never tells me about herself'. He tells his mother about 'things she likes to talk about and about his feelings'. If he has a problem in school he will discuss it with her. His mother likes to know everything about him and 'she likes when I tell her things'. He feels that he has his privacy.

Ethan believes that his mother has instilled in him self-confidence because 'if I get into trouble she'll tell me what I should do and tell me about the times she has gotten into trouble and how she coped with it. She gives me confidence and I know that if I get into trouble or anything, I can go to her.'

His mother has expectations of him:

> She wants me to learn sociology. She wants me to hold on to my money because she knows I will spend it and I will because I am like my brother. She has learned a lot through my brother so she knows I will make the same mistakes. If I wanted to do something she wouldn't stop me. She says that she loves me and doesn't care what I become when I grow up and that makes me feel that I can do whatever I want.

Ethan considers his mother to be a 'little pushy':

If she thinks I am doing something wrong then she will tell me not to and she will make sure that I don't. If I don't do as I am told, I'll be sent to my room and I'll be miserable and Mum and Dad will be angry at me. If I argue a lot I will leave the house to cool down.

Ethan is athletic – 'my mother encourages it' – and he has a lot of friends. He believes he is 'masculine and a leader' and his father is masculine because 'no one tells him what to do'.

His relationship with his father is close:

I talk to my father about things that interest him but he is not as 'feeling' as my mother. My mum is definitely affectionate and so is Dad, but he is not as open as my mum so I don't really like talking to him. Dad is very clever. I play on the computer with my father and when I was young, he would take me to the bank and stuff.

Ethan considers his father to be a good role-model because 'he doesn't smoke or swear'.

His parents are happily married and there is open communication between them: 'My mum always talks to my father about what she has done.' Both his parents make the family decisions. There is open communication in the family and 'sometimes there is arguing'. Sex has never been discussed because the 'family is shy'.

His mother doesn't have favourites and 'she loves us both the same. I know that she loves me because she tells me and I could tell.' Ethan identifies with his mother.

Ethan feels that he has to please his mother: 'If I get a bad mark in school, I won't tell her. If I get a good mark which I usually do, I tell her and she is happy and always reminds me that I got the good grade.'

Ethan says of his relationship with his mother, 'she levels with me and I level with her and we talk a lot. She shows me that she loves me and I show her that I love her.'

Interview twenty-five: Karen

British-born, forty-two-year-old Karen is married and the mother of two sons, Joe, twelve, and a younger son, nine. Joe wasn't breast-fed 'not from any choice of mine' and the younger son was breast-fed for 'quite a while, I can't remember how long'.

She has always been very maternal and 'was always sure she wanted a son. I did want a daughter too, but no big deal.' Having a son as a first-born was actually important 'partly in a nasty way, because there wasn't one in the family, there were only girls'.

Karen did not work outside the home when her sons were infants and spent time with them doing the 'usual things one does'. She read to them, carried them around and played with them. She was their sole carer but as they got older, she worked part-time from the house. Her working schedule 'has always been set up around the children and they come first. Even now, I try to cut down what I do in the evenings because of the children's needs.'

Karen does not remember their first day at school but recollects that she felt relieved when she took Joe to school:

> I would have this private time with the baby, I thought to myself. I did not feel this tremendous sense of loss but when the little one started, I felt that I must do something to fill my time and on the way back from taking him, I passed a junk shop and I was thinking that I must learn to play the piano or do something with all this time.

If Karen is honest with herself, she has expectations of her sons 'achieving and being reasonable, which they are not. I do expect it. I haven't got this idea that they'll be solicitors and doctors, but I would like them to do reasonably well, sufficiently so to be able to be independent, that life shouldn't be such a terrible struggle.'

Karen's sons please her 'but that doesn't mean they please me all the time. I mean, they can be horrendous, but they do please me. I do expect to be pleased because I'm very fond of them but I don't expect them to go out of their way to do so.' She is often not pleased by them when 'they are in a bad mood and when they are difficult or untidy': 'I grumble but it doesn't do a lot. It is not a very effective form of behaviour on my part because they don't do much about it. But I don't do it in a nagging way either, so I don't really expect much to change.'

Karen identifies very strongly with Joe: 'He thinks a lot of the time the way I do and when he is strong, demanding, horrible in a way, to me, there is a sense of relief because I don't feel he's stronger than I am. I thank goodness for it.'

Her younger son 'is a whole different ball game because he has learning difficulties and so I worry tremendously about his achievements. I just want him to survive and get to a position where he can be really independent.'

It is really important that her sons have strength but she does not encourage it 'because I am incredibly disgusted by certain things in society. They will hear me being very angry about certain things and speak endlessly about what pigs people are. So in a way, that is not encouraging strength because it is expecting them to give way to others and to think of the effect they have on people.' She likes her sons' personalities and their strengths even if it means they are being stubborn: 'I like signs that they are strong even if that makes them harder to live with.'

Karen does not know if she has instilled self-esteem in her sons and questions it a lot: 'I suppose that just by talking to them, listening, wanting to hear what they have to say, and by respecting them I have instilled self-esteem in them. But I sometimes wonder whether they have sufficient self-esteem. Whether I have sufficient self-esteem. I don't know.'

She is very close with her sons although the younger one does not like too much physical contact unless he wants it: 'He doesn't really like cuddles, but he does come to me for support and to hide in my arms. I feel awful when he doesn't accept my advances but I do try to respect his request, but it is very difficult.' Joe, 'is more cuddleable and at night he likes to have a little cuddle and hold my hand.'

Karen does not know her younger son:

I don't know if he is happy at school but he doesn't seem incredibly happy nor unhappy. I cannot tell, but nobody can tell what he is feeling. I feel that I am living with someone I don't know. I look forward to knowing him one day. It's part of his whole learning problem ... his whole mental state is somewhat closed off.

Her relationship with Joe is different: 'I don't feel that he hides his feelings from me and there is no reason that he should.' She added, 'If Joe is going through a bad phase, I am rather scared of how he's going to come home from school and I dread him walking in, in a foul mood.' She does not see him as an extension of herself because 'he is too complicated'.

Karen is 'as happily married as most people':

Marriage is a stupid institution but as stupid institutions go, it is better than not being married. We get on pretty well even though my husband misses the romantic bits because I think that as a man, he has missed out on having children. The big bug in our marriage is that I spend a lot of time on my children. I just recently said that I don't want to go out to the opera because I cannot cope with the tiredness and that's the issue between us.

Children at this age, especially a child with learning difficulties, take a lot of energy. They come first and my husband feels that it is unfair.

Karen believes that her children fulfil her need for mothering and 'if I look back to early stages of our marriage before the children came along, I did mother my husband more. Now that I have got children to mother my husband gets less mothering than he feels he would like. I think this is the crux of the problem between us.'

Karen does not think that there is open communication in the family and she and her husband avoid quarrels: 'We will drastically avoid confrontation and I tend to feel that it is he who mainly backs down. There are a lot of things that we don't say that other people might shout at each other, but we don't. We just sit on negative things.' Karen is pleased that she doesn't say what's on her mind because it is so unpleasant:

If I can bite back what I want to say, it's all for the good because it is only true for that moment. When I am depressed, it is only true for that moment, but not true the next moment and then it disappears. If I put out my anger into words it is permanent and I will regret it later.

According to Karen:

Sex is not something that isn't discussed, but it just isn't discussed! I mean, it is a joke, the word sex can come up while there is kissing on the screen in some programme and the children will say 'yuk'. I had some leaflets about talks on sexuality and I said I suppose Joe should go to these and passed him the leaflets.

Karen makes the decisions in the family. Her husband is involved in the home in the sense that he's around a lot. Her sons are 'warmly disposed towards their father but they don't take a lot of notice of him because he overreacts very easily. His method of guidance is that he will yell at them and then always apologize, which he probably shouldn't do as often.' Her sons are 'close' with their father, 'they are not remote in any way'. Karen believes that her husband does not have 'a very big influence on the children because he undermines himself'.

Karen confides her thoughts and 'that sort of thing' in her sons:

We talk so much. I don't think one could talk without confiding. I wouldn't tell them that I'm having a depression. I would try to keep that off their shoulders and not burden them with that sort of knowledge because it is too much trouble for them. I don't think they pick it up.

Her children are very susceptible and 'you just have to hint and they know what I am considering and what I think. One of the fears that I have is that by sharing a lot with them I am over-feminizing them in a sense, but I don't think I will because they are tough.' Karen believes her sons are masculine but 'I don't want to burden them with too much of a feminine approach because one doesn't know what that may influence. If they got into thinking my way maybe that would be a problem for them.'

Karen's parents divorced 'well after I had grown up and left home'. There was a lot of quarrelling and a lot of negativity at times: 'Looking back, they were very much in love at different times and had great affection for each other and they stayed well in touch after their divorce. I don't think it was a rotten relationship.'

Her relationship with her mother is very close: 'She is quite dominant and I'm just about able to separate myself from her. It is very difficult.' Karen never felt 'very adequate growing up and I still don't'. Her father was 'around but he wasn't there for anybody, not for me and not for my mother'. Her mother confided in her: 'Our relationship was very obvious, and it was very open, very clear.' Her mother was not a good role-model because 'she was too self-sacrificial, too intense and too raw in a way'.

Karen feels that she is repressed 'as a woman and because of her upbringing, because I was actually in the shadow of my mother'. Karen believes that women are 'actually deeper than men' because they have been repressed and that 'there is a strength and superiority in that'. She doesn't think that her sons 'take on board too much of my views but I suppose it must pass on in some way what I think'. She adds:

I worry that I might make my children not effeminate, but unmasculine, in the sense that they might not feel that they have to fight. You need to have that in this world and I am very delighted not to be quite in that forum. Neither my husband or I are ambitious people materially, and I fear that the children will be, not effeminate in the sense of sex, but just less ambitious maybe.

Karen thinks that she will feel a sense of loss when her sons marry: 'I shall think that I have to be incredibly nice and not resent their wives. It is like that old adage, "Your daughter is your daughter for all of your life but a son is only a son until he finds a wife".'

Karen worries about burdening her sons:

> I ask myself all of these questions about their upbringing and it makes for a tough existence. I have my own insecurities about bringing them up and about communicating that to them. Although I don't talk to them about it, I am communicating it in other ways. I dither.

She continues:

> My sons are my priority ... I just don't want to leave them. This is the time my children need me, they are dependent on me and I suppose there will come a time when they won't be needing me and they will be delighted for me to leave them alone.

Interview twenty-six: Joe

Twelve-year-old Joe, Karen's elder son, describes himself as 'very nice and clever. I use the word clever as opposed to sensitive.' He is enjoying his childhood and 'enjoying myself, but fun, I don't like fun. I sort of like pleasure but it's different. Fun is like going to the occasional theme park, but I don't want to do that too often.' For pleasure he 'reads and I like talking. I don't have hobbies because I think they are stupid because someone tells you that you should enjoy it and then you feel that you must. I don't want to do things like a robot.'

Joe was 'a social outcast. I am really stubborn which doesn't get me very many friends. I was very picky about friends and I still am. I just have different views from most people but I now have loads of friends since changing schools.' He doesn't like sports and has tried to 'steer clear of lots of games like football and rugby and I don't like swimming because the teacher is a bit of a tyrant. I don't like to do organized things and I try and beat the system. I know what I want. It is not that I am independent, I just don't like being told what to do.'

His mother is 'nice, clever and someone that I can trust'. He is close with his mother because 'we share the same kind of mind. We feel the same way about the same things and relate in the same way. Because of that, I think of her as my friend.' His mother shares the same views 'but you know, you can't go so away from society and I am much more looking for the truth and justice and she is looking for humanity and making everything right.'

He wouldn't change anything about his mother 'even when I am in a foul mood'. Joe feels that his relationship with his mother is something that 'can be broken and that if he doesn't try to keep it going, it can go wrong'.

Joe's mother has expectations of him:

> When I went to school she said to me that she'd be cross if I wasn't in all the top sets. She doesn't usually say things like that, and she really wouldn't have been cross or disappointed with me. She only said it because she knew I would be top of the class. I don't think her mind is like a chart, you've got to be this by this time, but obviously everyone has expectations of people and they are sometimes disappointed.

Joe wants to do something interesting when he grows up: 'I am not going to be cooped up in some office. I want to do work for animals and I want to enjoy myself and that's about it. Maybe fame. Maybe I'll be a naturalist but for sure it'll be fun and outdoors.' When Joe has had ambitions, he has always achieved them and 'they've been pretty high'.

His mother understands that he does not like to be patronized: 'I am a human being, not a child, so obviously she doesn't try and organize my life. I always ask for advice on small things and she tells me to do it myself. I just want to be treated normally and not like a child and my mother gives me that respect.'

Joe doesn't feel that he must please his mother but he tries to be 'perfectly all right and nice to her but I don't actually feel that its something conscious all the time, that I need to please her, but I always try to.' When he has caused his mother to be unhappy because he is in a bad mood, 'Mum will get really cross and then she shouts a lot and tells me off. When she is cross at me, I am cross at her. It makes me feel that she's doing me an injustice and that I was wrong. Then I say that I am sorry. Sometimes I get really depressed.'

Joe and his mother talk to each other about 'world issues and we might talk practically about issues like where we should go on holiday.' His mother doesn't tell him secrets 'because I don't really think she has any'. He has as much privacy as he needs but 'doesn't actually want any. I only want privacy from the outside world.' Joe can talk freely to his mother about his feelings: 'Last night I told my mother that I was depressed but that I felt better when I saw my friend who was even more depressed than me. She understood that.'

Joe occasionally sleeps in his parents' bed:

In the morning I decide I'm getting up and I make a start, but then I decide it's too cold and I don't have the energy to get back to my room so I stop at my parents' room. Their bed looks so warm that I just get in. I'd like to sleep in my dog's bed because I like my dog, he's cuddly.

Joe believes that his parents are happily married. There is open communication in the family but 'my father doesn't understand me so much and my brother always threatens to tell on me'. The facts of life were never discussed because 'I learned sex education in school'.

Joe loves his father but it isn't so deep: 'I talk to him but if I had a big, sort of deep problem, not homework or something, then I'd probably go to Mum. I don't talk so much with my dad about world problems and topical issues. The relationship with my dad is perfectly all right.'

Joe does not feel that he takes care of his mother:

My mother takes care of me and she knows what she is doing. I sort of feel that I take care of my dad. Mum and I are sort of trying to get Dad to be more fun because he is quite conventional and he is always reading the newspapers. Mum and I joke about him a lot because, well, in lots of ways we love him and everything, but he can be awfully incompetent. We joke about him together quite a lot in fact, but we don't complain ... he is always so nice to us. We don't complain about him, we joke about him.

Joe identifies 'more with my mum, much more. I have these controversial ideas and I don't get on well with people but I can identify with mum.'

Joe does not think that he has learned to be a man from his father: 'I have learned nothing from my father. Everyone sees all these American films about the father taking their sons into the forest but what should you learn? You don't usually learn from other people, you learn much more from life.'

Joe does not have a 'girlfriend'. He has this idea that he might even be a bachelor and never get married:

I don't like society and I find it annoying. I think I want to be a hermit when I grow up because society disgusts me. I am annoyed with what people do, and why they do it. I have some girl cousins and I find what they talk about quite trivial. There are more important things to think about. I don't want to land up too conventional because most people disgust me.

Joe has no idea about how his mother would feel if he got married but 'I don't think she'd be particularly worried if I didn't. She always laughs and says that she'd warn the person who marries me that I am a complete mess.'

According to Joe, his mother is slightly overprotective but 'she doesn't want me to feel that she is. She doesn't try to be over-protective but neither is she under-protective.'

Joe's definition of a Mamma's Boy is 'a son who is really looked after by his mummy, loves her and is really in touch with her. He is mocked by others.' He never uses the expression because 'I don't like it.'

Joe volunteered that he suspects that he might be a Mamma's Boy:

But even if I am, it doesn't really matter. It doesn't make any difference at all to any of my relationships with anyone. You're still the same person even if your mum is very protective and you're dependent. That's just your personality. It is you who decides if you're a Mamma's Boy or independent. It doesn't really matter at all.

GENERAL FINDINGS

What has emerged are discernible patterns, general points, recurring themes and linking similarities which have been indicated through examination of the cases.

It is suggested that the mothers of Mamma's Boys are unfulfilled by their marriages or relationships. Her expectations of her partner are unmet and she is the dominant force in the family even if it does not appear so – she uses her refined manipulation to achieve her end. These women have had powerful mothers themselves and have good reason to believe in 'phallic women' and, in effect, emulate their own mothers. It can be assumed that she unconsciously turns to her son to have her needs and expectations met in lieu of having them met by an adult partner. The mother of the Mamma's Boy does not work outside the home and especially not during her son's infancy – her main focus is on maintaining a 'traditional' role of motherhood. If she does work full or part-time, she is fraught with guilt.

Also implicit in the interviews is the idea that the mother of the Mamma's Boy did not have a satisfactory relationship with her own mother and in many cases it remains unreconciled into adulthood (examples; Interview eight, Barbara; Interview nineteen, Judith; Interview twenty-five, Karen). There is also a sense of inadequate individuation and separation in these women (examples: Interview eight, Barbara; Interview nineteen, Judith; Interview twenty-five, Karen) and problematic relationships with their fathers. Many of the mothers harbour unresolved conflict and ambivalence towards their parents.

According to Welldon (1988, p. 9), 'The main feature of perversion is that, symbolically, the individual through her perverse action tries to conquer a tremendous fear of losing her mother. As a baby she never felt safe with her mother, but instead at her most vulnerable, experiencing her mother as a very dangerous person. Consequently the underlying motivation in perversion is a hostile sadistic one.' Stoller writes (1975, p. 42), 'he is the cure of the lonely, hopeless sadness instilled in her by her cold and powerful mother and rejecting father.' Although Stoller is referring to the mothers of transsexuals, his theory holds true when applied to the mother of the Mamma's Boy.

Histories of some of the mothers suggest some degree of depression – Interview nine, Mary and Interview twenty-six, Karen. While most of the mothers did not discuss depression, there seems to be some undertones that it may exist. Others explicitly mention they had suffered from post-natal depression, as in the case of Barbara, Interview eight, and Marsha, Interview fourteen, which can be related to the discrepancies between the fantasies and expectations of being a mother held during pregnancy and the reality of being a mother once the child is born, the mother's self-esteem based solely on being a mother, the child as her single focus, and inadequate internal and/or external positive reinforcement. Other mothers acknowledge frustration at being the sole carer of their infant, which is accepted as a healthier and more balanced position to maintain (Acquarone, 1996). A mother's frustration, if not admitted, may be unconsciously taken out on her child in ways which are congruent with her conviction that she is conforming to a high standard of mothering, which is the case in the formation of the Mamma's Boy Syndrome.

For the most part, the mothers preferred and hoped to bear sons, indicating that they held males in higher regard than their own gender. Their preference for a son can be linked to societal expectations, the belief that their partner would favour a son, fulfilling their own parents' wish for a son they never had, continuation of the family line, and their unconscious fear of passing on their own insecurities and disturbances to a daughter. The mothers who were disappointed in not having a daughter held the belief that a daughter would never leave them – unconsciously, the Mamma's Boy is the 'chosen' son to achieve that same end. However, the mothers of both sons and daughters have better relationships with their sons, as in the cases of Interview seventeen, Liz, Interview fourteen, Marsha, and Interview twelve, Gloria. There is also evidence which suggests that there is a correlation between mothers who confide inappropriately in their sons and the likelihood that they are unable to allow their sons to separate fully.

Where open communication in the family was reported, there was evidence given to contradict this – sex was not discussed, important issues were not faced straightforwardly, and confrontation was avoided. In the families where sex was discussed, information was often not age-appropriate. In two cases of mother–son interviews (Interviews fifteen and sixteen, Terrence and Alex, and Interview twenty-six, Joe) the sons were not consulted as to whether they would partake in the study. They were told by their respective mothers that they would be interviewed and it was expected that they would comply. It can be deduced that these mothers would treat their sons in a similar manner in other aspects of their lives – they did not take their sons into consideration when making a decision for them and it is indicative of the influence they wield over their sons. Other mothers asked with genuine concern the type of questions that would be asked but gave the final decision whether to participate in the interview to their sons.

It is implied by many of the sons that they felt that their mothers' moods were inconsistent and unpredictable. It can be inferred from the interviews that these sons try not to instigate any negative change in her behaviour and would avoid conflict with her at any cost. These sons feel responsible for their mother's moods and are enmeshed in her feelings, attempting continuously to make her feel 'happy'. Often, the mother's mood was based on her son's and vice versa, which suggests that there is not adequate individuation and separation between mother and son. Many of the mothers could not cope with 'normal' separation from their sons and unconsciously attempted to impede their normal developmental stages of maturation. They felt anxiety and loss with their sons going off to school and admitted that they would feel a tremendous separation and loss when he would marry. Sons are infantilized as a means of mother not having to meet inevitable separation and, in some cases, sons sleeping with their mothers can be understood as a comfort to her rather than a conscious need of the sons.

In research undertaken by Dr Jerome Bach and his colleagues at the Bach Institute and the University of Minnesota (1988, p. 34), a second child will normally bond with, react to or identify with the mother. A second child will make decisions and hold values *vis-à-vis* the mother. A male second child will be an extension of the mother's unconscious needs or desires and become a man just like the one mother wished she could have married. According to Stoller, with regard to transsexualism (1975, p. 44), the transsexual boy is the youngest child in the family either permanently or for five or more years. Although there is no conclusive evidence to substantiate whether birth order has any bearing on a son becoming a Mamma's Boy, a tentative theory can be put forward as follows: given that a son is predisposed to an overbearing mother, he may suffer from the Mamma's Boy Syndrome if he is an only child (in which case his burden will be magnified), if he is the only son among sisters, or if he is a second child regardless of whether there are other sons in the family system. Intrapsychic factors of the 'chosen' son must also be considered.

Stoller (1975, p. 43) inadvertently became aware that mothers of transsexuals feel their infant to be beautiful with an intensity which persists unchanged through the years. His findings are relevant in understanding the similarities in behaviours and pathologies which exist between the mothers of transsexuals and Mamma's Boys. Two of the interviewed mothers referred to their sons in such a manner: Barbara (Interview eight) referred to her son as 'beautiful' and Marsha (Interview fourteen) referred to her son as 'pretty'. Carlos, cited in Chapter 1, remarked that his mother thinks he is 'beautiful'.

Evidence exists that many of the mothers were 'tomboys', who enjoyed that period of their lives. They related better to boys and identified with their fathers' strength. They are not reconciled with their own femininity and they grapple with mixed gender messages which were passed on to them from their own mothers. On delivering a male child these mothers have their unconscious fantasies of being a boy, which they gave up during their own latency period, reignited in disguised form. It can be postulated that in some cases (Interview fourteen, Marsha, and Interview one, Barry), mothers promoted and supported homosexuality in their sons as a means of vicarious wish-fulfilment.

Mamma's Boys identify more with their mothers and felt that they could not identify with their fathers. In cases, sons felt obliged to protect their mothers from emotional and physical abuse by their fathers (examples: Interview one, Barry, and the case of Fabio named in Chapter 1). In several instances there is an unspoken collusion between mother and son in the maligning of Father, as in Interview fifteen, Terrence, Interview twenty-six, Joe, and the case of Mark cited in Chapter 1. Fathers do not have a 'hands-on' approach to parenting and are physically or emotionally unavailable to their sons, which creates difficulty in their dis-identifying with Mother and counter-identifying with Father (Greenson, 1968, p. 370).

It is reported in some interviews that the sons as young children followed their mothers' routines around the house. There is also evidence which points to mildly obsessional mothers and their sons taking on some of that trait (Interview ten, Louise, and the cases of Mark and Fabio in Chapter 1). These mothers employ in obvious form the 'regulator' mode of mothering in which the mother expects the baby to adapt to herself and her routines (Raphael-Leff, 1991, p. 355). In the formation of the Mamma's Boy Syndrome there is vacillation between the regulator mode and the 'facilitator' mode, in which the mother is determined to be the sole source of goodness for her baby for whom she wishes to provide the ideal infancy (Raphael-Leff, 1991, p. 355). The mother of the Mamma's Boy in actuality 'provides' and simultaneously 'demands' with an extreme intensity and longevity which serve to enable her rather than her son.

From Interview fifteen, Terrence, and Fabio (Chapter 1) it is indicated that their fathers have had dependent relationships with their own mothers. It can be deduced that these men do not feel a need to interfere in their wives' involvement with their sons' lives. Their wives emulate their own mothers' behaviour. Some sons, although they had moved out of the parental home, were still dependent on their mothers. These sons still wanted and needed to be nurtured and cared for by their mothers – they went home for meals, to have their laundry washed, and lived in close proximity. Other sons reacted conversely and moved as far away as possible in order to escape their mothers' influence.

Marsha, Interview fourteen, and Laura, Interview ten, believe their sons are 'independent', independent by default, a result of their not bothering to fulfil their sons' needs. They waived their responsibilities in fear of not being able to make the right decisions in an authoritative and mature manner. Other mothers unknowingly relinquish the responsibilities of motherhood by seemingly treating their sons as friends and prematurely shouldering them with adult responsibilities. When mothers treat their sons as best friends or divest themselves of maternal responsibility, the son cannot feel contained. There is a lack of boundaries, of discipline (rather than punishment) and, in a sense, premature separation and unmet developmental needs, which make the sons cling even more desperately to their mothers. In wanting to feel contained by Mother, the son will act out as in the cases of Laura's son, Interview ten, and Lucy's younger son, Interview eleven, both of whom became dependent on drugs.

At the other extreme, mothers unconsciously expend too much effort directing their sons in virtually the same way that they were raised, namely, domination by their own mothers (Odom, 1990, p. 36). Continual demands were made on her as a child which she strained to meet. Whatever is deemed important to her, such as education, money, success, or being the best, is translated into demands on her son – it is highly important that her son excel at the cost of developing his own personality. This mother may seem to be loving, caring, and doting on her son, but she is overly disciplinarian, creating a man who will be haunted throughout his life by a sense of insecurity and failure as he feels unable to fulfil the expectations his mother set during childhood.

The reverse form of the MBS is suggested in Interview four, Conrad, Interview five, Gregory, and Interview six, Tom. Mother's seeming indifference as perceived by the sons produces the same effects as in the over-engulfed Mamma's Boy, with their need to please mother just as evident. A sense of duty towards Mother and an obligation to gratify her is evident in both forms of the Mamma's Boy Syndrome. Although many of the sons interviewed felt a mixture of love and hostility towards their mothers, which came through in the contradictory messages of their interviews, it was hard for the sons to admit, acknowledge and articulate directly their sense of reservation about the relationship. It is also apparent that when the mothers are frustrated, angered or their wants are dismissed, they react by withdrawing from their sons or behaving in a passive aggressive manner. These mothers employ direct or subtle threats of rejection and ridicule to make their sons conform to their expectations.

What is glaringly conspicuous from the interviews is that in the making of the Mamma's Boy mother offers 'love' based on the condition that her son meet her explicit or implied demands. By using the greatest weapon available to her, the threat of withdrawing her love, she surreptitiously weakens her son's threshold and programmes him to subjugate himself to her systematically. Mother becomes indelibly printed in his psyche as the map which guides him through and throughout his life.

Relevance and implications

Research on the Mamma's Boy Syndrome is significant not only for exposing it as a widespread disorder which is imposed on a son by his mother, but also for better understanding female and male perversion – in psychoanalytical terms, perversion does not carry moral implications but means a dysfunction of the sexual component of personality development (Welldon, 1988, p. 6). Although it may at first seem preposterous even to consider a link between the MBS and primary transsexualism – biologically and anatomically defined males who claim to have always believed themselves from as far back as they can remember to be female and act in feminine ways – it can be suggested that the MBS and transsexualism are merely two extremes found along the same continuum with homosexuality (which Mamma's Boys have a propensity towards), fetishism and transvestism.

Both the transsexual and the Mamma's Boy renounce their maleness, identity and power: the transsexual believes himself to be a female trapped within the wrong body while the Mamma's Boy is pressured into turning his power over to a female, his mother, and is 'trapped' by her overwhelming physical and emotional presence. Only the extent of the mother's psychopathology and overt manifestation of her perversion will determine the son's ultimate sexual and gender orientation.

Healthy mothering with the intention of bringing up a well-adjusted and self-actualized son and mothering a son in order to meet her own needs share several of the same components. Stoller (1975, p. 48) writes:

> In a happy mother–infant unit we expect to see a mother idealizing her infant, just as we expect a normal mother to feel herself anatomically more complete (in fantasy) on giving birth to a son. We expect to see moments of total openness of joyous communication between mother and infant. We expect to see a mother getting sensual pleasure from feeling her baby's skin up against hers. We expect to see a mother treating her infant not only as if he were a product of her body but as if he were still a part of it. In other words, we expect to see, if we are hoping for a baby's healthy development, that there will be times of perfect closeness and bliss. But we do not expect that she will *so* overvalue her son, *so* submerge her own desires and make such superhuman efforts to prevent any physical or emotional suffering. And, especially, we expect to see all this diminish with

time; we do not expect her to make this effort so unswervingly and keep it up for years.

What differentiates healthy mothering from selfish and perverse mothering is the need to keep the symbiotic process from ending. Stoller is writing in relation to the mothers of transsexuals; however, his description bears a striking resemblance to the warped needs and ultimate actions of the mother whose son is indisputably moulded into the role of a Mamma's Boy. What differentiates these two forms of mothering is the extent to which the mother uses her son for self-gratification, inhibits separation and individuation and prevents the development of her son's masculinity. The mother of the Mamma's Boy will treat her son as a male, albeit an emasculated one, whose sense of masculinity is formed through identification with his phallic mother or from the carefully prescribed and non-threatening masculine characteristics she deems suitable for him to acquire, while the mother of the transsexual will adamantly discourage any signs of masculinity in him by rewarding only his feminine virtues. When the son is left solely to his mother's devices without a father or adequate male role-model to protect him from Mother and with whom he can identify, the son's psychological and emotional well-being as well as his gender orientation, will be determined by his mother's own experience and well-being (there is a deliberate absence of discussion of the role of the father, since it is sufficient to say that it mirrors the absence of fathering given to his son, as well as the support given to his wife).

The Mamma's Boy Syndrome is pertinent not only for furthering the understanding of sexuality and gender-identity issues but for contributing to the recognition of the neglected area of female perversion.

CHAPTER FIVE

The Mamma's Boy's Relationships

PROFESSOR LEVY: *You will notice that what we are aiming at when we fall in love is a very strange paradox. The paradox consists of the fact that when we fall in love we are seeking to re-find all or some of the people to whom we were attached as children. On the other hand, we ask our beloved to correct all of the wrongs that those early parents or siblings inflicted upon us. So that love contains in it the contradiction. The attempt to return to the past and the attempt to undo the past.*

Woody Allen, *Crimes and Misdemeanors* (© 1989, Touchstone Pictures. All rights reserved.)

The Mamma's Boy's relationships are influenced by his mother, regardless of whether he is still living with her at the age of forty-five and asexual or has mustered up the courage to leave her to embark on seemingly 'healthy' heterosexual relationships – separation from Mother is an intrapsychic event independent of his physical separation. In the latter case, his afflictions may not seem as apparent or dire, but, indeed, Mother has coloured his way of being, the way he feels about himself and the way he will treat or be treated by women.

How have the Mamma's Boy's relationships been influenced by his mother? What are the messages he carries with him into adulthood which affect the way he feels about women, himself and his sexuality? Can the Mamma's Boy ever be fully free of his mother's influence? How does Mother react towards the 'other woman'? What are his expectations of women? Does having a relationship mean that he is unscathed by the MBS?

The Mamma's Boy who has dared to embrace the natural domain of relationships with a woman other than Mother will either identify with and take on the attitude of his mother or, conversely, attract to him someone with the same attitude as her. In either case, his actions are unconsciously motivated.

This chapter will explore and reveal the lingering influences that Mother has on her son's heterosexual relationships.

THE SUBSTITUTE MOTHER

If seemingly successful in pulling away from Mother's grip, the Mamma's Boy's new-found 'independence' will be developed within the limits of safety where he can remain a 'grown-up boy'. He will embark on a relationship with a woman – a girlfriend, partner or wife – who is in the image of his mother, 'a phallic woman' who will become his mother's replacement. He projects his masculine attributes onto her and attempts to compensate for what he lacks by seeking his ideal self-image in her.

Because the Mamma's Boy denies that his mother's treatment of him has had an influence on his behaviour, relationships with women, and on his sense of self-worth as a man, he is compelled to repeat the pattern – repetition compulsion – and attract to him a woman who will treat him as Mother did.

His deep sense of shame, low self-esteem and his internalized belief that he cannot cope on his own propel him to find a relationship which will emulate the one he shared with Mother. He will seek out a woman who will collude in keeping him a child, 'protect' and shelter him, mediate his life and make him feel complete. This scenario is familiar and comfortable for the Mamma's Boy, alleviates his separation anxiety, and provides him with a deluded sense that he has mastered his own life by breaking away from Mother. In truth, however, he has merely substituted one controlling mother for another; he goes through the motions of separation but remains close to Mother through reproducing the relationship with another woman.

The Mamma's Boy is incapable of participating in an equal relationship because his ability to trust has been impaired by the model of 'love' he was given by his 'trusted' mother. He moves away from real love (not that he would know what it is) and is attracted to an abusive, rejecting woman who will recreate the dynamics of his primary relationship. With his partner, as with his mother, he sets up a fantasy bond, idealizing her and taking on the belief that 'if only I tried harder, made more money, fulfilled her needs more consistently, maybe then, I would be loved'. He has been demanded to be sensitive to his mother's needs and, therefore, learns always to please as a requisite for being loved. He is comfortable relating to a woman in this manner and becomes dependent on her for approval.

Unconsciously, the Mamma's Boy remains submissive so that he can suppress his retaliatory feelings and destructive drives towards Mother, which he is at pains not to express. By acquiescing to his partner, he is neutralizing his aggression, which serves to maintain his tie to Mother. He is recreating the original masochistic relationship of the helpless child to the overpowering and cruel mother to whom he had to submit in order to survive (Socarides, 1978, p. 55).

His clinging to his abusive partner is based on infantile leanings (Socarides, 1978, p. 110). His developmental dependency needs were neglected as a child and he fears that he will be abandoned by his partner just as Mother so often threatened. He is fundamentally convinced that he cannot survive on his own because of the inferences he drew from Mother: 'No one can take care of you like your mother'; 'No one will love you like I do'; 'You don't need anyone else but me and besides, who would want you?'; 'You'll never be able to survive without me, you're incompetent and useless.' So when the Mamma's Boy has found a woman who will put up with his unworthiness he is so grateful that he clings to her 'for life'. He fears rejection and will consequently surrender to her control fully in order to ensure that he will not be abandoned.

The sexual component of his relationship with a 'new partner' is fraught with confusion due to the current of sexual innuendo and conflicting feelings which exist between mother and son. His erotic instincts and fantasies towards Mother are unconsciously retained and projected into a sanctioned and acceptable woman whom he perceives to be just like Mother, and with whom he can act out his desires without shame or guilt. In an interview with forty-two-year-old Tina, a highly successful and powerful businesswoman, she told of her relationship with Robert, eight years her junior: 'It was only the second time we had made love. At the height of passion he coyly whispered, "Can I come in you, Mummy?"'

This illustration aptly expresses the illusion of connection between mother and son which can be restored through sexual intercourse. Also, through sexual intercourse a personal experience and existence independent of Mother is created while simultaneously, and unconsciously, recreating the blissful union with Mother as the baby (penis) within. He has broken away from his mother but has united with his partner to become an extension of her, whom he now needs and clings to for his survival.

The Mamma's Boy is lulled into a false sense of maturity and independence by leaving Mother only to recreate the same dynamics with another woman who eliminates his pain of separation. Once defined by his mother, he is now defined by a woman who has become his 'loving' maternal figure. In essence, he has remained helpless, and is now at her mercy. By entering into a relationship with a phallic woman, his lack of independence and responsibility can remain unchallenged. He has ventured to leave Mother but is still not free from the constraints placed on him: his masculinity, sense of self and ability to be self-sufficient and directing are still influenced by his mother's treatment of him and unconsciously he punishes himself for his inadequacies through the reworking of the same dynamic in his adult relationships. Because of the unconscious repetition compulsion mechanism, he is getting exactly what he doesn't want: he chooses a woman who becomes synonymous with Mother and bonds with her out of helplessness and fear.

THE MASTER ATTITUDE

For the Mamma's Boy who has had to struggle for his apparent independence and separation from Mother, being in a relationship is tantamount to once again losing his autonomy. As already discussed in Chapter 2, the Mamma's Boy will not lash out against his mother upon whom his anger is directed, but will act out his frustration on other women, thereby keeping his mother and childhood idealized. He identifies with mother, obtains his masculinity from her, and re-enacts the role of the perpetrator as a defence against being controlled, engulfed and taken over by another woman. It is in this manner that he is able to hide from his reality: he remains powerless and unable to separate himself from the painful experiences and influences of Mother and, therefore, deceives himself by putting the onus on women whom he treats as dangerous and responsible for his insecurities.

The Mamma's Boy may become excessively domineering and aggressive towards women as a defence against his own sense of inadequacy and may revert to violence in order to prove his power. His aggression is designed to humiliate his partner in order to build up his own low self-esteem. Symbolically, through acting out his aggression on women, he is emasculating his mother and taking revenge. His aggression, provoked by his experience of Mother and displaced onto his relationship with a girlfriend, partner or wife, re-enacts the bullying of which he was the recipient; he now repeats the mother–child relationship with the reversal of roles and acts out his aggression on a woman as his mother did on him. His maltreatment of women deludes him with the feeling of victory (over his mother and all women), of being omnipotent and masculine, and converts his deep-rooted fear and sense of weakness into 'strength' which he uses against women so that he will not be found out: he is afraid of his mother and the power of all women.

The Mamma's Boy's experience of his overbearing mother has led him to believe that if he relies on a woman in the slightest, his independence will again be threatened. He has learned from his experience of Mother that intimacy is equated with control and closeness with fusion, and he fears being put in a position of vulnerability. Exposing his true self would reveal his lack of control over his own life and put him at his partner's mercy. Basically, he fears that if he gets too close to a woman, he will be re-engulfed, and his precarious identity depleted. He masks his emptiness and the fear he carries that of a little boy hiding from the power and wrath of Mother – by becoming the perpetrator, a seemingly self-assured and independent man who may not have control over his life, but who has the power to assume control of a woman's.

The Mamma's Boy cannot embark on an equal relationship because he needs to feel superior, otherwise he fears reverting back to his old pattern of surrendering his control to a woman. He will place excessive and unrealistic demands on his partner, be overly critical and deprecating, and basically emulate his mother's behaviour: he wants to be the master of his partner and make her subservient to his needs, unconsciously replicating the humiliating experience he encountered as a lap-dog to his mother.

The Mamma's Boy has conflicting notions about sexuality. He perceives sex as power and reassurance of his masculinity, proof to his mother, his partner and himself that he is a man. His sexual insecurity and hunger for love is demonstrated by his need to 'conquer' women, whom he relates to as debased sexual objects to be used. He has been objectified himself, and projects this onto his partner, a passive object without any power, whom he need not fear. He needs the woman to remain totally passive so that, in contrast, he can feel 'man enough' and assured of control.

His aggressive and libidinal wishes directed at Mother are taken out on this woman to obliterate the threat of engulfment. Sexual intimacy terrifies the Mamma's Boy as he fears being 'swallowed up' and made once again dependent, vulnerable and at a woman's mercy. As a reaction to his experience of Mother, he fears that all women will force closeness and dependency on him, which evokes sadistic feelings as a means of self-protection. His aggression is sexualized into sadistic and masochistic behaviour which allows him to engage in an intense relationship without the fear of intimacy and union (Glasser, 1985, p. 409); it is how he keeps the woman (object) at a safe distance. He has consciously decided never again to allow a woman to exert power over him and unconsciously degrades his partner, who is his mother figure.

As a man, his potency, self-esteem and worth, or lack of it, have been determined by Mother. So has his ability (or inability) to interact and sustain fulfilling relationships. The Mamma's Boy has struggled to assume an air of independence but he is not free: he is still trapped, confused and attached to Mother, as is evident in the corrupted model of behaviour which he replicates in his desire and fear of intimacy.

THE OTHER WOMAN

As a woman involved in a relationship with a Mamma's Boy, you will find yourself in a love triangle – you, your partner and his mother. Whether his mother is physically there or present as a ghost which haunts his present-day capacity to be fully committed in an adult relationship, she ultimately interferes with his ability to be intimate with a woman. He unconsciously needs his mother's consistency, ruinous though it is, which he has learned to depend on like a drug. The Mamma's Boy is emotionally unavailable to make a commitment because he is in denial about the control and impotence he feels about his life, his childhood experiences and his subservience to mother. While he maintains this denial, his mother will always be your rival for her son's affections and you may always remain the 'other woman', who will have to put up not only with being second-best but with his emotional unavailability, fear of intimacy, immaturity, lack of independence and inability to grow psychologically and in self-awareness. Furthermore, his overall feelings of powerlessness may unconsciously manifest themselves in sexual impotency as a means of releasing his suppressed anger and resentment towards his mother and women in general. As a form of retaliation, impotency serves to disable him from physically giving pleasure or 'performing', as he has been forced to do in other ways for Mother. Sexual impotency also safeguards the Mamma's Boy from intimacy with you, which he fears, and distances him from the possibility of re-engulfment.

A relationship with a Mamma's Boy is not an impossibility. Its quality, however, is questionable. You may start to feel resentment towards him as a result of his continuously siding with his mother rather than you and it is only a matter of time before you begin to lose respect for him because he allows his mother to control him. After a time, you may lose sexual interest in him because you begin to feel more like a mother than a lover in an equal relationship. It is his denial about his relationship with his mother which contributes to you acting out the role of his mother, whom he needs you to be. The Mamma's Boy may also suffer from inconsistent and unpredictable mood swings, bouts of rage and/or suffer from depression.

The Mamma's Boy may have all the equipment and trappings of a free and eligible man who is open to having a relationship, but closer examination of the mother–son relationship in which he has been since birth reveals that Mum is his number one priority and his most important relationship. If you are considering or are in a relationship with a Mamma's Boy, this may be playing out some of your unconscious needs. You may be frightened of intimacy and commitment and therefore seek a relationship with a Mamma's Boy who is already committed to another woman, his mother, or you may be repeating a pattern of abandonment by being involved with a Mamma's Boy who will ultimately not be there for you. In either case, you may suffer from low self-esteem and the belief that you don't deserve a partner all to yourself. You may need to be in control as a defence against the control and powerlessness you felt as a child (and as an adult) and, in a relationship with a Mamma's Boy, you hold the reins and have a willing victim who is comfortable being controlled. In a relationship with the damaged Mamma's Boy, you may attempt to mother him in a way which compensates for the faulty mothering he received as a child. Your hope is that he will overcome his past and change; this provides you with a sense of power and accomplishment. You may erroneously believe that you can come between him and his mother to win his affections, which is an unconscious attempt to re-work the Oedipal phase of your own development; you may even have been neglected as a child yourself, and feel that it can be repaired by becoming the partner of a Mamma's Boy, thereby earning what you perceive to be the loving concern of his mother.

Consider yourself warned: the Mamma's Boy equates love with control. You will either mirror the image of his mother or be the recipient of his passive aggression or forthright demonstrations of anger.

The two cited models of interaction that the Mamma's Boy may assume in his heterosexual relationships are by no means conclusive. There are many other ways in which he may relate to women, such as taking on the role of a 'Don Juan' or frequenting prostitutes to name but two. However, regardless of the Mamma's Boy's 'chosen' behaviour, what is common is his unconscious desire to find intimacy at an optimal distance.

'The core complex', as put forward by Glasser (1979), can be used to understand the Mamma's Boy's need for intimacy and his opposing fear of being engulfed. The core complex is a normal phase of development through which the infant has to pass. It is made up of the inter-related ingredients of a longing for intimate gratification and security and anxiety and fear of annihilation and abandonment by mother (Glasser, 1986, p. 10). The mother, then, is both a threat to his existence and the supplier of gratification. A conundrum is set up whereby she is both loved and hated, feared and desired, an object to be kept at a safe distance.

The Mamma's Boy has experienced his mother as engulfing and intrusive – his anxieties are no doubt well-founded – and this perception will be carried through into his relationships with women. As an adult, the core complex is expressed as a longing for 'union', 'merging', 'at-one-ness' (Glasser, 1985, p. 408) which is indicative of normal and loving desires. However, this state of intimacy is never achieved by the Mamma's Boy because it is reminiscent of his total possession by mother. He can never achieve real intimacy because, whenever the opportunity to be emotionally close and intimate with a woman arises, he fears a threat to his identity and withdraws. For him, merging has the characteristic of a permanent state and he fears that he will become indefinitely fused and suffer a permanent loss of self, which is equated with annihilation. Due to his fears and need for self-preservation, aggression is used to regulate distance between him and his partner to ensure against engulfment. In the case where the Mamma's Boy is in a relationship with a phallic woman, his aggression is turned inward as punishment for his neediness and dependency. Although he does not express his aggression outwardly, distance is nonetheless controlled by the masochistic relationship of which he is the subservient participant. Thus, intimacy is unachievable.

The Mamma's Boy, through heterosexual relationships, attempts to rid himself of the feelings of loneliness he has carried throughout his life. However, he fails to find relief in human contact since every woman is perceived as a symbol of his mother, who is capable of rejecting, controlling, abandoning, making him dependent and stripping him of his sense of self. The threats that haunted his childhood are petrified in his adult relationships and his desire for intimacy is superseded by fear.

As an infant, a male's first object–relationship is with the opposite sex, his mother, which might enable him later on in life to develop a sense of familiarity and ease in his relationships with women (Welldon, 1988, p. 45). However, for the Mamma's Boy, his 'ease', 'sensitivity' and ability to relate to women is due to a lack of fathering (male identification) and enmeshment with mother rather than a positive mother–son relationship. It is often remarked that the way a son behaves towards his mother reveals the manner in which he will behave towards women in his adult relationships. That is to say, 'If he is good to his mother, he will be good to his wife' (Landers, 1994, p. 5). Although this may be the case the underlying dynamics between mother and son are not taken into account: his fear of abandonment, Mother's passive-aggressiveness, manipulation and withdrawal of love, her subtle demands that he fulfil her needs, or his compliance as a means of survival.

George was a 'very good' son and close with his mother – Stella, his wife, knew it. He was also a very good husband and they were happily married, or so she believed. When he moved to London to marry Stella, he left his mother, father and two sisters in New York. She was unaware, however, that George was on the phone to his mother at least three times a day, as she later found out from his colleagues at the office. When Stella was eight months pregnant with their first child, George came home and announced that he was leaving her and moving back to New York, because his mother 'needed him'. He packed his suitcases, left his wife and filed for divorce. He never saw Stella again nor his new-born son. Stella now believes that 'a very good son is a euphemism for a son who is a Mamma's Boy. He gave up his responsibilities of being a husband, father and man and chose instead to remain the adored and dutiful son. It shouldn't have been a choice but his mother put the screws to him. I shouldn't have ignored the signals but I did.'

The Mamma's Boy, who has learned to please his mother in order to make her happy, may, in his adult relationships, unknowingly seek out needy women whom he can nurture and please. Having had little nurturing himself, he will give the love and attention to a woman that he wished he had received as a child, and identify with the mother he had always wanted his to be. Fundamentally, the Mamma's Boy draws these women to him because he has learned that he must serve and perform in order to be loved – he was rewarded for his 'good' behaviour with mother's 'love' and punished with its withdrawal if he did not comply. Being attracted to needy and damaged women in his adult relationships is comfortable – it allows him to get involved in their problems, taking the focus away from looking inside himself, and affords him a sense of self-sufficiency, accomplishment and worthiness. If a woman, in total contrast to his mother, is capable and independent, undemanding and unconditionally loving, he is thrown off-balance and made to feel redundant and worthless. He does not know how to interact with a woman who does not need or demand that he care for her and, furthermore, it would put him in a distressing position of reassessing his idealized relationship with mother.

The mother whose Mamma's Boy is leaving her for another woman, does not often accept the separation graciously – it is perceived as a betrayal and personal rejection. Eva, married to Peter, told me: 'His mother never liked me from the word go. I think she was always threatened by me because she knew that this relationship was serious.' According to Peter's mother, Eva was never pretty or fit enough even though she is a successful model. On Eva and Peter's wedding day, minutes before the ceremony was to begin, Peter's mother pulled Eva's father aside and began sobbing, telling him, 'Eva is taking my little boy away and because of her things will never be the same.' Eva told me in laughter, 'What did she expect my father to do? Agree with her that I was a horrible creature and call off the wedding because her only child was finally moving out after 32 years of listening to her problems and taking care of her needs ... I think not.'

Mother is being left for a younger woman, which brings up her own ageing, lack of achievement and self-imposed, limited way of life. With the loss of her son, the advantages that were once hers – status and power, companionship and caring – will be afforded to another woman and her purpose and position will be destroyed. She is left with the realization that she is all alone or, maybe worse, alone in a fruitless marriage.

For Mother, the 'other woman' brings up the Oedipal situation that she has never reconciled (Socarides, 1978, p. 19). Her son is perceived as her father and another woman (her son's partner or wife) as the mother who keeps her from him, thereby creating a triangular relationship in which Mother feels that she must compete for her son's love and attention. As Nancy disclosed in our interview, 'When I look at my wedding photos it is no wonder that me and Gary are divorced ... In all the pictures, Gary's mother has him pulled closely over to her with her arm around him like a grip. There I am standing alone on the other side of him as if I didn't belong at my own wedding. His mother wore a similar dress to mine and she even wore white.'

The mother of the Mamma's Boy can be overtly hostile and unaccepting of her son's partner in an attempt to break up their relationship and regain her son's attention. However, the more skilled mother will present herself as selfless and kind to her rival, to mask her manipulation and intrusiveness. It is the same subtle control used on her son in order to take over his life and obstruct his burgeoning freedom: now her aim is to penetrate the dyad of which she feels jealous and excluded. According to Alan D. Entin (quoted by Israeloff, 1992, p. 202), 'A husband's reluctance to confront his mother about her intrusions into his marriage may mean that he hasn't fully separated from her.'

On a parallel note, the 'mother-in-law', commonly mocked and ridiculed by men (in the same way that Mamma's Boys are caricatured by society), has been made to take the brunt of men's displaced aggression towards their own mothers. A man's mother can remain idealized and adored while the mother-in-law, deemed a socially sanctioned outlet, is injected with exaggerated and insufferable meddling qualities.

The aim of the Mamma's Boy in his adult relationships is to find the line between love and absorption. Unconsciously, he will re-enact his past history in his heterosexual relationships and remain the abused or become the abuser. As long as Mother remains idealized, and he remains ignorant of the effect she has on him, the pattern will repeat itself like a vicious circle and the Mamma's Boy will suffer intrapsychic conflict and loneliness pondering how to be free while at the same time remaining dependent on and dedicated to his image of mother.

CHAPTER SIX

Syndrome Check-list:
Are You a Mamma's Boy?

A man is mostly what his mother makes him.
Sir Richard Burton

The syndrome check-list is intended as a general catalogue of symptoms and behaviours which are indicative of the foundations upon which the Mamma's Boy Syndrome is built and perpetuated. If you have some of these symptoms, it does not necessarily mean that you are a Mamma's Boy – if your social and private life, relationships, self-esteem, personality development, gender identity and independence are undisturbed and Mother is not the most important person and relationship in your life (and vice versa), if Mother does not vehemently interfere in your leading your own differentiated life, and she does not relentlessly demand that you submit to her way of doing things, common sense says that the mother–son relationship may be sufficiently adequate or, at best, good enough to have allowed for your healthy development. Keep in mind that the Mamma's Boy Syndrome runs on a continuum from mild to extreme.

1. You were breast-fed for more than nine months.
According to research at the Parent Infant Clinic of London (Kahr, 1993), the psychic health of the mother will determine the duration of breast-feeding. Current work in infant psychotherapy has determined that a period of nine months is a sufficient length of time for breast-feeding.

2. You regularly slept in the same bed as your mother after the age of five.
A child can pick up his mother's unconscious needs, including the need to have you in bed with her. This need may be her unconscious wish to form a barrier between her and her husband, or, conversely,

to involve you in their sexual act, or to alleviate her loneliness. You are perceived as her substitute husband. You may have wanted to sleep with your mother in order to crush your insecurities of abandonment, as there is no firm representation in your mind of a consistent mother and you need to prove that she exists, that she is there. On your part, it may also be an unconscious desire to replace your father, whom you perceive as a rival for your mother's attention. Boundaries between you and your mother are not firmly drawn.

3. Your mother fails to accept your burgeoning sexuality or, conversely, is keen to know every aspect of your sexual life. You discuss intimate details with her.

Your mother does not accept you as a sexual being and does not admit that you are separate and growing up and apart from her. When Mother feels entitled to know every detail of your sexual life, she is maintaining an illusion that you are one and may receive vicarious fulfilment and delight from your sexual ventures. In both cases your sexuality is tied to Mother.

4. Mother dissuaded you from playing sports.

According to Bieber (1962), boys' masculine identity seems to be undermined by maternal overprotection and inhibition of rough-and-tumble play.

5. As a child you were dissuaded from playing with other children and forming relationships. You were told that no one was 'good enough' for you to associate with. Consequently, you felt isolated from your peers and alone.

Your mother depended on you and did not want to lose or share you, her one constant and committed companion. If you had formed other relationships, Mother would have felt threatened because you could make comparisons, receive feedback and discuss your relationship. She would no longer be your sole point of reference for a relationship. Often in dysfunctional families a sense of superiority is used to mask shame – this made you feel different and 'special' and that you didn't belong – you belong with mother with whom you feel comfortable. You were emotionally cut off from other relationships so that you would remain reliant on Mother for all your needs.

6. Mother made decisions for you without your consultation.

Your mother does not view you as distinct from herself and, therefore, does not take you into consideration when making decisions. She cannot accept that you have feelings, as that might tap into her own pain. If Mother is supportive of your choices and allows you to make your own decisions and mistakes, she may no longer perceive you as an extension of herself.

7. Your father was emotionally and/or physically absent while growing up. You feel you cannot identify with him.

Your father (or a father figure) was crucial in ensuring whether separation occurred between you and Mother. He abandoned his responsibilities by not intervening because he was emotionally and/or physically unavailable. Father must also serve as a figure with whom you can identify and acquire a masculine identity. If your father was aggressive, punitive or violent you could not identify with or emulate him. This left you instead identifying with your mother.

8. You are counted on to be Mother's escort at social events.

This may indicate that mother perceives you as her partner, the perfect man. You have been bred in the image of mother's perfect partner and she inappropriately takes pride in her creation.

9. As a child, your mother confided in you about adult matters.

This is inappropriate behaviour which encouraged you to assume adult responsibility prematurely. This behaviour is misconstrued as a 'special' position and keeps you unduly attached and responsible to Mother. You were needed to be available to your mother rather than her being available for you.

10. You cling to relationships which are destructive.

Because your needs were not met as a child, you are likely to cling to destructive relationships, situations and jobs as a defence against being abandoned and rejected.

11. You are often ill.

You are often ill, as you learned early on that in this way you were able to elicit Mother's sympathy, attention and care without demands being placed on you. When you are ill, Mother unconsciously satisfies your primitive needs which went unmet as an infant and child.

12. You still seek Mother's approval.

As a child, you were never able to obtain the praise and approval you needed from your mother. As an adult you are still trying to please her but are constantly disappointed over and again. You are still trying to prove yourself, that you are worthy of her acceptance and

love: you want to please her but to no avail. As an adult, you seek and
need approval from others.

13. You suffer from depression and feel powerless over your life.

As a result of your feelings of helplessness and inadequacy you feel
flawed and different. You feel you deserve the treatment you have
received from your mother and that it is somehow your fault, that you
are to blame. Instead of confronting and expressing the feelings you
have directed towards your mother, you internalize the hostility
(depression is anger expressed inwardly) and act it out in a self-
destructive manner in the form of depression.

14. You feel a sense of duty rather than love towards your mother.

This may be a result of the messages that were covertly passed on to
you: it is your duty to obey Mother and accept her will without
question because it is done in the name of love. You learned that it
was easier to comply with her unreasonable demands than to suffer
the guilt and fear of her loss. You learned to act lovingly – doing what
was asked or expected of you – rather than be loving towards her.

15. You avoid confrontation with Mother and asserting your views at any cost.

Effective and open communication were never a factor in your home
while growing up. Because you were not considered to be an
individual with thoughts and opinions of your own, confrontation was
viewed as a threat to mother's dominance over you and highlighted
your separateness. Problems were denied and avoided to maintain the
illusion of togetherness.

16. Your privacy was not respected.

When you are not regarded by Mother as a separate individual, she
cannot consider that you have a need for privacy or space of your
own. There are no boundaries which exist between you and Mother
and, therefore, there is no need for her to allow you privacy.

17. Your mother puts down your girlfriend or wife.

Your mother cannot cope with losing you to another woman. She
attempts to break up your relationship or create a wedge between you
and your partner in order to assume the position of the most
important woman in your life. If in disputes you take your mother's
side rather than your partner's, you are demonstrating that you are

not fully independent and separate from her. You are still trying to obtain her approval and love by allowing her to meddle in your life. There are no clear boundaries between you and your mother and she interferes in your adult relationships because she can. You fear your mother withdrawing her love completely from your life; there is no happy medium. You are still dependent on Mother to the detriment of having healthy adult relationships.

18. Your father was belittled by your mother. Your mother was the dominant force in the home who made all the decisions.

When Father and other men are belittled by your mother, you will unconsciously identify with her as a defence against being associated with those she attacks. You unconsciously do not form a relationship with your father as you yourself come to perceive men as victims. When Mother 'wears the pants' even if it is downplayed, it is she who holds the power over her husband and men. Identification with Mother assures you her alliance.

19. Your mother is a 'martyr'. You are her 'whole life'.

Your mother is self-sacrificing and she is sure to let you know. 'What I haven't done for you' is something to the effect uttered by Mother at a moment of displeasure or disappointment due to you not fulfilling her expectations. Her whole life is bound to yours and you are the centre of her focus. Her role as mother is determined by your success as she has invested in you all her unmet hopes and aspirations. She doesn't give unconditionally, but in order to be confirmed. She needs to know you are grateful.

20. You feel that you cannot depend on others.

As a result of your developmental dependency needs not being met and the threat of being abandoned by Mother with which you grew up, it is difficult to trust anyone to be consistent and dependable. It is difficult for you to create intimacy in your relationships because you fear betrayal. You will confirm this by unconsciously choosing a partner or friends who are abusive and who treat you in the same manner as Mother. Paradoxically, you believe that only Mother is dependable when in reality, your needs were disregarded so that she could rely on you.

21. You consider your mother to be unhappy in her marriage.

Marriage is the bedrock of the family system. When Mother is discontented within her marriage, or a single mother, there is a greater likelihood that she may turn to you to fill the gaping void left by the absence of an adult partner. You have been thrust into an inappropriate adult role before your time and become Mother's 'perfect partner'. The support she needs from a husband or partner is acquired from you and you become an adult without having had a childhood. You are no longer a son who has developmental needs which must be cared for, but an adult whom your mother needs and uses to feel complete.

22. Your mother's moods are inconsistent and her behaviour unreliable.

You never know what to expect. You walk on eggshells, feel jumpy and on the defensive in your mother's company. You dare not express yourself freely or provoke her in any way. You actually feel responsible for her moods and you constantly try to please her so that she will be happy. With magical child-like belief, you still feel that you actually have the power to make your mother happy: it is a role you have learned to take on. As a child it was unsafe to depend on Mother, her behaviour was inconsistent and her care contingent upon her mood, which was a threat to your survival.

23. You feel that you relate better to women than to men.

As a result of looking after your mother's needs, you relate better to women and feel a sense of familiarity with them. You are sensitive towards women to the extent that you take care of their feelings and wants instead of looking after yourself. You are attracted to women like your mother who are needy or alternatively, seductive and demanding. You have internalized a role of always being helpful and caring and never showing your anger or resentment. You are also more comfortable with women due to an underdeveloped identification with men.

24. You are hostile towards women.

You are unable to express your anger towards Mother and unconsciously take it out on women in your relationships. You are passive–aggressive or outwardly abusive; your moods are inconsistent because you unconsciously alternate between a desperate desire and desperate fear of being loved by a woman. You fear being controlled as you were by your mother and you harbour feelings of weakness and insecurity which you mask with aggression. You fear intimacy which for you is akin to being once again dependent and at the mercy of your mother. You recreate what was done to you by becoming the abuser.

25. You feel unable to cope with the main tasks of everyday life.

You have never learned to take care of yourself, you were never permitted to. Mother never allowed you to grow up and take charge of your life. Her over-protection has left you unprotected, unskilled and unable to cope with the basics of life. You still depend on Mother or alternatively you have attached yourself to a woman who has taken on her role: in either case, you remain powerless and dependent.

26. Your mother has unrealistic expectations of you. She demands perfection.

You represent your mother's unfulfilled dreams which, through you, can finally be achieved. She brought you up in her image and if you do not succeed, if you are imperfect, her flaws and vulnerabilities are exposed. She shames you for her imperfections. Meeting Mother's expectations and succeeding at what she deems appropriate are equated with securing her love and admiration. You fear losing Mother's love if you do not fulfil her expectations.

27. You perceive your mother as 'perfect'.

You have idealized your mother – no one can be perfect! As a child, you unconsciously created a fantasy bond to protect you with the illusion that your mother was there for you unconditionally. As an adult, the fantasy bond remains intact and you blame yourself rather than face up to your mother's imperfections. You are unable to evaluate your mother and your relationship realistically.

If you have answered *yes* to six or more of the questions, you must decide for yourself how much your mother interferes with your life, how much control she has over you, how hard it is to resist her, and how much you have been distressed and affected as a result.

I have purposely omitted to classify for the reader the degrees to which you, as a son, have been affected by the MBS – from mild to extreme – as it is a matter of personal awareness and acceptance that a problematic relationship exists between you and Mother.

The quality of your life may be greatly improved if you can become aware of and take the measures necessary to free yourself from the restraints of the Mamma's Boy Syndrome. Your behaviour is learned and developed. It can also change.

DETACHMENT CHECK-LIST: ARE YOU MOVING TOWARDS SEPARATION?

In order to find the keys which can unlock you from the Mamma's Boy Syndrome, you must first accept that you are imprisoned by it. Only then will you have the freedom to take the necessary steps towards escaping its effects and accepting autonomy and independence. You must negotiate a leaving – both physically and emotionally – to create the space between you and mother in which your separateness and individuality can be found.

In creating a map of the difficult yet rewarding process of self-actualization and independence there are positive steps you may choose, including consulting a qualified psychotherapist with whom you can develop a positive relationship. In a non-judgemental, non-threatening, accepting manner, with firm boundaries to contain you, you will be supported in understanding and resolving the dynamics of your relationship with Mother and the influences she has had upon you. The therapeutic relationship based on trust and respect will nurture your development and capacity to create a new reference point without the familiarity of demands being made of you, being told what to do or how to lead your life. By taking responsibility for your own growth and through making your own decisions, your self-worth and power will increase and you will learn new ways of being. However, this is no easy break – your therapist, unlike your mother, will not, and as a professional cannot, do it for you. He or she can only act as a catalyst while the ultimate change is up to you. Do you remain comfortable in the pain and, paradoxically, the pleasure which you know as a Mamma's Boy, or do you risk giving it up for the unknown, bitter-sweet experience of independence? If you do so choose, as frightening as it may seem, you can strive to:

- Break the idealizations you hold of Mother and the fantasy of being bonded to her.

- Redefine your relationship by creating firm boundaries and clear limitations.

- Focus on your own life and needs. Take responsibility for yourself – you are not liable for your mother's life.

- Learn to rely on your own sense of self-affirmation for approval.

- Unilaterally learn to alter the way you react towards Mother. Do not try to change her unless she has taken the steps to change herself. This is about *you*.

- Accept that your mother is a victim just as you were. Do not blame or hold her accountable for your problems.

- Value yourself and your needs – detach from your mother's beliefs and opinions of you.

- Rebuild your relationship with Mother based on choice rather than dependency. Only by being separate can you rebuild a healthy relationship.

- Create positive nurturing relationships with both women and men.

- Define yourself and discard your false self.

- Learn to trust yourself and others.

- Increase your self-worth by finding your own solutions and power.

- Build self-esteem.

- Take control of every aspect of your life.

Remember: You are resilient and have the capacity and free will to grow and evolve beyond the constraints of the Mamma's Boy Syndrome if you consciously choose.

Conclusion

The aim of life is no longer to grow up and assume life's burdens, but to remain attached to the nipple through which the milk of human kindness inexhaustibly flows.
Roger Scruton, *Fatherhood*, p. 73

I'd like to make a motion that we face reality.
Bob Newhart, *The Bob Newhart Show*

The mother–son relationship, instrumental in generating the Mamma's Boy Syndrome, is applauded, revered, encouraged and socially sanctioned. However, closer examination of this 'bond' has exposed it as simply a form of 'bondage' which Mother uses to shackle her son so that he exists only in relation to her: his every limited movement corresponds to her wishes and he cannot take a step towards separation without finding Mother attached to the end of the chain which binds them. In effect, Mother has manipulated a protective environment for herself at the expense of her son's development, sense of self and esteem, interpersonal relationships, and freedom. He cannot exist except in relation to Mother: he is yoked by her stiff demands.

Through excessive maternal preoccupation and an overwhelming gratification of her son's needs – partly out of love but mostly out of her fear of being left alone in the world – the Mamma's Boy is coerced into retaining his dependency on Mother long after the developmental point at which it is healthy or normal. The mother's own infantile fear of autonomy and separateness compels her to force upon her son a symbiotic relationship, which unconsciously, she wished she had had with her own mother. She denies her son the right to individuate so that she can deny her own inadequate sense of self and guarantee that she will always have him to feed off parasitically, to nurture, care for and fulfil her needs.

The Mamma's Boy is the receptacle for Mother's perverse tendencies which manifest themselves in the total control of her son, including the control and manipulation of his gender–identity acquisition. Her maternal instinct assumes a basic lack of empathy for her son, a driving need to cement an unhealthy and prolonged attachment, an excessive preoccupation which is out of sync with the son's appropriate needs for his age, and a quasi-pathological fear of him moving towards selfhood and separateness. As a result, the son's development is arrested and he remains throughout his life, as is his mother, in a state of incompletion. In this form of mothering, the mother of the Mamma's Boy exemplifies the unconscious enactment of female perversions.

The purpose of revealing the Mamma's Boy Syndrome is not to blame Mother – she is a victim as well, victim of her own unresolved experiences which are unconsciously translated into the 'smothering-mothering', over-involvement, intrusion and overbearing treatment of her son. However, what is intended is to have the power of motherhood recognized and the maternal halo removed from above her head. My intention is that no longer should the Mamma's Boy be merely considered the fictional subject of books, films and plays, e.g. Philip Roth's *Portnoy's Complaint* (1969), Hitchcock's *Psycho* (1960), or Cocteau's *Les Enfants terribles* (1938), to whom intrapsychic, psychological and emotional suffering is attributed. The MBS is a bona fide condition and not the non-threatening parody which society prefers to accept as a means of denying its reality.

The information and evidence presented in *Mum's the Word: The Mamma's Boy Syndrome Revealed* may not be at all palatable. Nevertheless, it should be digested in order to accept that over-mothering is not synonymous with good mothering or good-enough mothering. No longer should a Mamma's Boy – obedient, dutiful and caring to a fault – be representative of a mother's excellence. When a mother overvalues her son and burdens him with the responsibility of meeting her needs, when a mother lives vicariously through her son in order to negate the reality of her dismal life, when her son becomes the vehicle through whom she achieves and the repository for her expectations, when her son is needed as a partner and as her source of purpose in life, the likelihood is great that he will grow up to be a Mamma's Boy and, paradoxically, never grow up, remaining an appendage of his mother with little sense of who he is – if not in relation to her – with a lack of identity as a man or pride about his gender and sexuality.

The Mamma's Boy is by no means a press release for healthy mothering. Instead, the power of motherhood must be reassessed and her job performance re-evaluated: the Mamma's Boy Syndrome is the result of a perverse and abusive attachment which Mother never voluntarily severs.

Mum's the word ... silent and collusive.

Famous Men Who Have Experienced 'Smothering-Mothering'

Prime Minister Harold Macmillan: The youngest of three sons born to middle-class parents, the young Macmillan was dominated by his mother Nellie, who was determined that he be the best at everything. He grew up shy and withdrawn and in a perpetual state of anxiety. He remained awkward and reserved, especially with women. With his mother's firm backing he married Dorothy Cavendish, a daughter of the Duke of Devonshire. Not surprisingly, Dorothy hated her mother-in-law since Macmillan, who adored his mother, always took her side in disputes between the two women (Hudson, 1996, p. 47).

Peter Sellers: The famous actor, whose real name was Richard, was a substitute child for a first son called Peter who died in infancy. He was the only child of an ambitious, dominating, possessive, Jewish theatrical mother who completely overshadowed her gentle, totally ineffective and meek husband. Peter Sellers 'was spoiled rotten, and learned, early on, the art of throwing tantrums to get his own way'. He never made friends of his own age and as a consequence he and his mother were unhealthily close: 'She overwhelmed Peter. When they kissed, mother and son, it wasn't pleasant' (Barber, 1994, p. 1).

Lennox Lewis: The world heavyweight boxing champion of the world says he'd be nowhere without his mother Violet, who dictates everything from his diet to whom he dates. In his autobiography, Lewis writes, 'My mum is always good when it comes to weeding out certain girls in my life and giving me her motherly advice ... I trust my mum's opinion because you may have many girls but you only have one mother' (Lewis and Steeples, 1993, p. 56). Lennox was brought up solely by his mother, who says of their relationship, 'I suppose that is why Lennox and I are so close, because he is all I had to cling to ... I poured all my love on Lennox. I don't know if it was wrong of me to do that, to show him so much love' (Lewis and Steeples, 1993, p. 6).

L. P. Hartley: The famous novelist was born in 1895, the middle child of three and the only boy, to a prosperous middle-class family. His father, a solicitor, seems to have played little part in young Leslie Poles's upbringing and from birth he was cocooned in 'the warm, comforting, adoring embrace of women' – his nurse Bubby for the first few years, his affectionate but dominant older sister, and his mother Bessie, an intense neurotic woman so terrified that her infants might catch diseases in the cold that she coddled Leslie to distraction. When he was sent to boarding school at the age of twelve, on the decision of his father, Bessie deluged her son with anxious letters which he answered in kind: 'Yes, Mother, I shall put on my Thermogen wool so as not to catch a chill ... Yes, Mother, I will be sure to take rhubarb and a mustard-plaster.' Until her death in 1948, mother and son corresponded at least three times a week.

The novelist [Lord] David Cecil and Hartley became inseparable and it is Cecil to whom he gave his heart, although there is no evidence that it was anything other than a platonic relationship, with sexual attraction always present but suppressed. He spent most of his life entertaining and being entertained by titled ladies. When he proposed marriage to a Miss Joan Mews who accepted, he promptly drew back and had some kind of a nervous collapse (Hudson, 1996a, pp. 32–3).

Alexander Portnoy: The fictional character of Philip Roth's novel *Portnoy's Complaint* (1967) is an unmarried thirty-three-year-old who recounts to Spielvogel, his fictitious analyst, his childhood memories of his overbearing mother who vied 'with twenty other Jewish women to be the patron saint of self-sacrifice' (p. 18), his emasculated father, and his preoccupation with his penis. A disorder is named after him,

Portnoy's Complaint, which embodies a number of sexual perversions – a lack of sexual gratification, feelings of shame and the fear of retribution by means of castration. According to Spielvogel, many of his symptoms can be traced to 'the bonds obtaining in the mother–child relationship'.

Princes William and Harry: The sons of Diana, Princess of Wales, are at risk of being smothered by their mother as a means of easing the loneliness of her situation as a divorced wife. It is through her son Prince William that one day she will be able to exert her power as an influence behind the throne.

According to Parsons and Seward (1994, p. 48), 'William has become a mummy's boy, rarely leaving the Princess's side when he is with her. And when he is at school he finds the slightest excuse to telephone her.'

Lyndon B. Johnson: The President of the United States (1963–69), Johnson was the favoured son of five children born to a dominant mother. In the book *Lyndon Johnson and the American Dream* (Kearns, 1976), it is stated, 'My mother soon discovered that my daddy was not a man to discuss higher things. To her mind his life was vulgar and ignorant ... she felt very much alone ... Then I came along and suddenly everything was alright again. I could do all the things she never did.'

His mother was compelled to renew on her son's behalf all the plans and projects she had given up for herself – he would fulfil the dreams she had never carried out, he would become the important person she had failed to be. In the recounting of his early years, Johnson spoke almost exclusively of his mother and only mentioned his father to enumerate his failings as a husband. However, Lyndon never experienced his mother's love as a steady or reliable force, but as a conditional reward, alternately given and taken away. When he failed to satisfy her desires he experienced not simply criticism but a complete withdrawal of affection. His mother had her own way of showing her displeasure – 'not to yell or even to scold, but to greet her son at all times with an impassive stare ... He knew by his mother's withdrawal that he had not lived up to the splendid vision she had held of him as a boy' (Kearns, 1976, Chapter 1).

Charles Dance: The actor Charles Dance grew up feeling frustrated by his mother's overwhelming need for attention, 'She was the sort of woman whose embrace became as tight and constrictive as an iron vice. I found home life overwhelmingly claustrophobic.'

His mother's father went off and left his overworked wife, his mother and her three brothers struggling to survive and, as a result, 'I think my mother was desperate to make the family that she created a lot happier than the one she had been a part of, and she tried much too hard.' 'When I think about my mother,' Dance writes, 'I don't remember her ever being happy ... She seemed to be frustrated by her life, she was always banging on about making sacrifices, with lots of sighing and weeping. There are times when, like my mother, I am prone to feel a bit sorry for myself, especially when I go through periods of being out of work. And I am prone to depression from time to time, and she used to get quite depressed' (Danziger, 1996a, p. 21).

Jacob: The biblical character Jacob was the second and favoured son of Rebecca. It was she who decided that, of her two sons, Jacob, not her older son Esau, would lead the clan. Rebecca created the plan in which Jacob collaborated to deceive Isaac, his father, into blessing him instead of Esau, his favourite son. 'My son, obey my word as I command you ... so that he may bless you before he dies ... Upon me be your curse, my son; only obey my word ...' (Genesis 27:5–20; Brichto, 1994, pp. 105–6).

Orson Welles: George Orson Welles, the legendary actor and director, was born on 6 May 1915, the second and much-favoured son of Richard and Beatrice. He was heaped with adulation and fulfilled his parents', especially his mother's, expectations: 'He would master whatever skills were required of him to keep him at the side of his beautiful, tough mother.' With his mother separated in 1919 from his alcoholic father, Beatrice continued her single-handed education of Orson and turned to him for stimulation. 'What she was looking for was a companion, someone she could talk to on her own level.' Until his mother's death when he was nine years old, he had her undivided attention – a focus full of demand. He was expected and required to be intelligent, amusing, considerate, sympathetic and grown-up (Callow, 1995, p. 1).

The Duke of Clarence and Prince George: Their mother, Queen Alexandra, the wife of Edward VII, 'made children her consolation' and was overly possessive of them to compensate for her husband's philandering (Hall, 1991, p. 243). The elder of her two sons, Prince Eddy as the Duke was known, was thought to be homosexual and it was even rumoured that he was Jack the Ripper, the infamous slayer of prostitutes (Hall, 1991, p. 53). Engaged to marry Princess May of Teck, he died at the age of twenty-eight before their marriage could take place. According to the historian Elizabeth Longford ('Gay Abandon', 1994), the Duke would not have pursued 'those proclivities' (speaking of his homosexuality) had he become King as the Princess's 'strength of character would have put a stop to all that'. Instead, she married the Duke's younger brother, Prince George, whom Queen Alexandra was heartbroken to lose to another woman: 'It is sad to think we shall never be able to be together and travel in the same way –– yet there is a bond between us, that of mother and child, which nothing can diminish' (Hall, 1991, p. 241).

Laurence Marks: Laurence Marks, television sitcom writer, was pulled out of school two months before he was due to sit his O-levels by his mother, who did not tell him she was doing so: 'I still have a dream where I have continued at school, taken A-levels and gone to Oxford. That is what I believe would have happened with different, more encouraging, parents.' His mother pulled his sister out of school at fifteen and his brother at fourteen in just the same way. He imagines his mother did this because of 'her anger and envy at seeing all her brothers go to university. Because she was a woman in an Orthodox Jewish household, her job was to make sure the house was tidy and she never got the academic advantages, although she was just as bright ... She was so embittered she didn't get an education that she was going to make sure her children didn't either, which is very perverse' (Danziger, 1996b, p. 22).

Michael Keating: The third child of Gloria Hunniford came to London alone with her when she was offered her Radio Two show. He was eleven and they became very close: 'She had no one to talk to except me so I was suddenly exposed to adult emotions and insecurities,' he explains. 'There were times when Mum cried and I felt very protective of her. The two of us have an incredible bond. She'd discuss her emotions and cry on my shoulder.'

After his parents' separation, his mother would always discuss her subsequent relationships with him and say: 'You're the most important thing. If you don't like him, tell me and I'll finish it tomorrow.' Michael acknowledges, 'I know that because the bond between us is so strong, I'll have to make a psychological break one day [he is twenty-two at this time], especially when it comes to girlfriends. It could be frustrating for a partner that she doesn't have more influence on me than my mother, even though Mum would never infringe on our relationship consciously' (Honan, 1993, pp. 6-7).

King Solomon: He had a throne set by his side for his mother, Bathsheba (I Kings 2:19).

Kirk Douglas: The actor was born Issur Danielovitch to Jewish parents who escaped the ghettos of Russia for the slums of Albany, New York. His father worked as a rag-picker and his mother never learned to read and write but struggled to bring up her one son and six daughters. His father, who spent his spare time drinking with his mates, never gave him the love, praise and comradeship he craved and Douglas could never identify with him.

Douglas was unofficially adopted by a schoolmistress who also seduced him. When he left for college, as he tells in his autobiography *The Ragman's Son*, his mother said to him in Yiddish, 'A boy is a boy, but a girl is drek [shit]'. He was shocked by her words. In an interview with Lynn Barber, Douglas was asked about his 'notoriously Neanderthal attitude towards women' and said that he liked women. 'Women have always played an important part in my life. I've always liked capable women. I've always liked intelligent women.' Of his six sisters he says, 'I love my sisters, but I'm not close to them, not very close, because their affection is overwhelming' (Barber, 1991, pp. 93-101).

J. Edgar Hoover: The director of the US Federal Bureau of Investigation (FBI) for half a century, Edgar was the fourth child, separated by twelve years from his next youngest sibling, and conceived when his parents were still mourning the death of his infant sister. His father, Dickerson, was a modest government printmaker who was weak and suffered from mental illness in later life. His mother, Annie, came from a privileged upbringing and saw herself as a 'lady' with pretensions to a certain social status. Edgar was 'rather more than the apple of his mother's eye' (Summers, 1993, p. 433) and her hopes that her husband would rise above his origins had vanished by the time Edgar was born. Instead, she put great expectations on Edgar; he was 'pushed' by his forceful mother and came to believe that only greater achievement could make him 'good' — he had to perform not just well but perfectly (p. 434). According to psychiatrists (pp. 434–5), Edgar missed a stage of normal childhood development, namely, the end of total dependence on the mother, a bond with a supportive father, and the discovery of an independent personality. He was both attracted and repelled by women, idealized mother figures and lusted after the degraded woman. Allegedly, he was a homosexual and transvestite (Summers, 1993, pp. 435–6).

APPENDIX

Questionnaires

SONS

Age:
Do you have any brothers or sisters?
Nationality:
Marital status: at what age did you marry? (if applicable)
Parents' marital status:

Tell me about your relationship with your mother.

Was she your sole carer?

Were you breast-fed?

Tell me how you spent time with your mother, i.e. playing with her.

Did she work outside the home?

Did you sleep in your parents' bed?

Tell me about your mother. Describe her.

Tell me about your mother's relationship with her own mother.

Do you think your mother was happy in her role as mother?

Did your mother confide in you?

Tell me about the closeness between you and your mother. Who maintains it?

Describe your first day at school.

Were you athletic?

Tell me about the ways your mother encouraged you.

Describe how you think you may please your mother.

Describe your father.

Tell me about playing with him, spending time with him.

Tell me what you have learned from your father about being a man.

Describe your relationship with your father.

Tell me about the ways your mother instilled self-esteem in you.

Tell me about your siblings. Are you close to them?

Do you think your siblings have the same experience of your parents as you?

Are you your mother's favourite?

Describe your parents' marriage.

Tell me about decision-making in your family.

Tell me about the communication in your family. Was it open?

Tell me about how the topic of sex was dealt with.

Tell me what sexuality means to you.

Tell me about the messages you were given about sexuality.

Tell me about the expectations your mother has of you.

Describe how you live up/don't live up to her expectations.

Do you believe your mother preferred to have a son?

Tell me what masculinity means to you.

Tell me about your father: is he masculine? What about yourself?

Tell me about your father as a role-model.

Tell me about your relationships with women/men.

Tell me about the similarities between your mother and your partner.

Tell me about your fantasy of an ideal mother.

What does femininity mean to you?

Where do you live in relation to your mother/parents?

At what age did you leave home?

Tell me about the role religion played in your family.

Tell me who you identify with, your mother or father?

What is your definition of a 'Mamma's Boy'?

MOTHERS

Age:
How many brothers and sisters do you have?
Your marital status:
How many children do you have? Their ages and sex:
Parents' marital status:
Nationality:

Tell me about your fantasies of having a son.

Tell me about your expectations. Does he live up to them?

Were your children breast-fed? How long?

Tell me about what kind of mother you wanted to be.

Tell me about your pregnancies.

Tell me about your relationship with your son.

Do you confide in him?

Tell me about your marriage: your relationship with your husband/partner.

Tell me about your parents: were they happily married?

Describe the communication in your family.

Did you work outside the home when your son was an infant?

Tell me about the time you spent with your son. Tell me about how you felt about it.

Were you the sole carer?

Tell me about the closeness in your relationship with your son: your husband.

What is your definition of masculinity? Tell me about your son, your husband, your father.

Describe the decision-making in your family.

Is your husband involved in the home, in decision-making, with your children?

Tell me about the relationship between your son and his father.

Tell me about your relationship with your mother. Did she confide in you?

Tell me about your mother, your father. Who do you identify with?

What is your definition of femininity? How would you describe your mother, yourself?

Tell me about your mother as a role-model.

Describe your relationship with your father.

Tell me what sexuality means to you.

Tell me about the messages you think you may have passed on to your son about sexuality. Was it openly discussed?

Tell me about your son's first day at school. How did you feel?

Tell me how you encourage your son, his independence, his self-esteem.

Do you think it is easier to be a man or a woman?

Did your son ever sleep in your bed?

What age was your son when he left home? How did you feel?

Where does your son live in relation to you?

Tell me what role religion plays in your family, if any.

Describe your son.

Tell me how you think you will feel when your son gets married.

Describe the ways in which you have been a role-model for your son, for the type of woman you would want him to marry.

What is your definition of a 'Mamma's Boy'?

Bibliography

Abdela, L. (1995) 'When marriage is slavery'. *Cosmopolitan*, September, p. 67.

Acquarone, S. (1996) Personal communication, 17 February.

Allen, W. (1989) 'Oedipus Wrecks', from *New York Stories*. Touchstone Pictures.

Allen, W. (1990) *Crimes and Misdemeanors*, in L. Sunshine (ed.) (1993), *The Illustrated Woody Allen Reader*. London: Jonathan Cape.

Alta, in an interview by Jennifer Stone in *City Miner*, San Francisco. Reprinted in J. Arcana (ed.), *Every Mother's Son*. New York: Anchor Press/Doubleday, p. 140.

Arcana, J. (1983) *Every Mother's Son*. New York: Anchor Press/Doubleday.

Archer, J. and Lloyd, B. (1985) *Sex and Gender*. New York: Cambridge University Press.

Bach, J., Anderson, A. *et al.* (1988) 'A systems model of family ordinal position', in J. Bradshaw (ed.), *Bradshaw On: The Family*, Deerfield Beach, FL: Health Communications, p. 33.

Barber, L. (1991) *Mostly Men*. New York: Viking, pp. 93–101.

Barber, L. (1994) 'Funny Peculiar'. *Sunday Times*, 1 May, Section 7, p. 1.

Bibring, E. (1953) 'The mechanisms of depression', in P. Greenacre (ed.), *Affective Disorders*. New York: International Universities Press.

Bieber, I. (1962) *Homosexuality: A Psychoanalytic Study*. New York: Basic Books.

Brichto, S. (1994) *Funny ... You Don't Look Jewish*. Northampton, MA: Pilkington Press Ltd.

Burn, L. (1990) *Greek Myths – The Legendary Past*. London: The British Museum Press.

Callow, S. (1995) 'Little Lord Orson'. *Sunday Times*, 5 February, News Review section 3, p. 1.

Danziger, D. (1996a) 'I so wanted to push my mother away', in series: The Best of Times, the Worst of Times. *Daily Mail*, 29 January, p. 21.

Danziger, D. (1996b) 'My hate-filled school days', in series: The Best of Times, the Worst of Times. *Daily Mail*, 5 February, p. 22.

deMause, L. (1974) *The History of Childhood*. London: Souvenir Press.

deMause, L. (1990) 'The history of child assault'. *Journal of Psychohistory*, 18, 11–29.

deMause, L. (1991) 'The universality of incest'. *Journal of Psychohistory*, 19, 123–64.

de Saussure, R. (1929) 'Homosexual fixations in neurotic women', in C. W. Socarides (1978), *Homosexuality*. New York: Jason Aronson, pp. 547–601.

Franchetti, M. (1995) 'Chinese babies waste away in "dying rooms".' *Sunday Times*, 11 June, p. 23.

Freud, S. (1897) 'Extracts from the Fliess papers'. Standard edition, Vol.1, pp. 240–73. London: Hogarth Press.

Freud, S. (1905) *Three Essays on the Theory of Sexuality*. Standard edition, Vol. 7, pp. 125–45. London: Hogarth Press.

Freud, S. (1910) 'A special type of choice of object made by men' (Contributions to the psychology of love I). Standard edition, Vol. 11, pp. 163–75. London: Hogarth Press.

Freud, S. (1923) 'The Ego and the Id', Standard edition, Vol. 19, pp. 3–66. London: Hogarth Press. Reprinted in J. Archer and B. Lloyd (1985), *Sex and Gender*. New York: Cambridge University Press.

Friel, J. (1991) *The Grown-up Man*. Deerfield Beach, FL: Health Communications.

Fromm, E. (1957) *The Art of Loving*. London: George Allen & Unwin.

'Gay Abandon' (1994), 'Londoner's Diary'. *Evening Standard*, 16 June, p. 8.

Glasser, M. (1979) 'Some aspects of the role of aggression in the perversions', in I. Rosen (ed.), *Sexual Deviation*, 2nd edn. Oxford: Oxford University Press, pp. 278–305.

Glasser, M. (1985) 'The weak spot: some observations on male sexuality'. *International Journal of Psycho-Analysis*, 66, 405–14.

Glasser, M. (1986) 'Identification in the perversions'. *International Journal of Psycho-Analysis*, 67, 9–17.

Goldenson, R.M. (ed.) (1984) *Longman Dictionary of Psychology and Psychiatry*. New York: Longman.

Granoff, W. and Perrier, F. (1980) *El Problema de la Perversion en la Mujer*. Barcelona: Editorial Critica.

Greenacre, P. (1979) 'Fetishism', in I. Rosen (ed.), *Sexual Deviation*, 2nd edn. Oxford: Oxford University Press, pp. 79–108.

Greenson, R. (1968) 'Dis-identifying from mother: its special importance for the boy'. *International Journal of Psycho-Analysis*, 49, 370–4.

Hall, U. (1991) *The Private Lives of Britain's Royal Women*. London: Michael O'Mara Books.

Harding, E.M. (1971) *Woman's Mysteries*. New York: C.G. Jung Foundation.

Honan, C. (1993) 'Will Michael ever leave Gloria for another woman?' *Daily Mail Weekend*, The Saturday Interview, 16 October, London, pp. 6–7.

Hudson, C. (1996a) 'He wrote of passionate love, but was tortured by his own secret sexuality'. *Daily Mail*, 10 February, pp. 32–3.

Hudson, C. (1996b) 'Revenge of the cuckold'. *Evening Standard* (London), 11 March, p. 47.

Israeloff, R. (1992) 'The sweet ogre: learning to live with your mother-in-law'. *Cosmopolitan*, March, pp. 200–2.

Jones, M. (1992) 'Learning to be a father', in S. French (ed.), *Fatherhood*. London: Virago Press.

Jung, C.G. (1983) *Memories, Dreams, Reflections*. Recorded and edited by A. Jaffe. London: Flamingo.

Kahr, B. (1993) Personal communication, 25 May.

Kahr, B. (1994a) 'The historical foundations of ritual abuse: an excavation of ancient infanticide', in V. Sinason, *Treating Survivors of Satanist Abuse*. London: Routledge.

Kahr, B. (1994b) Personal communication, 3 May.

Kearns, D. (1976) *Lyndon Johnson and the American Dream*. New York: Harper.

Kiverstein, A. (1993) 'If you give birth to depression'. *Jewish Chronicle* (London), 24 September.

Kramer, S. (1980) 'Object-coercive doubting: a pathological defensive response to maternal incest'. *Journal of the American Psychoanalytical Association*, **31**, 325–51 .

Landers, A. (1994) 'Mama's boys make best husbands, wives say'. *The Gazette* (Montreal), 5 May, p. 5.

Laplanche, J. and Pontalis, J.B. (1973) *The Language of Psychoanalysis*. London: Hogarth/Institute of Psycho-Analysis.

Lemkau, J. and Landau, C. (1986) 'The selfless syndrome: assessment and treatment considerations'. *Psychotherapy*, **23** (2), 227–33.

Lemoine-Luccioni, E. (1987) *The Dividing of Women or Woman's Lot*. London: Free Association Books.

Lewis, L. and Steeples, J. (1993) *Lewis: The Autobiography of the WBC Heavyweight Champion of the World*. London: Faber and Faber.

Mahler, M.S. and Gosliner, B.J. (1955) 'On symbiotic child psychosis: genetic dynamic and restitutive aspects', in *The Psychoanalytic Study of the Child*, Vol. 10. New York: International Universities Press, pp. 195–212.

Mahler, M.S., Pine, F. and Bergman, A. (1975) *The Psychological Birth of the Human Infant*. New York: Basic Books.

Mernissi, F. (1973) 'The effects of modernization of the male–female dynamics in a Muslim society: Morocco'. Ann Arbor, MI: University Microfilms. Quoted in C. Safilios-Rothschild (1977), *Love, Sex, and Sex Roles*. Englewood Cliffs, NJ: Prentice-Hall, p. 30.

Moss, H. A. (1970) 'Sex, age and the state as determinants of the mother–infant interaction', in K. Danzinger (ed.), *Readings in Child Socialization*. Oxford: Pergamon Press.

Odom, G. R. (1990) *Mothers, Leadership, and Success*. Houston: Polybius Press.

Orgel, S. and Shengold, L. (1968) 'The fatal gifts of Medea'. *International Journal of Psycho-Analysis*, **49**, 379–83.

Parsons, J. and Seward, I. (1994) 'Why the young princes are growing up in different ways'. *Mail on Sunday*, 23 January, p. 48.

Pines, D. (1993) *A Woman's Unconscious Use of Her Body: A Psychoanalytical Perspective*. London: Virago Press.

Raphael-Leff, J. (1991) *Psychological Processes of Child Bearing*. London: Chapman and Hall .

Rebelsky, F. and Hanks, C. (1971) 'Fathers' verbal interaction with infants in the first three months of life'. *Child Development*, **42**, 63–8.

Rich, A. (1977) *Of Woman Born*. London: Virago Press.

Richler, M. (1992) 'His balls', in S. French (ed.), *Fatherhood*. London: Virago Press.

Roith, E. (1988) *The Riddle of Freud: Jewish Influences on His Theory of Female Sexuality*. London: Tavistock.

Rosen, I. (1979) 'The general psychoanalytical theory of perversion: a critical and clinical review', in I. Rosen (ed.), *Sexual Deviation*, 2nd edn. Oxford: Oxford University Press, pp. 29–64.

Roth, P. (1967) *Portnoy's Complaint*. London: Penguin Books, 1986.

Safilios-Rothschild, C. (1977) *Love, Sex, and Sex Roles*. Englewood Cliffs, NJ: Prentice-Hall.

Schindler, U.H. (1982) 'Fetish', in H.J. Eysenck, W. Arnold and R. Meili (eds), *Encyclopedia of Psychology*. New York: Continuum.

Scruton, R. (1992) 'The loneliness of the long-distance father', in S. French (ed.), *Fatherhood*. London: Virago Press.

Shepherd, N. (1993) 'The fair sex – and the unfair'. *Jewish Chronicle* (London), 24 September, p. 29.

Socarides, C.W. (1968) 'A provisional theory of aetiology in male homosexuality: a case of preoedipal origin'. *International Journal of Psycho Analysis*, 49, 27–36.

Socarides, C.W. (1978) *Homosexuality*. New York: Jason Aronson.

Socarides, C.W. (1982) 'Abdicating father, homosexual sons: psychoanalytic observations on the contribution of the father to the development of male homosexuality', in S.H. Cath, A.R. Gurwith and J.M. Ross (eds), *Father and Child: Developmental and Clinical Perspectives*. Boston: Little Brown, pp. 509–21.

Socarides, C.W. (1988) *The Preoedipal Origin and Psychoanalytic Therapy of Sexual Perversions*. Madison, CT: International Universities Press.

Stoll, C. (1978) *Female and Male: Socialization, Social Roles and Social Structure*. Dubuque, IA: William C. Brown.

Stoller, R.J. (1975) *The Transsexual Experiment*. London: The Hogarth Press/Institute of Psycho-Analysis.

Summers, A. (1993) *Official and Confidential: The Secret Life of J. Edgar Hoover*. London: Victor Gollancz.

'We need career mothers says Pope'. *Daily Mail*, 7 December 1995, p. 17.

Welldon, E.V. (1988) *Mother Madonna Whore – The Idealization and Denigration of Motherhood*. New York: The Guilford Press.

Wildmare, L. (1980) 'Raising a male child'. *Women*, 7 (1).

Winnicott, D. (1953) 'Transitional objects and transitional phenomena'. *International Journal of Psycho-Analysis*, 34, 89.

Index